D0465018

CHUTZPAH

CHUTZPAH

WHY ISRAEL IS A HUB OF INNOVATION AND ENTREPRENEURSHIP

INBAL ARIELI

WITHDRAWN

HARPER
BUSINESS

An Imprint of HarperCollins*Publishers*

CHUTZPAH. Copyright © 2019 by Inbal Arieli. All rights reserved. Printed in the United States of America. No part of this book may be used or reproduced in any manner whatsoever without written permission except in the case of brief quotations embodied in critical articles and reviews. For information, address HarperCollins Publishers, 195 Broadway, New York, NY 10007.

HarperCollins books may be purchased for educational, business, or sales promotional use. For information, please email the Special Markets Department at SPsales@harpercollins.com.

FIRST EDITION

Designed by Fritz Metsch

Library of Congress Cataloging-in-Publication Data has been applied for.

ISBN 978-0-06-288303-2

19 20 21 22 23   LSC   10 9 8 7 6 5 4 3 2 1

TO MY LOVED SONS:

Yonatan, Daniel, and Yarden

Children must be taught how to think, not what to think.

—MARGARET MEAD

CONTENTS

STAGE V: RENEWAL

INTRODUCTION

"It's impossible!"

Most people would give up when they're told something is impossible to achieve. But try saying "It's impossible" to an Israeli. The result would be an excited, dreamy, motivated journey to achieving maybe not the original goal, but something close enough. Probably better than initially envisioned.

At the root of this approach is the Israeli chutzpah, a determined approach to life, which might seem to some as rude and opinionated, or, to others, seen in a more positive light, as preferring directness to political correctness for the sake of achieving one's goals. With the right amount of chutzpah, anything is possible. Whether you are a seven-year-old kid insisting on speaking out at a family dinner or an experienced business executive proposing a creative solution to a commercial transaction, you are instilled with the chutzpah power—determined, courageous, and optimistic that anything can be achieved.

This spice of chutzpah is manifested across the board, in all aspects of Israeli life. It's also an essential part of the success of Israel as a tech nation. You may have heard someone call Israel the "Start-Up Nation." It's a moniker that fits: Israel has the highest density of start-ups in the world and is ranked first outside of the United States as a global hub of entrepreneurship.

People ask me all the time: "What makes Israel such a cradle of innovation?" or "Why are Israelis constantly busy with new initiatives?" I've heard many different explanations, ranging from the influence of Israel's technologically advanced military to the effect of the long-standing Jewish traditions of study and questioning. Those explanations, while not without merit, are too narrow. What I've come to understand is that it is the unique way Israelis are brought up, within a tribe-like community and with a childhood full of challenges and risks, that is at the root of Israelis' entrepreneurial culture. That, and a lot of chutzpah we all share.

For the last twenty years I have been immersed in the Israeli entrepreneurial ecosystem and have been gathering insights, data, and stories. I have spent my career working with serial entrepreneurs and nurturing some of the most talented Israeli youth. I did this during my service in the Israel Defense Forces' elite Unit 8200; through running accelerators and tech talent incubators; while taking on senior leadership roles in global technology companies; by becoming an entrepreneur myself; and by being a mom to three curious boys.

Over the years, I have observed the roots of Israeli entrepreneurship deepen and identified the key factors necessary for this process. All these experiences have solidified my conviction that innovation and entrepreneurship do not originate in one magical moment, nor are they the province of a select few born with an "innovative gene," but rather they are a product of a specific set of skills, ideally nurtured from a very young age.

Granted, I'm an Israeli mother, so perhaps I am a bit biased, but I think the answer to why Israel is such a laboratory of innovation and entrepreneurship begins with the way Israelis raise their children.

From the moment they can raise their heads, we encourage our sons and daughters to explore the world around them, freely and without fear or constraint, which is much easier said than done! I realized when I had my first son, Yonatan, that while I couldn't expect not to worry about him, what I could do was not pass that anxiety and fear onto my son. What made the decision easier was that I had many moms around me who made the same choice. We saw our role as not just keeping our kids safe or teaching them what we knew, but also fostering in them real independence.

Giving my son that gift meant knowing how to get out of his way, letting him fall and explore even where it wasn't totally safe, and, when he was ready, helping him process and make meaning of his experiences. What I'm describing is not conditional independence; it is absolute, and it is difficult.

This freedom extends and grows as our kids age; it is embedded in our institutions and in our culture. As I'll show in the coming pages, Israel is not a very risk-averse society; our willingness to make mistakes and, even more important, allow our children to, builds resiliency and creativity, and eventually amazing inventions.

Warren Buffett once said: "If you're going to the Middle East to look for oil, you can skip Israel. If you're looking for brains, look no further. Israel has shown that it has a disproportionate amount of brains and energy."[1]

Today, Israel has the highest concentration of start-ups per capita worldwide, with more than one start-up for every two thousand people. Which means that Israel, with a population of just over eight million citizens, a country roughly half the size of Lake Michigan, is home to more than five thousand Israeli start-ups, alongside an additional thousand mature tech companies.

Israel is ranked third out of 138 countries in the World Economic Forum Innovation Rating, boasting a long list of innovations: from cherry tomatoes to drip irrigation; from the first capsule endoscopy solution to the first software for online chat; from the USB flash drive to Waze, a GPS-based geographical navigation application program for smartphones. And so many more.

Israel has the globe's highest R&D expenditure in terms of percentage of GDP and leads the OECD in the number of scientists and researchers per number of employees. Since 1966, twelve Israelis have been awarded Nobel Prizes in an array of fields including chemistry, economics, literature, and peace. A unique example is Professor Ada Yonath of the Weizmann Institute of Science, who was awarded the 2009 Nobel Prize in Chemistry, along with her colleagues Venkatraman Ramakrishnan and Thomas Steitz, for their groundbreaking work on the protein-producing part of the cell known as the ribosome, which led to treatments for leukemia, glaucoma, and HIV, as well as antidepressant medications. Professor Yonath was the first female Israeli Nobel laureate, the first woman from the Middle East to win in a scientific field, and the first woman in forty-five years to win the prize for chemistry.

This tiny country's inventory of achievements in the tech and entrepreneurship space, within but a few decades, is long and impressive. Israel attracts more venture capital per capita than any other country in the world, surpassing the United States, Canada, and European strongholds. Despite the challenging geopolitical environment, confidence among investors vis-à-vis Israeli high-tech companies is extremely high, second only to the United States; to date, there are more than one hundred venture capital and private equity firms operating in Israel and actively investing in Israeli companies. Eighty-five percent of these investments come from abroad—mostly the United States but with growing representation from Asian investors. And as of 2018, Israel has the highest representation of companies listed on Nasdaq, following only the global giants of the United States and China. It also hosts more than three hundred multinationals—from Apple to Intel, Facebook and Google, Dropbox and PayPal—who have opened R&D offices in Israel and are leveraging local talent.

These accomplishments have positioned Israel—its tech innovation and entrepreneurial ecosystem—as the leading innovation hub outside of the United States, and, as a result, it has been dubbed the "Start-Up Nation" and "Silicon Vadi."

As a robust economic center for innovation and entrepreneurship, Israel also has been ranked sixth out of fifty countries in the Family Life Index, which measures factors such as access to affordable and quality education, leisure activities, and family well-being. A final, fun figure: Israel has more museums per capita than any other country in the world.

Anyone who has spent time in Israel can sense that what is unique about this place is more than just the brainpower Warren Buffet was talking about. People in Israel live for the moment. We are full of energy and grow up in organized chaos. We encourage our children to be audacious and imaginative, to follow their dreams. But it comes at a price.

I was picking up my son Yarden from school one day when I ran into Yonatan Adiri, a years-long friend and neighbor, who was waiting for his daughter, Carmel.

Yonatan was the first-ever CTO of an Israeli president, Shimon Peres. More than he actually needed a CTO, Peres, at the time, was of the opinion that someone like Yonatan was a hidden force—a person of great talent who is good to have around. In this role, Yonatan led Israel's tech diplomacy with heads of state from the White House in Washington to the Blue House in Korea. He was also responsible for the president's long-term agenda on transformative technologies such as neuroscience, immunotherapy, stem cells, and bioinformatics. Before he became one of Peres's hidden powers, Yonatan had already managed to be an integral part of the Tannenbaum and Hezbollah prisoner exchange deal in 2004 in his capacity as captain (res) in the Israeli army's diplomatic-military unit, earn a master's in political science and law from Tel Aviv University, and serve as the senior policy consultant for Reut Institute, all before he turned twenty-four. Nowadays, Yonatan is focused on Healthy.io, which he founded and leads as

CEO. Healthy.io is a revolutionary company, founded on a remarkably simple solution for urinalysis using just a practical home kit and a smartphone. The start-up has grown to be a leading company in the field of digital health care, winning landmark FDA approval for its smartphone camera unit scanner. His leadership in the technology and diplomacy sphere was recognized by the World Economic Forum, which selected him, at the age of thirty, as one of the hundred "Young Global Leaders" and recently chose his start-up, Healthy.io, as a member of the select "Technology Pioneer" group that includes the likes of Google, Uber, Dropbox, Kickstarter, and more. Not surprisingly, Yonatan was recently nominated by *Time* magazine as one of the fifty most influential people in health care for 2018.

Like me, Yonatan has three kids. As we were walking toward our homes, our kids running ahead of us, we got to talking about what it was like growing up in Israel when we were kids and what it's like now raising children here. Yonatan told me that being the youngest of four accomplished siblings actually freed him of the burden of having to prove himself. "That's ironic," I said jokingly, "considering you'd completed your bachelor's degree by the time you were seventeen." He smiled. "It's true. I achieved a lot at a young age, but I wasn't pushed to do it. My father immigrated to Israel from Tehran at the age of seven. Faced with the adversity of radical immigration—he had a very resolute approach to life— whatever you do, do it right. He didn't wish for my siblings and me to be anything more than good people."[2]

We sat on a bench by a crowded snack bar where a group of people were talking loudly while reading the daily newspaper. "There's nothing like a bit of drama to start a quiet afternoon," he joked.

"Definitely," I answered in jest. "I was just starting to worry that my levels of stress and fuss are going down." I decided to raise an issue I'd been contemplating ever since I began writing this book. "Why is it, do you think, that Israelis are so easily dragged into intense, often aggressive debates with complete strangers, yet it is so difficult for us to handle banal, nonemergency situations calmly?"

"It's an interesting point," Yonatan said. "We Israelis are exceptionally efficient under pressure. Our military is among the most effective and professional in the world, and we are able to execute an action plan in no time, going from an idea to starting a company, raising significant capital, putting together teams, and launching in a matter of months. But we tend to interpret everything as an emergency, and we invest tremendous resources in dealing with situations that are really not that extreme, which is far from efficient. We're always putting out fires, even when there aren't any."

This got me thinking: Could the Israeli quality of handling stress be a double-edged sword? On the one hand, we have perfected the art of dealing with crises. On the other hand, we're always expecting the worst to happen, which puts us under enormous strain at all times.

I wanted to get at the cultural side effects of growing up and living in an extremely intense environment such as Israel. "Beyond the fact that everyone is stressed," I said to Yonatan, "too many people get involved in every situation."

"Definitely," he said. "It's like each person feels it is their responsibility to handle the situation, to offer their opinion, and to make sure it's being heard, without realizing they are just making things harder."

"It's true," I said. "We're always so ready to respond, always on our toes, that when something, anything, happens, we immediately go into emergency mode, creating unnecessary chaos."

The "all opinions count the same" is a great tactic for handling emergencies because it is the quickest way to make sure all opinions and options have been taken into consideration; when a decision needs to be made, it is quick but not impulsive. But Yo-natan was also right. We tend to interpret everything as an emer-gency, which gets us to a state of analysis paralysis. Too many people get involved, each one absolutely certain they're an expert and knows exactly what needs to be done. Then everyone tries to advance their own point of view. "We're diluting experts," Yo-natan said, "with so many opinions supposedly equal—analysis paralysis soon follows."

There's a logical explanation to this behavior, I thought. The geo-political circumstances and our national history have nurtured a culture that is extremely efficient, exceptionally alert and respon-sive, and highly innovational—when you don't have time to think you just act, and this results in impressively resourceful solutions to all kinds of life puzzles. It also makes for great entrepreneurs. But at the same time, it means we're always on edge, ready to pounce at the first sign of trouble.

Long-term planning and real-time decision making are often seen as necessary yet contradictory entrepreneurial skills. Entre-preneurs must be able to envision a route and plan ahead. But once the business is up and running, they must rely on ad hockery to take them to the top: things don't always go as planned, and one must learn to deal with it. Strategic planning that precedes the foundation is as much a part of scaling up a business as the real-time management of it. That means reacting to what happens or is needed at a particular time, rather than planning in a way that suits all possible situations. In the developing world of artificial in-telligence computing, ad hockery means applying arbitrary rules that are sometimes included in artificially intelligent software to simulate the unexpectedness in human reasoning. Ad hockery is also about improvising on the go.

Israelis train their ad hockery skills from early childhood, which is why we're always in the game, making on-the-spot deci-sions about our next step, our muscles constantly active. But we lack the foresight, the strategic as opposed to the tactical thinking, that has helped build hundred-year-old institutions and cooperatives in other parts of the world. Always thinking in terms of tomorrow, never in terms of decades, has made it difficult for us to scale up. We're great entrepreneurs, but unfortunately not many of us are great managers of scaled operations, yet.

"Cut us some slack," Yonatan said when I shared these thoughts with him the next day. "We've just been busy training specific muscles like asking questions, challenging assumptions, creativity, resourcefulness, and lots of other skills that make for wonderful entrepreneurs. But it doesn't mean we can't train other parts, just as those who've been training their scaling-up, long-term planning, and other skills, all crucial for running a successful business, have been doing. We need to brush off skills that were honed over so many years—which prioritized instinct over planning. We might be a little rusty, but it's nothing that a little practice won't fix."

Later that evening I got to thinking, *Is it all really about practice? Can our ability to handle crises really be explained away as hereditary, or is it a skill that we've developed, a muscle we've trained since childhood? And as such, can it be learned later in life, or in different settings?*

We tend to think of an entrepreneur, someone like Yonatan Adiri, as somebody with a brilliant idea. In reality, there are millions of brilliant ideas, services, and products that never see the light of day. An idea, while at the heart of every entrepreneurial venture, can originate from anywhere.

If you had met Yariv Bash, Kfir Damari, and Yonatan Winetraub in 2008, before they decided to participate in the Google Lunar XPRIZE to land a spacecraft on the moon, you probably would have warned them that their idea was unreasonable, that their goal was unachievable, and that the whole venture was laughable. The Google Lunar XPRIZE challenge was for privately funded teams to build a robotic spacecraft that would land on the moon and send back a high-definition selfie video and image. It comes as no surprise that, for a venture whose cost was estimated at no less than $300 million, the $20 million prize did not prove profitable. One by one, the competing teams from around the world dropped out until eventually Google announced the cancellation of the competition. Competition or no competition, only one team kept going: the Israeli team. Fortunately, Yariv, Kfir, and Yonatan were born and raised on the unstoppable value of chutzpah. Ten years later, Israel's Beresheet—SpaceIL's unmanned spider-like spacecraft—made tiny Israel the fourth nation ever to have launched a lunar project, after the United States, Russia, and China, and the first with a private lander shipped to the moon, on a budget of less than US $100 million, a fraction of the standard budgets that the governments of the United States, China, and Russia have used for their respective programs.

Even the sky was not the limit for their idea and chutzpah.

Chutzpah means participating in a competition but having completely different goals in mind than the ones set by the organizers of the competition. Although Google sparked the idea, for SpaceIL, the main goal was never really to put a vessel on the moon and have it take a selfie, as the competition dictated; instead, it was to establish an educational program with which even greater things could be achieved. Beresheet's selfie on the moon is just the motivating driver. SpaceIL, founded as a nonprofit organization and funded primarily by philanthropists, now works to promote scientific and technological education in Israel. They have already reached tens of thousands of children who are beginning to take an interest in aerospace, astrophysics, and related fields, with programs ranging from extracurricular activities at school to volunteering opportunities at SpaceIL.

Chutzpah means taking on a massive project with no prior

relevant expertise and without having worked out all the details. The founders themselves had no deep expertise in aerospace. Yonatan, now a graduate student at Stanford, is completing a doctorate in cancer research; Kfir is the chief product and strategy officer at Tabookey, a cybersecurity start-up; and Yariv is chief executive officer of Flytrex, a company that employs drones to deliver consumer goods. Why did they all suddenly decide to become aerospace entrepreneurs? They thought it would be fun to take on a new challenge.

Chutzpah is to make do with what you've got and figure things out as they come. To make it to the moon, Beresheet had to take a two-month, four-million-mile route; slowly adjust its orbit, stretching to the outermost point until the moon's gravity pulled it into lunar orbit; and eventually land at the Sea of Serenity. The moon, mind you, is only a quarter of a million miles away, but budgetary constraints forced Beresheet to take the long way while piggybacking on the Indonesian telecom satellite PSN-6.

Chutzpah is inspiring people and getting them on board with an idea, no matter how crazy it may sound. It is believing in the journey and in the unexpected results it will bring. It's saying *yalla*, let's dive in and see where we end up. Let's aspire and inspire. Let's achieve unrealistic goals and turn them into reality.

On April 11, 2019, as Beresheet began its descent, Israelis held a collective breath. Beresheet broadcasted a selfie against the backdrop of moon, showing Israel's flag and the words "Small country, big dreams." But at the last seconds of the landing, the main engine stopped, and Beresheet crashed to the moon's surface. Despite the failure, and thanks to their resilience in continuing to Beresheet 2, SpaceIL and its founders have taught us an important lesson about chutzpah and the potential this quality holds.

So, while an idea is necessary, it is in no way the sum total of entrepreneurship. Entrepreneurship is the ability to execute an idea, to bring it to life. In the process of bringing any idea to life, entrepreneurs are required to use a variety of skills, some of which they may not be used to practicing. According to the World Economic Forum, social skills—such as persuasion, emotional intelligence, and teaching others—are increasingly in demand.

I think of these skills the way I think of our physical anatomy: we all have the same muscles in our bodies, but we use them differently. Some people choose to train and reinforce different muscles than others. If you were encouraged from a young age to ask questions and challenge assumptions, your curiosity muscle would be well trained. You would be in tune with that muscle and know how to use it. But even if you didn't practice a specific sport as a child, that doesn't mean you cannot take it up later in life. The same applies to your soft skills, critical to entrepreneurship: it's never too late to start practicing, strengthening, and nurturing your entrepreneurial skills. Like your muscles, these skills lie deep inside—you just need to be aware of them and set an intention to use them. This book will show you how. Time to unveil your own chutzpah!

I invite you to join me on a journey through a typical Israeli childhood. Along the way, we'll observe its surprising yet strong resemblance to the life cycle of a modern business: from discovery and exploration of your target market and value proposition, to the actual validation of your business's raison d'être—from the trial-and-error process of creating efficiency, aiming to support potential scale and sustainability of a global business, to, eventually, the renewal and reinvention of your business.

Israeli society, like industries around the world, comprises many different types. So, the experiences and attitudes I will describe might differ in some respects from one Israeli to another. However, the takeaways and principles I will introduce you to, arising from the experience of wide swaths of Israeli society, can be relevant to any individual holding, or aiming to hold, business or entrepreneurial positions.

Jack Ma, Alibaba's founder, who recently visited Israel, mentioned that the two most important things he learned in Israel were "innovation, and chutzpah: the courage to challenge."[3]

Having visited Israel or not, think of this book as a workout for your own chutzpah and entrepreneurial muscles. *Yalla*,* let's begin to connect with, cultivate, and strengthen them together!

---

* Yalla—Literally, "Let's go!" Most commonly used as "Let's go" or "Hurry up." An expression of eagerness to get down to brass tacks. Can also express haste, impatience, enthusiasm, or simple practicality. Originally from Egyptian, popularized through vernacular use in Egyptian, Persian, Turkish, and Hebrew film, television, and slang.

DISCOVERY

HOW DO YOU think of discovery? Is it the act of finding something that no one else knows? Or maybe just something you did not know? For me, it's that "aha" moment when dots are suddenly connected in a way I did not envision before, when I realize something new, to me. I have had few moments like this in my professional and personal life. I know that if you had been watching me at those moments, you would have seen my eyes brighten, the pleasure of discovery written all over my face. I strongly believe most of us are genuinely excited when discovering new ideas and new solutions.

In my years of experience working with business executives and early-stage entrepreneurs, I have realized that their discoveries typically arise out of necessity. They either face a problem themselves or recognize one for others. And once they somehow connect the dots, it's like magic! They become obsessed with their idea. And that's where the hard work begins, since discovery on its own is simply not enough.

Which is why, once I've had that "aha" moment, I start asking myself a litany of questions: Is my discovery relevant to others as well? To whom? Can I assess what it will take to achieve an efficient solution, a better-performing product or service than what already exists? What would I need to overcome? Do I have all the necessary resources? Am I going to try to do this all by myself? Who do I want with me on this journey? Do I really want to take the risk and pay the opportunity costs involved in this project? Do I have all the information I need? And so many more. I assault myself with these questions, and the more order I try to bring to the process at this stage, the lower my energies drop, and the less interest I have in my new discovery.

Now think of how kids react to new discoveries: the light in their eyes, their high level of energy and enthusiasm when they have their own aha moments. Only they don't ask themselves too many questions. They act intuitively. They don't stop to worry. They collect whatever resources they can find—most typically their friends—and start *doing* and *moving*, clearing obstacles along the way, in a fluidly ad hoc process. And the more they achieve, the brighter the light in their eyes.

Why don't we learn from them?

1

PLAYING WITH JUNK

In the 1950s, on Kibbutz Sde Eliyahu, a small socialist cooperative situated in the north of Israel not far from the Jordanian border, a young German immigrant developed a unique educational approach for her preschool.

At the time, Sde Eliyahu was a settlement poor in financial resources but rich in ideology. Malka Haas was tasked with equipping the kibbutz's first preschool, on a very small budget. Haas came up with a creative solution, which quickly became the standard for Israeli early childhood education facilities.

Instead of purchasing expensive, mass-produced toys, Haas appropriated objects from the homes, fields, and workshops of the kibbutz, filling the preschool's yard with objects, which in their better days had been used by the adults on the kibbutz. Thus, the junkyard concept was born and from it an entire educational philosophy grew: playing with junk. To this day, throughout Israel, you can find junkyards in day-care facilities, preschools, and kindergartens.

Were you to visit one, you would find a fenced-in yard containing old furniture, tractors, ladders, beds, tires, barrels, old stoves, pans, teacups, cutlery, fabrics, wicker baskets, paint cans, paper, straw, etc. Aesthetically pleasing it is not.

But if you were to watch the children at play, you would notice a few things: First, that they love their time in the junkyard. Some use several items at the same time; others focus on a specific object. Most kids play together, though few feel at ease playing by themselves. They are extremely active, focused on the doing. It seems like they could play for hours and hours, moving and using these objects. Second, you would notice that their engrossment and creativity flow in a way you won't see when children are playing with structured toys. You'd see them manipulate things, maybe break them, and come up with numerous uses for a single object, only a few of which might correspond to its original purpose. They are not bound to guidelines or best practices. They do not have to rely on someone else's prior experience. It's theirs to discover and act upon, creating whatever they want to. An old microwave turns into a space shuttle dashboard, operated by a four-year-old girl, her friends the shuttle's crew; a car tire becomes a stage for a special mirror dance by two boys; the keys of a keyboard are disassembled by a group of four kids and turned into magic stones with special powers.

In the junkyard, children find themselves immersed in the world of adults, on the one hand, while having the freedom to experiment with it, on the other. By playing freely with old appliances and household items, children explore their inner workings and material qualities, and in the process gain perspective on cause and effect.

But playing with junk is much more than just experimenting with materials. As Malka Haas explains, it "involves the whole person: muscles and senses, emotion and intellect, individual growth and social interaction."[1] In the junkyard, children are able to re-create the human interactions they observe in grown-ups, acting out the relationships, social status, gender roles, or any other human activity they observe in their daily lives.

As I described in the Introduction, I believe that Israeli children, like all children, start building their creative muscles from the beginning. But where young children in many other cultures are cushioned and sheltered and may have less opportunities to practice these muscles freely, the Israeli preschooler is set loose among potentially dangerous, inappropriate objects. This gives them the opportunity to work those muscles more, developing social and creative skills from a young age. And you don't have to just take my word for it. Researchers Isobel van der Kuip and Ingrid Verheul have found that, given that children's personalities are especially "malleable in early childhood, initial education can play an important role in the development of personality traits or, more [specifically], entrepreneurial qualities."[2]

So how exactly does playing with broken computer hardware and discarded coatracks build entrepreneurial skills? You might be surprised, but playing in a junkyard helps build an impressive set of skills necessary for entrepreneurial endeavors: risk management, independence, conflict resolution, and teamwork, among others. Let me explain how.

HISTORY-MAKING POWER

Unlike standard play environments, where objects are often stationary, have clearly defined purposes, and are imitations of real objects, the Playing with Junk approach empowers children. Even at the young age of two, Israeli children playing in a junkyard have what Valerie Polakow, a professor of educational psychology, calls "history-making power": they are capable of transforming their environment.

Israeli children aren't playing within an environment but substantially changing it. They take the metal barrels, car tires, and sheets of plywood and move them around to build houses or castles or vehicles. Imagine a 4x4 car made out of baby car seats balanced on a coffee table, complete with headlights fashioned from large tin cans and a real steering wheel. Later, the car is taken apart to make room for an operating table or launchpad. Building and making changes to their environment is extremely empowering for children. Within this setting, each child has the opportunity to become a creative entrepreneur.

IS THAT SAFE? RISK MANAGEMENT AND PLAY

I can testify that believing in my children's abilities and encouraging their independence has been one of the most difficult and important challenges I've faced as a mom of three boys. But raising them in Israel has made it not only unavoidable but easier.

Anyone new to Israel who encounters a junkyard in a preschool is immediately horrified. Dilapidated tractors, concrete sewage pipes, bricks—the yard looks like one big liability. But letting young children climb chairs, handle heavy wooden objects, and play with rusting pots and pans gives them a chance to experience and evaluate risks. Managing such risks is another empowering experience for children lucky enough to have a junkyard at their disposal. It's true that children may get hurt while playing. But getting hurt is an integral part of living. Life entails all kinds of risks.

As adults, we are able to deal with the risks and avoid getting hurt because we have developed skills and techniques for risk management. Through practice, children learn to handle risks, to be careful, and to know the boundary between what is too dangerous and what is possible. Entrusting our children's safety to themselves shows them that we trust them so they can trust themselves. It is an extremely powerful message to give them.

This is not to say that an Israeli junkyard is a free-for-all. Ground rules are set in place, but as long as they adhere to these rules, the children are free to play. The rules tend to be general enough to be applied in many different scenarios: always check the stability of your structure; make sure to put stops under functioning wheels; a rope is tied only around one child's waist; objects are thrown only to empty spaces. These safety instructions complement a child's spontaneous behavior rather than correcting it.

COOPERATION AND CONFLICT RESOLUTION

Moving around household appliances is quite a task for preschoolers and kindergartners. It demands that children cooperate and work together toward a common goal. Malka Haas remembered a scene of an old door being carried by four tiny girls. Feeling the weight of the door through their bodies helped them to quickly realize that they could only carry this heavy item together. In an interview with the artist Amnon Zilber about his youth playing in a kibbutz junkyard, he mentioned how this type of collaboration exists only when there is a physical task that a child must accomplish in collaboration with the other children, acting together as a unified and adaptive group. "These were complicated assignments," he recalls. "I remember that when we would succeed, it would give tremendous satisfaction as a group. . . . And the fact is that to this day I remember the experience as empowering."[3]

To tackle such grandiose projects, the children also need to learn to solve conflicts. In the junkyard, children learn to acknowledge and adjust to the needs, wants, and limitations of others. Often their own wishes collide with their playmates'. These difficult, messy situations constitute learning opportunities. In the junkyard, children are challenged to find a creative solution that is acceptable to all. And things can get very complex when children are engineering tunnels in the dirt to funnel rainwater through vacuum hoses.

WHY SHOULD ENTREPRENEURS PLAY WITH JUNK?

Playing with Junk is not a teaching tutorial. It is a philosophical approach to the education of children, one that enables them to test their abilities, learn to cooperate with others, be creative, and practice life as an adult. Israeli children are not taught to be entrepreneurs but, rather, they are encouraged to develop skills that can later be identified as skills among successful entrepreneurs.

2

BALAGAN

When I was four years old my family moved abroad for three years. I was admitted to a preschool in Geneva, where we lived. I have a very strong memory from my first day of the kind teacher who took me by the hand and introduced me to the other kids. I did not speak the language, but their smiles were enough to make me feel welcome. She showed me where to put my bag and lunch box. She then took me to the playground, pointing out the familiar structures of the swing, the carousel, and the slide.

When we approached the slide, my teacher called another girl to demonstrate for me how the process works: the girl climbed up the ladder, and only when she reached the top of the slide did my teacher give me a sign that it was my turn to climb. By the time I reached the top of the ladder, my friend had reached the bottom of the slide. My teacher made it clear: that was my cue to slide down myself. And so on. The process is safe. It's organized. It's fun. But while the slide was familiar to me from Israel, the process was completely different.

If you spend half an hour at a typical Israeli playground observing the children, you may be struck by the chaos. Like in most places, you will see children climbing up the ladder and then sliding down. However, you will also see children walking up slides instead of sliding down them, scaling the peripherals of jungle gyms instead of using the ladders, standing on the swings, running without caution, yelling, and never waiting in line.

What is striking is that the adults rarely interfere with the children's play. As opposed to my teacher in Geneva, they offer no instruction as to how one should climb a structure or use a slide, nor do they correct children who choose to use the playground equipment in what might be considered an unconventional manner. The lack of interference is indicative of two strong characteristics of Israeli culture: a high tolerance for unconventionality and *balagan*.

Balagan, a word borrowed from Russian that has taken on a quintessentially Israeli meaning, is a state of mess, in which things have no preordained order. People, and even entire systems, act spontaneously. In Israel, there is a lot of *balagan* and, surprisingly, this has proven to be a good thing.

For Israelis, *balagan* is a way of life, not only among children. Unlike the common perception of disorder as a disruptive force, in Israel *balagan* reveals itself as an incredibly flexible and accommodating system. Instead of following strict rules regarding social behavior and play, *balagan* fosters ambiguity, encouraging the development of skills necessary for dealing with the unpredictability of life. Though this may seem counterintuitive, if it were not for *balagan*, how would we ever learn to deal with conflict and disagreement?

THERE'S ALWAYS ANOTHER WAY

From an early age, children are taught social conventions pertaining to every aspect of their lives—family dynamics, social relationships, and even play. They are taught that certain toys are intended for certain games, that specific objects belong to select domains, and that there is a right way to do things, including playing with other children. For example, when on the playground, one child should not push another, cut in line, or yell;

objects available should be used the way they were meant to be—slides for sliding and ladders for climbing. This approach is not without its merits. Arguably, it helps raise people who are polite, organized, and considerate.

But there are other ways. With *balagan*, children learn that there is no predetermined order. Who is to say that you shouldn't climb a slide? Or that social interactions should always be polite? The lack of a system, such as obedience, that organizes social and individual behavior allows for freedom of expression and comfort with ambiguity. Freedom of expression is nurtured when there are no defined borders limiting a child's ability to express his emotions, needs, and desires. Ambiguity is inevitable, because the scene is always unpredictable, forcing the child to handle surprises.

I believe that children can learn a lot from living with disorder. In my view, *balagan* promotes in both children and adults creativity, problem solving, and independence—three highly effective characteristics of entrepreneurs. I often challenge my teams, colleagues, and kids to shake up the usual order of things, to spice it up with a bit of chaos.

HOW *BALAGAN* WORKS

I'll acknowledge that, even for Israelis, *balagan* might not immediately suggest "freedom of thought" and "creativity." But, as with the benefits of playing with junk, here, too, there's science to back up the association. Recent experiments looking at the effects of disorderly environments on behavior concluded that while orderly environments encourage conventional behavior, messy ones stimulate the generation of new insights. Studies of children's creativity by Shirley Berretta and Gayle Privette have shown that flexible play as opposed to structured play encourages greater creative thinking.

Unstructured play—whether standing in line or the use of

certain toys—creates ambiguity: there is no way of knowing what will happen next. This is not only socially and intellectually challenging, it can also be more enjoyable, bringing an element of surprise into the play environment. In an organized system, a new child will automatically join the end of the line. No interaction is necessary between the children, as rules dictate proper behavior for this situation. In the absence of such a system, when another child wants to join in, the other children are suddenly forced to adapt and relate. They must consider the new child's desires, needs, and abilities. With no rules to fall back on, they resolve the situation themselves. In other words, social situations laden with ambiguity help develop a child's problem-solving skills, not to mention their self-confidence and ability to persist in the face of adversity.

Tel Aviv, where we live, is on the shore of the Mediterranean. We often go to the beach as a family, and my kids have always loved playing in the sand, building castles and digging tunnels for the seawater to pass through. I have recently noticed something interesting: most tourists visiting Tel Aviv's beaches equip their kids with colorful sets of plastic forms: the tower of a castle, the shape of a pyramid, a sea star. Their kids manage to build impressive structures using only these templates. But Israeli kids usually bring a bucket and a shovel and make do with those. With no template to follow, you'll find these kids creating more unusual, free-style structures. Perhaps unsurprisingly, when you provide children with pre-designed tools, they use them; but when you give them more basic tools and the freedom to create whatever they want, you're in store for surprises.

MESSY IS THE NEW BLACK

Balagan is a commonly used term in Israeli life and manifests itself in almost every arena: from waiting in the supermarket line, to getting on a bus, to visiting a governmental office or participating in a political demonstration. With fewer social conventions and organized social behavior, *balagan* instigates conflicts and frustrations, but it also demands on-the-spot solutions for very particular situations.

Albert Einstein famously said, "If a cluttered desk is a sign of a cluttered mind, of what, then, is an empty desk a sign?"[1] Studies such as Penelope Green's of the *New York Times* support this view, demonstrating that "messy desks are the vivid signatures of people with creative, limber minds," who, not incidentally, earn more than those who maintain neat "office landscapes."[2] Jerrold Pollak, a neuropsychologist, is quoted by Green to argue that "[t]otal organization is a futile attempt to deny and control the unpredictability of life."

Both Green and Pollak have a point. As an entrepreneur myself, I see many benefits to being disorganized at particular stages of the entrepreneurial journey. When I work with groups of early-stage entrepreneurs, I always ask them to make a point of sitting in a different spot every day. Instead of controlling their microenvironment by adopting an assigned seat, alongside colleagues they feel comfortable with, I challenge them to switch places. They suddenly see each other from a different angle; they have a fresh view and hear sounds slightly differently from various spots in the room; they have proximity to different peers, which creates opportunities for new connections and impressions. This simple exercise trains them to deal with some uncertainty and has proven to enrich their experience in these group sessions.

If life is naturally disorganized, wouldn't developing the skills necessary to deal with its unpredictability be more effective than trying to create order? When you think about it, disorder is incredibly flexible and adaptable, unlike order, which is fragile and can be destroyed by any deviation from its well-defined boundaries. *Balagan* encourages adapting and adopting new and unforeseen parameters. It encourages our children and ourselves to continuously reconsider our deepest biases and assumptions regarding the "organization of things" and allows us to consider alternative possibilities.

In their book *A Perfect Mess*, Eric Abrahamson and David H. Freedman argue that "moderately disorganized people, institutions, and systems frequently turn out to be more efficient, more resilient, more creative, and in general more effective than highly organized ones."[3] Pioneering research into the effects of various environments showed that clutter was associated with efficient decision-making capabilities.

Messiness, Janice Denegri-Knott and Elizabeth Parsons add, is not symptomatic of a "messy mind," it actually produces "better" thinking. *Balagan*, they say, encourages us to constantly reconsider our "deepest held biases and assumptions regarding how things should be organized, and equips us to consider other possibilities," whether it is found in its simplest form, in a child's word, or in the home and workplace.[4] Isn't that what entrepreneurship is all about?

3

PLAYING WITH FIRE

Lighting bonfires is a fun practice enjoyed by children throughout the world. While some cultures maintain a protective and risk-averse approach to the handling of fire by children, Israeli parents actually encourage kids to take charge of the entire situation.

Weeks before the Jewish holiday of Lag B'Omer, Israeli children begin to prepare. Unprompted by their elders, they take full responsibility for gathering wood, choosing a campsite, buying food, and spreading the word. If they don't begin to prepare weeks in advance, there will be no wood left with which to light a fire and all the good spots will be taken. On the night of Lag B'Omer, they clear the site, light the fire, and do everything they can to make it last through the night. Their parents? They are either somewhere in the background or fast asleep in their beds.

EVERYONE ENJOYS BONFIRES

My kids adore this holiday. For them and their friends, it is a three-to four-week project. It is a complex and taxing project that requires physical strength, resourcefulness, patience, and collaboration. While they take pride in their final product—the bonfire—kids do not typically make a fuss about the process. In fact, if praised by their parents or other adults for their accomplishments, they would often dismiss the compliment with a shrug and say, "Oh, *katan alay.*" *Katan alay* is the Hebrew equivalent of "no sweat." It is used to make something praiseworthy seem like a piece of cake. Literally, the phrase means "it's small on me," and can be modified to have a more general meaning (e.g., *baktana* [small]). The motives for using a diminutive idiom to refer to what at their age is a significant achievement are unclear. Perhaps it is a sophisticated way of building up confidence for a task that is complex, difficult, or tiring. Not quite the pep talk you would expect.

The first objective in the four-week holiday project is to collect wood, and a lot of it. But we live in Tel Aviv, and you will not find many forests here. No Israeli parent would actually buy wood for their kids to burn. So where can the kids find the wood they need? Some will venture out to a nearby copse or search garbage collection areas for old tables and chairs; they will look behind shops or schools or pretty much any other local spot they can imagine that will have what they're looking for. But for most of them, the answer is simple: they go where they're guaranteed to find lots of wood, for free. Construction sites.

As crazy as it sounds, during the weeks leading up to Lag B'Omer, you'll see groups of kids trespassing on construction sites across the country. They collect wooden pallets, broken-down crates, beams, and whatever else they can scavenge. But then they face another problem: How will they transport this treasure to the bonfire site? A bike isn't big enough; they don't have trollies or wheelbarrows; Mom and Dad aren't going to fill their cars with splinters and debris. The best practice is . . . supermarket carts.

Imagine the streets of New York or Boston filled with groups of kids pushing supermarket carts piled high with wood they "liberated" from construction sites. That's the reality here in Israel for most of the month of May. It's normal to see them in the streets, going about their business. No one interferes or reprimands them. We know that after the climax of the project, the night of the

bonfires, they will return the cart to its legal owner, the supermarket.

The next thing these bands of kids must do is stake their claim
to a spot on which to build their bonfire. In our neighborhood, the
only sandy open space left is a strip that runs behind a large gas
station. For dozens of years, that's where the neighborhood kids
have lit their bonfires.

The evening of Lag B'Omer is a remarkable sight: It's barely
dusk and already the empty lot is full of bonfires, children mill-
ing around them. Some fires are small, just large enough to roast
a marshmallow. There are also one or two large fires—the wood
piled into the shape of a teepee the height of a grown man. In
the background, adults can be found sitting around and mingling,
eating watermelon or corn on the cob. This is not unique to our
neighborhood. This is how the holiday of Lag B'Omer is celebrated
throughout Israel.

While bonfires bring people together and fill the night with
light and warmth, they are approached differently in different
cultures. In the United States, for example, campfires follow clear
and strict rules that are meant to balance safety with fun. The
typical American child is expected to know certain ground rules
by heart before even approaching a fire: "You don't play around
the campfire," says Chris Gay, who for over twenty years was a
Girl Scout leader and camp volunteer in southeast Michigan.
"You don't run. You don't pass things around. Clothing should
be fitted; no hoodies with loose strings, or nylon, which is highly
flammable. The ground itself is important, too: Within three
or four feet of a campsite fire pit, rake away any leaves and
branches, which stray cinders could ignite." Gay explains that
the method to building the safest, most stable bonfire is in the
shape of an A, which is the job of the supervising adult. Kids
should always keep a three- to four-foot distance from the fire,
where chairs or benches should be placed—and, it is important

to be clear, Gay says, "The only time they come up to (the fire) is for cooking."[1]

If she were ever to visit an Israeli Lag B'Omer campfire, Gay would probably have a heart attack.

TYPICAL ISRAEL

On the big day, groups of children gather before sunset and start stacking the wood they collected. If the kids are out of elementary school, their parents will probably be there just for the first couple of hours. The kids start lighting the fires when it gets dark, and the parents sit back and let the kids figure it out. It is a group.effort and no child is left without a job to do, whether it is to collect wood chips and weeds, light a match, or to gently blow on the first flames until they catch. Their responsibility continues throughout the night, as they plan how to ration their wood stock so that it will last until dawn. They need to decide when to put in the aluminum-wrapped potatoes, and they must carefully put the fire out when the night comes to its end.

The reward for their hard work is absolute freedom and unlimited fun, as they sit around the fire, talk and play games, or sing songs. Just imagine how it must feel for children to be given the responsibility of caring for the fire and their own safety, coming up with hours of activities, spending an entire night awake and outdoors, and being with friends without the presence of a parent. This annual ceremony is one of my best memories of my childhood and it's definitely the favorite holiday of my three boys.

IS THIS REALLY A GOOD IDEA?

Many would probably criticize this practice. After all, fire can be dangerous, and children should not be entrusted with their own safety. Guidelines and best practices evolve for a reason. However, Israelis prefer to learn from their own experiences rather than through explicit teaching. By allowing our children to learn the right way to deal with the dangers of the world, such as fire, on their own, we believe they learn more valuable lessons. First, they learn that, like many things, fire can be dangerous but, if treated correctly, does not have to be. Second, the world is theirs to explore, and their parents cannot be with them every step of their way.

Israelis' entire approach toward the holiday of Lag B'Omer encourages capability, independence, freedom, and the courage to experiment. At an American campfire, an adult would probably advise a child against throwing a cardboard box onto the fire, warning him that it will fill the air with unbearable smoke. At an Israeli bonfire, children not under the watchful eye of experienced adults might more readily throw a cardboard box onto the fire and see what happens. After experiencing the smoke themselves, they will definitely never do it again.

Much like when "playing with junk," here, too, children are given the freedom to experiment with materials, learning firsthand how the world works. This kind of responsible freedom is a gift given to them by their parents, but it also teaches them valuable lessons about the responsibility that comes with such freedom. They are learning to handle the unpredictability associated with groups of kids building bonfires, to take an instrumental part in an important community tradition, and to work with their peers toward a shared goal. Overall, it's an opportunity for children to strengthen their individual sense of capability and freedom while also connecting to their group identity.

INTO THE WILD

It's not just on holidays like Lag B'Omer that Israeli children, including very young ones, spend unstructured time outdoors.

Throughout the year, children alone or in groups entertain themselves outdoors, often unsupervised. My children, starting from
when they were around five years old, were largely free to roam
the neighborhood. On a typical evening, as we're getting dinner
ready to put on the table, I send my eldest son, now seventeen, to
round up his younger siblings from around the neighborhood. He
knows they could be anywhere: at the school yard—which is open
for the kids to play during all hours; at the playgrounds; at the
commercial center. He doesn't know exactly where they are, but
he's confident he'll find them eventually. It may sound irresponsible to not check up on your children or know their whereabouts,
but in Israel, playing outdoors without supervision is a norm.
Playing is not the only thing they do by themselves outdoors: my
nine-year-old is responsible for taking our dog for a walk when he
gets back from school, while his older brothers are responsible for
the morning and evening shifts.

The challenges, both physical and mental, offered by playing
outdoors are part of the reason it's encouraged. In Scandinavian
countries, outdoor exercise has been incorporated into the education system. Scandinavian preschoolers between the ages of three
and six can go to "Forest Kindergartens." These kindergartens
are held almost exclusively outdoors, come rain, snow, or shine.
In Denmark, for example, 10 percent of all preschools are run
entirely outdoors.

Compared to kindergartens in other Western countries, this
model is groundbreaking. In the United States, for example,
Ke'Tara Wells, a journalist in Texas, found that "children spend
just about 7 minutes a day on outdoor activities, up to 40 percent
of U.S. school districts have reduced or eliminated recess time for
kids, and many schools keep children inside when temperatures
get below freezing."[2]

Not so in Forest Kindergartens such as in Finland or other
north European countries, where even in subzero temperatures

children can be seen climbing trees, sharpening sticks for knives, wandering into the snowcapped woods, and working together on various activities. Outdoor kindergartens have also reached Israel, albeit to a much smaller extent. In the first Israeli outdoor kindergarten in the desert town of Mitzpe Ramon, for example, five- and six-year-olds learn how to build a fire and make pita bread on a *saj*. Unlike in most preschools, the children here are encouraged to be truly independent: they take care of their own physical well-being, adapt to the weather, maintain a high level of physical activity, and, with the help of their imagination, create a magical and wonderful world among the trees.

These kinds of experiences are even more typical after school. In Israel, where summers are warm and dry and last from April to October, and winters are generally mild, children spend the bulk of their free time outdoors. As when playing with junk or with fire, children are given general safety guidelines and are then free to explore their surroundings. If the sun is blazing and the air is dry, they are taught to take the proper precautions, but neither their actions nor their imaginations are limited.

One might argue that Israel's physical warmth, in turn, helps create a "warm culture." A study conducted in the United States by Lawrence E. Williams and John A. Bargh, professors of marketing and psychology, found that "experiences of physical warmth . . . increase feelings of interpersonal warmth."[3] Indeed, Israel is a very physical culture. Communication involves lots of gesturing and touching (excluding the Orthodox Jewish community), which can be crucial in projecting understanding and a willingness to cooperate. As I will show in more detail in the coming chapters, Israel's close, interpersonal climate stands at the core of its start-up ecosystem and is one reason for Israel's success as a start-up nation.

As I pondered the creative spirit, organized chaos, and experimentation, I was reminded of Micha Kaufman, cofounder and CEO of Fiverr, which allows entrepreneurs, start-ups, and established businesses to get things done for their businesses by tapping into the world's largest marketplace for freelance services.

Micha's story begins in 1967 on a boat that originates in Argentina and is en route to Israel. A young couple filled with patriotism are convinced they're about to step off the boat and don their khakis for the Israeli military in a significant regional war. Of course, they had no way of knowing that the Six-Day War would be over in just six days. And so, upon docking, rather than join the army, they settled on a kibbutz with nothing but their two guitars—after all, their belongings were stolen on the way to Israel. Micha and his younger brother were born in the kibbutz. Micha remembers his father driving the tractor and plowing the fields. He recalls sitting next to him on the tractor's wing, and the hours upon hours of work at the kibbutz workshop, where his dad fixed appliances and objects. Five-year-old Micha sat by his side, watching him, learning how to weld, cut, and occasionally even help him. Micha also remembers the communal children's sleeping area, which was common on Israeli kibbutzim until the eighties. His memories are of a chaotic environment; unruly children jumping around, shoving one another; noise. Surprisingly, he remembers those evenings and nights away from his parents as a positive experience. Similarly, the proximity to the sea—its fresh air and endless space—greatly influenced Micha's childhood. Micha has very good memories of his early days on the kibbutz, characterized by a freedom of spirit, hours and hours wandering the sunny fields, fixing and creating new appliances at the workshop, and a strong sense of social belonging and collective identity among the children.

However, disillusioned by the radically communal way of life of the kibbutz, his parents eventually decided to leave—much to his regret. Empty-handed once again, with only slightly more than their two guitars, the couple started a new chapter in the city. Micha's father had a hard time finding work at first as an engineer and finally found himself working as a draftsman in a semiconductor company. They led the simple life of a young couple struggling to make a living and raise a family. Micha remembers the family's first car, an old Simca he and his dad used to fix every weekend. These moments reminded him of his early days at the kibbutz workshop. And indeed, within only a few years, Micha's father's dedication and talent led him to become the company's CEO and one of Israel's most prominent executives in the semiconductor industry.

Micha did not enjoy his mornings at elementary school. He was bored, branded a "troublemaker" by the teachers, a kid who "is not fulfilling his potential."[4] By fourth grade, when Micha was only ten years old, he had already started missing school in favor of playing basketball with friends and wandering the open area surrounding the hills of Haifa. He loved working with his hands: fixing, assembling, creating. He and his friends used to build homemade firecrackers for fun! They used gunpowder from their parents' military bullets and sulfur from matches, assembling old, unused parts to create new objects. "I call it technology education by experimentation," he tells me. He wasn't afraid; on the contrary, he remembers sensing that everything would be okay, that he could achieve whatever he wanted and that he was capable. Being brought up with the passionate risk takers that were his parents, it's no wonder Micha went on to become the serial entrepreneur he is today.

Micha's own story continued at Haifa University, where he studied law and specialized in intellectual property. But as doers like Micha aren't meant to sit behind desks, Micha soon decided to turn the page and start again.

In 2003, Micha founded Keynesis together with his partner, a Russian researcher whom he'd never met in person. The company provided security software for the banking and aviation industries and was successful from the moment it launched. More than anything, Keynesis was born out of the need for a fresh start and a self-written narrative, so typical of the Kaufman family. Micha's first entrepreneurial success, however, was short-lived. A couple of years later, he founded Invisia, a patent-development start-up that focused on vision improvement, and then in 2005 he founded Spotback.com, whose technology mirrored those of Outbrain and Taboola today. Going up against experienced, better-funded competitors, particularly in the case of Spotback.com, led to the company's imminent demise. Failing at his ventures but learning that not all stories have happy endings, Micha sat down to write his best seller.

In 2007, Micha initiated the Accelerate think tank, which aimed to create a space for brainstorming with like-minded experts and tech influencers about the future of software and the Internet. In 2009, a call between himself and Shai Wininger saw the idea of an online marketplace for freelance services emerge. Micha remembers the call from Shai, one out of many, many others, starting with: *"Listen, I have this idea..."* Usually, they would listen to each other, talk for few minutes, and move on. But this call felt different. The following morning Micha was still thinking about Shai's idea. And so was Shai. They felt this idea had a different kind of merit. Micha asked for a couple of days to come up with a solid business model. He wanted to make sure he was investing his resources and time in a position with huge potential and a positive impact on countless people. He took a few days to explore the concept and idea; the more he thought about it, the clearer he saw it—this could turn into a big company and bring value to a huge market.

Micha and Shai went on to build Fiverr, which today is one of the world's leading marketplaces for creative freelance services. Fiverr has revolutionized the old-school business of working with freelancers offline by creating a marketplace that allows anyone to order a digital service from its marketplace with a click of a button. Fiverr's "service as a product" or the "productization of services" is transforming the way we understand commerce and our role as service providers and consumers.

The success of Fiverr is largely due to a simple yet powerful idea—combination, or in Hebrew, *combina*. By combining the digital space with actual service givers, Fiverr provides an answer to a problem that used to be difficult to solve and often more expensive than it had to be. *Combina*, indeed deriving from "combination," means coming up with a nonofficial solution to a problem. It has the connotation of bypassing a bureaucratically laden system or authority that is just getting in the way. Connecting consumers with service providers the way Fiverr does may be unconventional, but it is hard to think of a more efficient, convenient solution.

This most recent—but certainly not final—chapter in Micha's life was built on the foundations of his past successes and failures, starting from his early childhood. "A lot of what turned me into the entrepreneur I am," he told me recently, "is the inspiration I got from my parents, and the support they provided me as a child, to explore my curiosity, doing things my way."

Micha can be proud of his parents. Another well-known parent practices the same approach. Jeff Bezos, the founder, chairman, CEO, and president of Amazon, who is currently the world's wealthiest person, and no doubt an extraordinary entrepreneur, is also the father of four young children. He testified that he "let his four kids play with knives at age 4 and power tools since age 7 or 8."[5] Why, exactly? he was asked. "Because allowing them to take risks and be self-reliant teaches resourcefulness—a key trait both in business and in daily life," he answered.

VALIDATION

FOR A START-UP or any business, thorough validation of their offering to the market is critical. The discovery of a need and of a solution to address that need is not enough to ensure success. Further steps are required in order to grow and establish actual market credibility.

Any business seeking to validate their model must focus diligently on achieving a good product—market fit, a process that starts with letting go of the theoretical demand entrepreneurs may have written in their business plans. They need to ascertain the actual demand for their product or service in the markets.

This is when opening oneself to collecting feedback and input from outside your business becomes essential; when it is critical to be receptive to signals from the target market; when revisiting your assumptions and hypotheses is beneficial; when you might need to reassess the boundaries and constraints you initially defined, such as: Who is my target audience? What is the most effective business model? What is my competitive advantage? What do I do when I realize my assumptions were all wrong?

In the validation stage, entrepreneurs will want to turn their attention to some new muscles: openness to criticism, testing limits, resilience, experimentation, and maybe the most important one—tolerance of failure.

Reflecting on the Israeli childhood journey, I realized that we start working exactly these muscles at a very young age, resulting in flexible, agile, resourceful, and collaborative children.

4

IN HEBREW, THERE IS AN "I" IN "WE"

Out of the ashes of the Holocaust rose the State of Israel. Founded in 1948, Israel was one of the many countries created in the wake of World War II. European Jews who had survived the Holocaust, now refugees, came by the boatload to the ports of Haifa and Jaffa. They were joined by Jews fleeing anti-Semitism in the surrounding Arab countries, Iran, and North Africa. Waiting for them were men and women who had come to Palestine from all over the world with dreams of creating a Jewish state.

The building of the State of Israel was an arduous task. One famous Israeli children's song describes how it happened:

MY LAND OF ISRAEL
by Datia Ben Dor[1]

My land of Israel is beautiful and blooming
Who built and who planted?
All of us together!
I built a house in the land of Israel
So we have a land
And we have a house in the land of Israel. . . .

Throughout the song, different speakers present their personal contributions:

I planted a tree . . . ; I paved a road . . . ; I built a bridge.

Each of these lines is answered by a chorus of voices, which sings:

So we have a country,
we have a tree,
we have a road.

To the question: "Who built and who planted?"
The answer is: "All of us together!"
"My Land of Israel" is known by heart by every Israeli boy and girl. It is taught in schools throughout Israel, usually in preparation for Independence Day. I learned that song when I was in preschool, and so did my kids. Through this song, we learned how Israel was built through the joint effort of individuals, each doing a specific task but all together creating a country and a culture.

This simple children's song, still taught in schools today, is both symbolic and insightful. It expresses a unique aspect of Israeli society: the positive tension that exists between the group and the individual. It's been that way from the beginning.

Soon after the country's founding, my mother emigrated from Poland. My father was an immigrant from Egypt, arriving during the same period. They met at Ben-Gurion University in Beersheba, in the south of Israel. The truth is, they did not have much in common; they came from very different cultures, didn't share a native language, and had wildly different upbringings. But they fell in love. And they did have a common goal that united them beyond their personal love for each other: they wanted to build their home and family in the new State of Israel, alongside immigrants from seventy different nationalities who shared the same vision.

All these immigrants needed to learn a new language—a

shared language with which to craft their individual futures and their shared destiny. In Hebrew, the root of the word for "I" is *an*; this is also the base of the word for "we" or "us." ("I" is *ani*; "we" is *anu* or *anachnu*.) The "I" and the "we" are inextricably linked here. I like to think that in Israel, as in the Hebrew language, we've managed to turn the old adage "there is no 'I' in 'we'" on its head.

POSITIVE TENSION

Cultures are often divided into two types: individualistic or collectivist, with most leaning toward one or the other. In individualistic cultures, it's up to each person to provide for their own and their families' material and emotional needs; in collectivist cultures, individuals are quickly and thoroughly integrated into strong, cohesive in-groups. Countries in Western Europe and the United States are generally individualistic. In these countries, personal achievements and the individual's rights are of primary importance. In contrast, countries like Guatemala, China, Japan, and South Korea are at the other end of the spectrum. In these countries, unselfish behavior, the importance of the extended family, and cooperation are highly valued.

However, just because a culture is individualistic, or collectivist, does not eliminate the tension between the two values. Everyone has the human need both to feel a sense of group belonging and to establish themselves as differentiated individuals. Our personal identities—made up of idiosyncratic attitudes, memories, and behaviors—and our social identities—derived from the groups to which we belong—develop hand in hand, but with differing balances between the two.

According to Matthew Hornsey, a psychology professor at the University of Queensland, in individualistic societies, "the self is usually prioritized above the group, and group membership is valuable to the extent that it allows freedom of personal expression."[2]

Unlike in collectivist cultures, where being nonconformist and rejecting group pressure is perceived as a sign of immaturity, here it is seen as a virtue.

One who knows how to balance the tension between the individual and collective basic human needs is Benny Levin. If ever there was a true sabra in Israel, it is Benny. A sabra is any Jewish person born in Israel, a rare breed just fifty years ago. What is even more incredible is that Benny's parents, and even grandparents, were sabras. They were born in Israel before the establishment of the state. Benny's grandfather was the first winemaker in the area; he worked at Carmel Winery and later was a successful exporter. Benny was born in the same house that his mother was born in and that her father had received from the famous Baron Edmond de Rothschild. He was born to the quintessential Israeli family and went on to have the quintessential Israeli childhood.

Benny was a Tzofim (Israeli scouts) cadet, turned guide, turned supervisor. After high school he went on a unique Israel Defense Forces (IDF) track called Atuda, a program that lets high school graduates defer their drafts, attend university, and then join the army as officers (doctors, engineers, etc.). Benny studied electronics engineering and then served in Unit 8200 of the elite IDF Intelligence Corps.

But while many Atuda alumni turn their IDF service into a military career, Benny decided, after serving as a technology officer for fourteen years, to gather seven friends from the unit, and together they set off on a different path. In typical Israeli fashion, they went on a business venture, not knowing what they wanted to do, just that they wanted to do it, and do it together. Making the most of their significant set of skills, in 1986 they founded Nice Systems, a software company that became an Israeli technology mammoth. Benny left Nice after fifteen years as the company's CEO, not because he grew tired of working but because he realized it was time to pass the torch. In 2001 he cofounded dbMotion, a company that specializes in helping health-care organizations leverage their data assets, a real pioneer in health-care data management, where he took the chairman position. In 2013, the company was acquired by Allscripts for hundreds of millions of dollars.

It was at this point in time that Benny realized he has been a part of a team all his life, from very early childhood through his military service and all through his career. He decided to quit the aspect of the business world that only deals with exit strategies and turn to the social sector. He has been involved in the fields of health care, education, and employment ever since. Together with Shlomo Dovrat, Eric Benhamou, Itzik Danziger, and Nir Barkat, all successful entrepreneurs, Benny founded Israel Venture Network—IVN—in 2001. The platform's first project was providing practical management tools to school managers and municipalities. This was unique. Not only was Benny involving the third sector with the world of technology and business, he was finally making the most of all the skills he had acquired throughout his childhood, military service, and business career. IVN now boasts over fifty social business portfolios, including youth-at-risk projects, people with disabilities, and economically disadvantaged populations, promoting employment and reducing poverty in the ultra-Orthodox sector; addressing special needs communities; and so on—an exemplary fusion of business acumen, technological knowledge, and social goals. If you wish to meet him today, you will most probably be asked to visit the youth villages Benny is chairing, helping underprivileged kids, strengthening their sense of belonging, and equipping them with the skills needed for the future. All of Benny's projects are centered on the idea of a team, of the meaning and power of belonging to a group. JDOCU, his latest project, involves a group of philanthropists/amateur photographers who travel to remote areas in the world, documenting isolated Jewish communities. Upon landing back in Israel, he returns to his own little team—his wife of forty-one years, their two children, and their six grandchildren.

As I suggested above, Israeli society seems to have created a more balanced blend of individualist and collectivist cultures. This is not to say that the tension between the individual and the collective does not exist, merely that both values coexist without stepping on each other's toes.

But it is when the individual's and group's goals align that you really see projects take off. On their last day of school, my nine-year-old son's class was informed that they would be responsible for the ceremony marking the opening of the following school year. You can imagine their excitement: they would be standing onstage on the first day of school, performing, singing, dancing, and welcoming the first-graders coming to school for the first time.

They remembered how they had felt only three years before: excited, probably even frightened on their first day as first-graders. Now, they had a common goal, a project they'd have to work on during their summer vacation, or at least for the last week of summer vacation. And here's the surprise: their teacher told them they could all participate, and it was up to them to decide how. Instead of informing them who would do what, they were to tell *her* what they were going to do. Some wanted to emcee the event; others to be responsible for the audio; some wanted to dance or sing—so they get to pick the songs and come up with the dances. As a group, they were responsible for pulling it off, with the support of each other and of their teacher, but within that framework, there was plenty of space for their individualism to develop and to shine.

GROUP DIVERSITY

You may be wondering where this positive tension comes from. I would argue that it stems from the diversity of Israel's population. As one of the most heterogeneous countries in the world, Israel has a population that consists primarily of immigrants from more than seventy different countries, making diversity one of the country's greatest assets. In fact, in 2014, 25 percent of the Jewish-Israeli population consisted of immigrants, 35 percent were children of immigrants, and another 40 percent were second-generation Israeli. This culturally diverse population is one of the reasons it is so hard to answer the question: "Who is the Israeli?" It's because there is no one type of Israeli. There are Moroccans, Russians, Polish, Ethiopians, Americans, Egyptians, Ukrainians, Uzbeks, and the list goes on.

It is well documented that group diversity is a hotbed for creativity and innovation. Each individual brings the traditions, knowledge, and qualities of his or her country of origin to the new one, thus enriching its population. On a national level, diversity has a tremendous, positive influence on a country's culture and economy.

It is enough to look at the numerous successful American companies that were founded by immigrants or their children. According to a report by the New American Economy Research Fund, first- and second-generation immigrants make up 40 percent of Fortune 500 companies. Mind you, these are not small companies. "Many of America's greatest brands—Apple, Google, AT&T, Budweiser, Colgate, eBay, General Electric, IBM, and McDonald's to name just a few—owe their origin to a founder who was an immigrant or the child of an immigrant."[3]

As in America, Israel's immigrant society is closely connected to its successful start-up culture. There are a number of reasons for this. For starters, immigrants are inherently risk takers and hard workers. They make the brave decision to leave their home countries and familiar communities to set off on their own. Upon arriving in a new land, immigrants find themselves in an unfamiliar environment to which they must quickly adapt. This requires them to react rapidly and take on challenges outside their comfort zone. In Israel, this kind of personal ambition is often channeled into collective projects and goals.

Like my parents nearly seventy years ago, immigrants to Israel usually share a vision: to take an active part in the construction of Israel, to inhabit the land and be part of the culture that is formed upon it. Their group identity is built upon a shared goal.

As is the case with many great entrepreneurs, Kira Radinsky's journey began in a foreign country and ended with her in Israel with not much more than the clothes on her back. It was 1990 in the Ukraine when the Radinsky family women—including four-year-old Kira, her mom, aunt, and grandmother—decided to pack their bags and immigrate to Israel. After an arduous journey that involved armed Hungarian soldiers shoving people onto an airplane, Kira and her family finally landed in Israel, without their luggage.[4]

They arrived right on time for the Gulf War. With no belongings, no gas masks, and the sound of sirens in the background, Kira and her aunt went to the beach. "What do you want to be when you grow up?" her aunt asked her. Kira sank her feet into the sand and said, "A scientist, of course." That didn't surprise her aunt. Kira had grown up in a family of engineers, where intellectual excellence was a way of life that allowed a level of prominence in the Ukraine's mediocre lifestyle.

At fifteen, Kira was already a student at the Technion, from which she graduated with honors. At eighteen, she joined an intelligence unit in the Israel Defense Forces, where she and her team received the Israel Defense Prize for developing a technology that was later used in the 2006 Lebanon War. Her days in the military, including the screening processes, introduced her to a different environment than she was used to. For the first time, she was faced with topics she knew nothing about. Armed with the knowledge that she could learn anything and fast, she began teaching herself. It was the first time she wasn't the best in her class. This both challenged and motivated her. Barely a year following her discharge from the military, she was already completing her master's and heading toward her doctorate in computer science. This was a natural step for Kira, the immigrant child who was taught to admire intellectual excellence.

At twenty-three years of age, Kira married her childhood friend (who wooed her at age eight by solving a complex mathematical problem) and was eager to release the explorer inside her. Kira quickly became a well-known and respected academic and an employee in Microsoft's Research Department. As part of her PhD work, Kira developed an algorithm-based prediction program. She fed enormous amounts of data to a machine that analyzed it based on time-lapse patterns, and could then produce patterns of prediction. It was successful. The data, which included 150 years of news, social media, search-engine results, and more, enabled Kira to predict momentous events, including the extreme wave of violence that swept Sudan after the rise of gas prices in 2013, and the cholera outbreak in Cuba, 130 years after the last outbreak had been recorded. Her mom, aunt, and grandmother were so proud of her scientific achievements. They were therefore extremely surprised, not to mention disappointed, when Kira told them she was leaving Microsoft and moving on to expand the limits of her discovery. "Let's see where else this could work," she thought. Inspired by the Israeli mind-set of risk taking, exploration, and big dreams, she stepped out of her comfort zone. And, lo and behold, in 2012, together with Yaron Zakai-Or, Kira founded SalesPredict, an economy prediction platform. The company, where Kira works to this day, was acquired by eBay in 2016 for $40 million.

The implications of Kira's contribution to the field of predictive analytics are immeasurable. Applying human thinking patterns to a machine that has the capacity to analyze infinite amounts of data can transform any field, from e-commerce to medicine to politics. The successful experiments Kira performed raise serious questions about the future of artificial intelligence and how we currently leverage the massive amounts of data available to us.

Like all the women in her family, Kira is now a self-made success and a working mother of a girl and a baby boy. Regarding her future, it screams success. But for her mom, aunt, and grandmother, there are things that can't be 100 percent predicted. One thing is for sure: Kira is encouraging her two-year-old daughter to dream big, whatever her dreams may be. "I'm not telling her how and what to do. I want her to be independent," Kira says.

THE BENEFITS OF THE GANG

Did you ever stay up late as a child, hiding under a blanket with a flashlight, reading a Nancy Drew or Hardy Boys mystery? For Israeli children it is the Hasamba series that keeps them awake long after bedtime. Similar to Nancy Drew and the Hardy Boys, the main characters in Hasamba are children who solve mysteries and crimes. Hasamba is a Hebrew acronym for "an absolutely, definitely secret gang." The adventures of the Hasamba gang first appeared in 1949 and it quickly became one of the most popular children's book series in Hebrew, selling over a million copies. However, unlike its American counterpart, these are stories about a group of children who fight crime together, not just one or two children. This small detail represents a huge cultural difference.

Childhood in Israel is oriented toward group cooperation, community building, and maintaining and expanding social networks. Consequently, the "gang" becomes extremely important. In English, the word *gang* generally carries a negative connotation. Translated into Hebrew, a gang is *chavura* (plural, *chavurot*) and its connotations couldn't be more positive. A *chavura* is a group of young adults or children who spend most of their free time together. They know each other from school, from extracurricular activities, or from the neighborhood. In Israel, *chavurot* form the social network of children and oftentimes adults.

Remember the junkyard at preschool? Or the Lag B'Omer bon-fire events? Where children optimize their fun by collaborating and working in teams? These are just specific examples of how most childhood moments in Israel are experienced within a group. Daniel, my fourteen-year-old son, has his own gang—a group of friends who have been together since kindergarten. Starting when they were in first grade, they would meet up almost every after-noon to play soccer on the school field, not as part of an organized after-school activity with an instructor but on their own. One of them was responsible for bringing the ball. But others might bring one just in case he forgot. Somehow it worked.

By the time they were in third and fourth grade, they would on occasion open their group to other kids, boys and girls. But while these "outsiders" would come and go, the core members of the gang remained constant, creating a strong support group for one another. In the fifth and sixth grades, they each started ex-panding their friendships, beyond the gang. But, somehow, they also made a point of continuing to see each other, even when they moved on to junior high and each went to a different school. To this day, the gang plays an important role in Daniel's life. He told me recently: "Mommy, they are like brothers to me. I always know they are there for me if I need them. And I feel very comfortable just being around them."

Paul Graham, start-up guru and founder of Y Combinator, says that "friendship" is among the five most important elements he seeks in founders of start-ups: "Empirically it seems to be hard to start a start-up with just one founder. Most of the big successes have two or three. And the relationship between the founders has to be strong. They must genuinely like one another, and work well together."[5] In fact, 95 percent of the individuals who try to start a business have either involved others to some significant capacity or intend to in the near future. About 50 percent of ventures start in teams, with entrepreneurs mainly drawing on their core social networks during the founding stages.

Like with Daniel's gang, you want to surround yourself with potentially long-term partners as cofounders, ones you can really trust. This is the case for me and my cofounder/co-CEO at our company, Synthesis. We met more than twenty years ago, at university. We established a strong friendship, although most of the time we lived in different countries. As individuals, we bring different strengths and weaknesses to our partnership. But we have learned how to work together, toward a common goal and a shared vision. We found a balance that optimizes our collaboration. And every now and again, we recalibrate it.

5

FREE TO BE

It's Monday, 1:30 p.m. I'm at the office, at a team meeting. My cell phone rings and I recognize the number—it's Yarden, my nine-year-old son. I ask my colleagues to excuse me, telling them it's my son calling, and answer the phone. "Hi, Mommy. Can Roni come over?" School just ended for the day, and Yarden, like most of his friends, will walk home, a distance of about nine hundred feet, by himself. He has the key to the house, and once he gets home, first thing, he needs to take Moon, our dog, for a short walk. By the time he and Moon return, Daniel, his thirteen-year-old brother, will have arrived home from junior high. They will heat up the lunch I prepared for them that morning, do their home-work, watch TV, or go outside to play with friends. "Of course, Yarden," I answer, "just don't forget Moon. There's chicken and rice for lunch, and please make sure to make yourself a fresh salad. Roni is more than welcome to join you, okay?" I hang up and turn back to my colleagues and the business at hand.

This story is very familiar to most Israelis. Commonly, both parents work, and often come home at 6:00 or even 7:00 p.m., which means children spend entire afternoons by themselves, unsuper-vised. By force of necessity, children must learn to take responsi-bility for themselves, which provides a great sense of achievement and pride. In 1986, Roger Hart, a child-rights academic, conducted an experiment in rural New England in which he tracked the movements of eighty-six children in the local elementary school, to create what he called a "geography of children," including actual maps that would show where and how far the children typically roamed away from home. The experiment revealed to Hart that for "the children, each little addition to their free range—being allowed to cross a paved road or go to the center of town—was a sign of growing up. The kids took special pride in knowing how to get places, and in finding shortcuts that adults wouldn't normally use."[1]

More than just circumstance, being able to walk around freely, without supervision and, most important, without a fixed plan on where you're going, is something Israelis regard as a positive personality trait. In Hebrew, this quality is called *leezrom* (literally, "to go with the flow"). *Leezrom* may seem like something that just comes naturally to some, but when it becomes a cultural phenomenon, consistently fostered from early childhood, it takes on a deeper meaning. For Israelis, it's a way of life. *Leezrom* requires one to be prepared for the unplanned and to accept it with open arms. More than simply being spontaneous, it is a powerful and enjoyable view on life and all its unexpectedness.

So while this empowering approach to child rearing has vanished from many Western countries, Israel has held its ground. It's worth noting, however, that, as with most other aspects of Israeli culture, giving children freedom and encouraging them *leezrom* is not a thought-out philosophy. On the contrary, it is born out of the necessities of life in Israel, though it isn't wholly unique to it.

CHILDREN ON THEIR OWN

Various cultures around the world encourage children to take on responsibilities, whether out of necessity or principle. In the Netherlands, for example, children sometimes go from door to door offering simple cleaning services in exchange for one euro (*"Heitje voor een Karweitje"*). In other countries, it is natural for kids to walk home from school by themselves, or to hang out with their friends in the neighborhood, especially if they live in a village or a suburban area.

However, in countries like the United States, China, and France, giving children this amount of freedom is a very unfamiliar parenting strategy (albeit for very different reasons). With all the dangers one is exposed to and the overemphasis of tragedies in the media, it is not surprising that parents become anxious about their child's safety.

Although it is understandable, some caution that the result of this parenting approach is children who grow up to be adults who are incapable of dealing with the risks and possibilities the world has to offer. "Parents' most important task is to help young people to become independent and autonomous. When we infantilize our young, we stifle their development," says Robert Epstein, visiting scholar at the University of California at San Diego, and West Coast editor of *Psychology Today*.[2] The concern is not just that children with limited freedom and risk-taking possibilities may lack the confidence to function independently in the adult world later. What is more pressing is that they are not motivated to do so.

If children are always instructed regarding their academic activity, play, and social behavior, their motivation for success may not be their own. The motivation to succeed and to develop a social life will stem from their parents, as opposed to from the child himself. Dr. John Mark Froiland, currently clinical assistant professor in educational psychology in the College of Education at Purdue University, explains: "When it does come from the parent, the motivation is related to the parent's ideas and desires, as opposed to the child's. Naturally, the child, in later life, will be less inclined to think on his own or to set goals for himself to pursue.

If the motivation is intrinsic it is necessarily far more powerful than if it is external and is forced upon the child."[3]

Since parents understand the importance of achieving good grades in school, many tend to overencourage behavior that is aimed at doing just that. The result of this, however, is often the opposite of the intended outcome. For example, in a 1989 study conducted by the child psychologists Richard Fabes and colleagues, it appeared that "rewarding children for helping sort pieces of paper for sick children undermined their subsequent helping behavior." This suggests that rewarding behavior in the moment may not be a good strategy for encouraging that behavior long-term. A similar study from 1983 performed on older students found that "payments undermined undergraduates' sense of moral obligation to help a blind person, and this in turn deterred helpful behavior toward this person."[4] Indeed, for both children and adults, being able to choose an action as opposed to being told to do it is one of the strongest determining factors in decision making.

CALL ME YAEL

When Yarden, my nine-year-old, leaves school at 1:30, heading home by himself, he will walk down the main corridor of his school. If his school principal happens to step out of her office at that moment, he will wave to her and say, "Bye, Yael." A straightforward, informal, casual bye-bye. Yael will smile at him and say, "Bye, Yarden. Enjoy your afternoon." She knows all the kids by name. And the children address her, as well as all their teachers, by their first names as well.

Aside from its informality, which I do think is significant in ways I'll get into later, the typical classroom experience in Israel looks much like what you'd find around the world. Children are expected to consume knowledge in order to regurgitate it later in an exam; to answer questions someone else has already solved. On the global scale, Israel is falling behind in the academic achievements of its youth. According to PISA (Program for International Student Assessment), Israel is at the bottom 40 percent when it comes to mathematics and science. Out of the seventy-two countries that participated in the PISA test in 2015, Israel came in fortieth place. Israel consistently lags behind countries like China, Singapore, Japan, South Korea, Switzerland, and Austria, while surpassing countries like Peru, Indonesia, Qatar, and Colombia. Yet, Israel has the highest density of start-ups per capita in the world and is ranked number three in innovation, according to the World Economic Forum. How is it that a country so successful in tech entrepreneurship, requiring extensive usage of mathematics, science, finance, and business, can be so far behind in its math and science formal education?

The answer to this question lies in the difference between what is necessary to do well in academic environments versus what is required to succeed as an entrepreneur and innovator. Keep in mind: the changes that are overtaking the industrial world are so extreme, and happen so fast, many industry observers term them the Fourth Industrial Revolution. According to the World Economic Forum, "current technological trends are bringing about an unprecedented rate of change in the core curriculum content of many academic fields, with nearly 50 percent of subject knowledge acquired during the first year of a four-year technical degree outdated by the time students graduate."[5]

So, the academic training we're providing young people is largely useless. But, in any event, the assumption that excellence in education translates into scientific innovation and business prowess is not necessarily correct. In Israel counterexamples abound.

Guy Ruvio, a successful Israeli cyber-automotive entrepreneur, recalls that he used to skip class a lot:

Those days I used to walk around the Hebrew University, looking for interesting things. One day I saw an unsolved

problem written on the board in one of the faculties—
network optimization. I told myself I'm not going back to
school until I figure this out. After some time, I came up
with a possible direction, which I thought could be interesting. I didn't even know the term *start-up* at the time but
finally I went to my computer teacher. I hadn't been going
to class, but I told him I had this idea and suggested we
work on it together. He agreed, and we started building the
network. In the end it didn't take off but still I remember it
as one of the most significant projects I was part of.[6]

Guy was used to thinking of teachers as approachable figures;
after all, he'd been calling them by their first names since he
was a boy. Perhaps this was part of what allowed him to make a
proposal others may have been too timid to attempt. Still, Guy's
teacher would have been well within his rights if he'd said that
Guy needed to come to class before they could talk about working
on a project together, but he didn't. He was open to a young man,
one who was dismissive of the official education system norms, and
took a chance on him. Guy's passion for mathematics and networks
never ceased and brought him to explore the cyberspace that he
became an expert at, eventually merging the start-up he founded,
TowerSec Automotive Cybersecurity, with the world's leading
automotive giant Harman.

THE IMPORTANCE OF GETTING STUCK

There's an old Hebrew saying that when it comes to self-defense,
one should always try to beat their attacker to the punch, a principle that Adi Sharabani has dedicated his life to.

Every step he took brought Adi closer to becoming an industry leader in the field of application security, and a specialist in

preemptive protection systems. He dedicated many years to the IDF as a security consultant and education adviser. After earning a bachelor of science in mathematics and physics from Tel Aviv University and doing research there, he moved into the business realm. Adi joined IBM through the acquisition of Watchfire—a Canadian start-up leveraging Israeli technology—and after a few years he was tasked to oversee the security of IBM software products. In 2012, Adi cofounded and was CEO of Skycure, a start-up company that redefined the mobile threat defense industry. The company was later acquired by global security tech leader Symantec, where Adi is now senior vice president. Over the years he perfected his methods and accumulated over twenty-five patents in the security space.

In the spirit of planning ahead, Adi is also a key educational figure. Besides being a regular contributor to the RSA conference, the world's largest IT security conference, which attracts more than forty thousand visitors every year; a high school teacher; and an education adviser; Adi has also helped establish cybersecurity education as a national mission. He is instrumental in constructing the vision of and implementing the cyber defense curriculum for Israeli high school students majoring in cybersecurity. "The earlier we start," he says, "the better."[7]

Israel, like many other nations, has developed an array of informal educational institutions and programs with the help of people like Adi. Their novel and shared approach to education is that they all tend to value the learning process over the practical knowledge gained. Adi explains: "What we do in these programs is take a child's ability and make him run with it. The purpose is not to teach the kids a certain skill in the sense of 'how-to.' The purpose is the vector, the movement, the progress itself as opposed to the final goal." According to Adi, the secret of the popularity and success of such programs is to allow, no, actually, to *make* the children get stuck:

We are not really interested in teaching children to take
a skill that they acquired and apply it to another field. Instead, we are focused on increasing the ability to create new
skills in realms we are not really aware of today. That is a
hard task, and our practice shows that the way to do that
is by bringing the children to a place where they are truly
stuck, do not know the answer, and no one will give it to
them. . . . Therefore, true growth, true teaching, comes from
that place of not knowing the solution, trying to figure out
an answer regardless of whether you find it or not.

Gilad, a seventeen-year-old from Ashdod, describes a typical
experience in one of these enrichment programs: "We are given
basic coding skills and then they throw us into the deep end. We
are challenged by complex assignments such as building a chess
game, without instructions, in an autodidactic way. This year my
group is working on a car-robot that drives according to certain
calculations and knows how to scan and map the area to which it
wants to go, manually and automatically."

And like in Israeli schools, the programs contradict the image
of the teacher as the ultimate authority figure. Teachers aren't
seen as necessarily expert and inexhaustible sources of knowledge. Adi recalls:

When we first started the cyber program, we thought that
it would be a good trigger to start the do-it-yourself process
of thought because the amount of knowledge you need to
have before you get stuck is rather small. When we started
training schoolteachers, it looked like it was going to be a
complete flop for the simple reason that the teachers did not
have enough experience and expertise in the cyber field. But
what happened then was fascinating. It created scenarios in
which the teachers looked the kids in the eyes and honestly

said, "I don't know." And this suddenly brings us back to a place where teachers and students are actually having a conversation; they are brainstorming and enabling the process of getting stuck. One does not simply feed data to the other, rather they both grow together, and they reach places no one has ever thought of. The teacher, in this approach, is not a funnel of facts but a conveyor of methodology.

If the purpose of education is the transfer of knowledge, then programs that refuse to give their students free knowledge are groundbreaking—and, apparently, effective.

Assessment methods in these programs are also radical. Rather than measuring the students' successes, the instructors measure their failures as a better indicator of their learning. "If you managed to solve twenty exercises, I, as an educator, have wasted your time. Since you already knew how to solve [the exercises], you made no progress, you've learned nothing."

An Israeli educational institute that promotes an interdisciplinary approach to learning is the Young Persons' Institute for the Promotion of Creativity and Excellence–The Erika Landau Institute. An alternative educational institution for gifted children, its purpose is to nurture creativity, social skills, and independent thinking.

Erika Landau, its founder, developed a unique educational approach that encourages learning through hands-on experiences in a multitude of fields. Landau believed that "the purpose of education is not to know but to experience."[8] The things we remember best, according to her, are those we experienced firsthand. Professor Ran Balicer, a graduate of the institute, explains the rationale behind this approach:

It is no longer enough to be an expert. It's not enough to be very, very skilled in one thing. . . . The exceptionally talented people today, those who make real, profound changes in our world, are not those who are extremely good at their profession but those who can connect the tastes from different worlds. This is the essence of this institution. It raises children and young adults whose way of thinking is of making unusual connections, of doubting, daring conventional wisdom, daring to dig deep and to investigate, and never accepting "No" or "This can't be done" as the end of the road but only as the beginning of a new path, a new challenge: "So how do we make it a yes?"[9]

Professor Balicer still does not accept a no. Today he is a public health physician and researcher; the founding director of the Clalit Research Institute, an award-winning data-driven health innovation center; and director of Health Policy Planning at Clalit—Israel's largest health-care organization. In these roles, he is responsible for strategic planning and development of innovative organization-wide interventions for improving health-care quality, reducing disparities, and introducing novel data and artificial intelligence–driven tools into health-care practice to increase care effectiveness.

Israeli children may not score high on standardized tests, but they are certainly not falling behind. It is the learning process and not the test result that is crucial. It is not so much what our children know but rather how they came to know it.

In the business context, results are important. But not exclusively. The processes, the capabilities, the opportunities, the confidence to try, get stuck, and overcome—these are no less important for a business to succeed over time. So, let your colleagues spend time defining their own goals, let them tackle big challenges, let them get stuck, and don't feel like you need to have all the answers.

6

FAILURE IS AN OPTION

The year is 1965 and three generations gather in a two-hundred-square-foot living room in Ramat Gan, Israel: Avraham, the family's elder, a transcriber by profession, is leaning over his craft; his son, Baruch, a mechanic, is rummaging through his toolbox; and ten-year-old Dov Moran, the family's successor, is fixated on digital watch parts he ordered by mail from a company advertising in the last page of *Mad* magazine, trying to fix them or to build another from a few good working watches. Surrounded by both the past and the future, this small living room is where Dov took his first steps in his journey to inventing the USB memory stick and becoming one of Israel's most notable industry leaders.

Despite an early childhood clash with the education system (notably the kindergarten teacher who assured his mother that Dov was "not ready" for first grade), Dov quickly demonstrated outstanding academic skills. At age sixteen, he'd sat through computer programming courses at Tel Aviv University. Being first in his class (even now he claims that he did not deserve the award he received for this achievement), it was only natural for Dov to pursue a programming career. However, as his family would have told him, men plan, and God laughs. And so he found himself graduating from the Technion with a degree in electrical engineering and later serving in the Israeli Navy as a commander of the advanced microprocessing department.

Reaching such academic heights was not easy for Dov. Indeed, anxiety and fear of risk were an inseparable part of Dov's childhood. His father and grandfather were the only members of the family who escaped the horrors of war-torn Europe to come to Israel and start anew. And his mother, Bina, escaped to Israel from Blonie, Poland. Being a child of Holocaust survivors meant growing up in a constant state of angst. Even a walk to the local library proved a test of resilience for his parents, who couldn't help but follow their son quietly from the other side of the street.

Considering his childhood, it's perhaps ironic that Dov became one of Israel's top risk takers. But if we look at his father, we see an honest man who worked until the day he passed away, ninety years old and tall as an oak. And if we look at his grandfather, who shared a room with Dov for most of his childhood and saw Dov's education as his final, perhaps most successful life project (accompanying him throughout his early life until the day he first wore his navy uniform), then we realize there's nothing ironic about Dov's success. He is a man who grew up in a house that was painfully aware of risk but bravely pursued a better future.

In 1989 Dov founded M-Systems, a global leader in the flash data storage market. Together with his team, he invented the USB flash drive and scaled the company to enjoy $1 billion in revenue. In 2006, it was acquired by SanDisk for $1.55 billion, the largest acquisition Israel had seen. In 2007, Dov founded Modu. By 2011, its intellectual property was acquired by Google. And the infinite list of accomplishments continues. From Kidoz to GlucoMe and Comigo, RapidAPI to Grove Ventures, his name features on forty patents, beyond the technologies that were acquired. Dov was also the chairman of Tower Semiconductor, a semiconductor device fabrication company based in the northern part of Israel.

When asked about his greatest success, he points to his leading a turnaround of this company, taking it from near bankruptcy to a great success, valued at Nasdaq at several billion dollars. He has left a footprint on every aspect of Israel's tech industry, as CEO, founder, board member, investor, and inspirational mentor and figurehead.

Dov's story is unique in that it doesn't fully belong to him. His narrative is part of his parents' story, his grandfather's story, their families, and their families before them. It is a story of generations and of people who built a nation against all odds.

My path crossed Dov's in late 2006 when I joined the founding team of Modu. At the time, there was hype surrounding Modu in Israel and it showed much promise. In a very short period of time, Modu raised more than $120 million, recruited over two hundred employees, opened subsidiaries around the world, and developed and manufactured two consumer products that were marketed under Modu's brand. All the elements for success were there. And yet, only three years after its founding, the company closed its doors.

This was an extremely difficult time for my colleagues and me. We believed in the company and its products and were proven wrong. But here's an interesting fact: many of Modu's two hundred employees went on to establish their own start-ups, including me. Out of the ashes of one big failure, dozens of new business ventures sprouted. How were those who'd given so much of their time, energy, and resources only to see their work go down the drain not discouraged? Rather, they decided to invest more energy, take more risks, and start ventures of their own. This is a bold move, since 90 percent of start-ups fail and the 10 percent of start-ups that make it get close to falling apart along the way.

What motivates people who've failed—like myself and my colleagues at Modu—to try again? For me, it was perceiving Modu's failure as an opportunity for professional growth—a motivating

factor rather than a discouraging one. Now, I believed, I know
what not to do. Next time I'll have a better chance of success.

THE UPSIDE OF FAILURE

The idea that failure affords a learning opportunity is crucial for
any entrepreneurial mind-set. In many cultures, however, failure
is avoided at all cost. As we saw in the previous chapter, many
parents attempt to protect their children from any kind of failure.

However, numerous psychologists today warn that those who
were deprived of failure in their childhood will pay the price in
their adult life. Having never experienced failure, they haven't
acquired the skills necessary to deal with it, emotionally or practically. Instead of viewing failure as an opportunity to reflect on
what went wrong and to learn to improve next time, they view
failure as an innate part of their selfhood and, therefore, find it
extremely hard to overcome. In Israel, failure is most often viewed
as both an inevitable part of life and as something that can be and
needs to be overcome.

Today it sounds inconceivable but, up until 1993, there was
only one television channel in Israel. It was appropriately called
"The Israeli Television" and dutifully watched by every Israeli
family who owned a TV set. In 1978, an Israeli television show
called *Zehu Ze!* (*That's It!*) was first broadcast and immediately
became a hit. One of the show's most famous characters is Yatzek.
Sporting a bucket hat, Israeli flag, accordion, and gunslinger mus-
tache (Israeli culture can sometimes be a bit strange), Yatzek travels around Israel. At the end of every episode, Yatzek falls—from
a tree, into a river, from the back of a horse, and even into a cow
patty. Immediately afterward, he gets up and says: "Don't worry,
kids, Yatzek always falls and gets back up." A whole generation of
Israeli children grew up with the strong message of: "Don't worry.
When you fall, you can always get back up."

I DIDN'T FAIL, MY PROJECT DID

Don't get me wrong. Israeli culture does not encourage failure. Rather, it is somehow more tolerant and knows how to accept failure in such a way that we keep getting back up, trying, moving forward, and advancing.

Psychologist Steven Berglas promotes the idea that failure can be overcome if it is looked at from a different perspective. "The key to dealing with failure," Berglas says, "is differentiating between global and restricted attributions of failure. . . . If you make a global attribution—'The business failed because I suck'—then the failure will be devastating. But if you make a restricted attribution—'It failed because the Japanese were dumping product and I lost my VP of information systems at a crucial juncture'—then it won't be so destructive. It has to do with storytelling, and it's how you differentiate self from situation."[1] Berglas also adds that people who have interests other than business, anything from religion, to community service, to skydiving, tend to have an easier time making restricted attributions and shrugging off setbacks. This is because their sense of self-esteem is derived from multiple sources.

There are two main takeaways from what Berglas is describing. First is that how you handle failure depends on your perspective, on the story you tell yourself. Retracing the steps to understand what went wrong and why may help you build a story of failure that is restrictive, isolating what specific things led to the failure of the project. Failure can be told as something that happens to you and not something that you are. The second thing that we can learn from Berglas is that having a strong, supportive community life and other interests makes it easier to see failure as a constructive experience as opposed to something that defines you.

Jerry Useem, an editor at the *Atlantic*, writes: "There are three things to know about failure: 1. It happens. 2. It can be destructive in ways you've never imagined. 3. Believe it or not, there's a right way to do it."[2] According to Useem, the "right" way to fail is to learn from the experience. The first step is to separate the failure from the person. Failure is something you did or that happened to you, not something that defines you. The second step is to view failure as something positive—a learning opportunity.

Personally, I encourage a hands-on approach in anything that has to do with learning experiences. The best way to learn, I believe, is through personal experience. This idea is especially relevant for failure. One has to fail in order to learn, in order to grow. Modu's employees, having been part of an organization that failed, could reflect on the mistakes that were made. After Modu's failure, they had a better understanding of what they should and shouldn't do in their own entrepreneurial endeavors. They learned. And since the entrepreneur and the business are two separate entities, the entrepreneur can go on to create subsequent businesses.

IT'S NEVER TOO EARLY TO FAIL

I've missed more than 9,000 shots in my career. I've lost almost 300 games. Twenty-six times, I've been trusted to take the game-winning shot and missed. I've failed over and over and over again in my life. And that is why I succeed.[3]

—MICHAEL JORDAN

In recent years, there has been a growing phenomenon of rewarding children for everything they do, regardless of whether or not they have succeeded. This is especially evident in youth athletics teams, where everyone is considered a winner simply by virtue of participating. Not everyone agrees with this approach. Laura Miele, a writer for *Psychology Today*, argues that "contrary to what many would think, having an 'everyone's a winner' mentality in my daughter's youth softball league did not come as good news to me. In order to level the playing field, rules were altered to prevent children from striking out, getting tagged out, etc."[4] It seems that competitiveness is slowly gaining a bad reputation. But what happens once we eliminate the possibility of failing? We deprive our children of a powerful learning experience.

Failing is emotionally hard, which is why the motivation of those who went through it is incomparable to those who haven't. Failure, in many cases, is instrumental to meaningful success.

Parents who protect their children from failure when they're young often find themselves doing so into adulthood. Robert Epstein, whom we heard from in the previous chapter, recalls: "I've seen parents come to campus protesting a low grade. When I caught one student cheating on a paper, his mom called and demanded I let him write a new paper." Steve Rothberg, president and founder of the CollegeRecruiter.com career site, reports that "parents are writing resumes, applying to jobs and even attending interviews."[5]

We must ask ourselves whether we are depriving children of one of life's most valuable lessons when we save them from failure. As parents, watching your child fail can be painful. However, children are constantly learning. Every experience is registered and functions as a model for future behavior and understanding of the world. Why shouldn't games, sports, or anything else be considered a learning opportunity, an occasion to train and reinforce some of our soft skills?

Speaking of coping skills, the emotional aspect of failure is perhaps the hardest part to deal with. But like other skills we've been examining in this book, dealing with failure is one that can be acquired and practiced. Ashley Merryman, the author of the *New York Times* essay "Losing Is Good For You," referenced a Stanford psychology study that found that children who receive praise for effort rather than for achievement are more likely to see skills as something that can be improved, rather than an innate trait. This, of course, has everything to do with being an entrepreneur;

after all, it's not just about talent or luck, it's about trying, failing, improving, adapting, and, finally, making it.

Heidi Grant Halvorson, a social psychologist, mentions that when we try to eliminate failure we also eliminate a lot of our creative ability. Never failing has the disadvantage of not being able to handle new, challenging situations. "We start worrying about making mistakes," she explains, "because mistakes mean that we lack ability, and this creates a lot of anxiety and frustration. Anxiety and frustration, in turn, undermine performance by compromising our working memory, disrupting the many cognitive processes we rely on for creative and analytical thinking."[6] Trying to reach perfection in everything we do also results in our inability to behave in a way that drives us to explore, gain new knowledge, and learn new skills, or, in other words, to innovate. This last point is crucial. If we are constantly concerned about failing, we hardly ever allow ourselves to try. This is the perfect recipe for ruining the entrepreneurial spirit, which, given that 90 percent of all start-ups fail, very much relies on risk taking.

Considering the practical lessons both adults and children learn from failure, the emotional growth they achieve by failing, and the healthy state of mind they adopt after having failed and tried again, it is safe to say that failure is one of the entrepreneur's most valuable experiences. Failure is an important, positive part of life, and not something that cannot be overcome.

On a personal level, I admit, I fail at least once a day, whether it's in my personal life as a mother of three young boys or as a businesswoman. From this, I've learned that one of the things that really makes me happy is that my children are growing up in Israel, where we have the unique ability, as a culture, to look at any event, success or failure, head-on, discuss, and learn from it. As Vince Lombardi, legendary head coach of the Green Bay Packers, said, "It's not whether you get knocked down; it's whether you get up."[7]

EFFICIENCY

DISCOVERY IS ALWAYS exciting. It feels like all options are open, like there are no boundaries or constraints. We are in love with our ideas, which are great, at least in theory. We are confident that our proposed solutions will work and make a difference.

As we make progress along the business journey, we meet reality. Through market validation, we realize that our assumptions were not all accurate. Our plans were not practical. Does this mean we failed? Or is this an essential part of our learning experience, on the path toward improving our offering? We definitely need to adjust, recalibrate, and refine our value proposition.

But we don't have all the right answers. And we can't predict the future. What we can do is better assess our own personal, and business, strengths and weaknesses, the resources we have, and master our execution and delivery skills.

We must now become more efficient in everything we do.

With limited resources, we have no choice but to be resourceful. This is when we can use our creativity muscles, to make more from less. This is when we can test our own boundaries, simply out of necessity and a constantly changing business environment, to push ourselves to achieve more than we imagined we ever could.

7

CERTAIN UNCERTAINTY

"Mommy, do I have to go to school today? I am afraid. What if the terrorist comes to our school?" Yarden asked me when he was six years old.

"Don't worry, dear," I answered, "You are safe at school." As crazy as it sounds, I do believe my kids were safe at school—although at the time, an armed terrorist was hiding somewhere in Tel Aviv after he had attacked and murdered civilians not forty-eight hours earlier, on New Year's Day, in the center of Tel Aviv. And to make things even more distressing, the attacker's cell phone was found only 170 feet from our home, where he left it before he went to execute his terrible plan. You might think I am irresponsible. But my response was the norm, at least among Israelis.

I have come to believe that learning to cope with uncertainty, and developing skills to adapt to changing circumstances, is in the DNA of Israeli society. This is something our kids learn at an early age. In the summer of 2014, my boys were five, nine, and twelve. Like most working parents, I find the two long, hot months of summer vacation challenging. That summer, as usual, I had signed my children up for summer activities to keep them entertained. A week into the summer vacation, on July 7, 2014, war broke out between Israel and the Gaza Strip. By the end of

August, Palestinian militants had fired 4,844 rockets and 1,734 mortar shells toward Israel, with the majority of Israel's populace within range.

Where we live in Tel Aviv, we had a minute and half to find shelter once the rocket sirens went off. Summer activities, and work for the parents, continued as usual, despite the rocket fire. Parents, myself included, dropped their children off at camp in the morning on the way to work. We knew that, most likely, at some point during the day the children would be forced to stop their arts and crafts projects or games and run to a bomb shelter.

One day that same summer, Yonatan, who was almost twelve then, asked me if he could invite his friends to our home. I agreed, without hesitation. We have a security room, like most Israeli homes, so if a siren were to go off the kids would all join us there, which is exactly what happened. A dozen twelve-year-old kids, two adults, and a dog, all together in the security room of our home. We joked, sang, and talked while the sirens blared. Three minutes after the sirens had stopped, my kids would be able to go back to whatever they had been doing. For my children, despite the rocket fire, it was summer as usual.

LIVING WITH THE UNKNOWN

The geopolitical climate in Israel makes it a challenging country to live in, to say the least. It requires a high tolerance for unpredictability. There are thousands of Israeli children for whom running to a bomb shelter is a normal, albeit stressful and inconveniencing, part of the day. This is particularly true for those who live in the southwest city of Sderot, which borders the Gaza Strip. For more than a decade, Sderot and neighboring settlements have suffered from routine rocket barrages from the Gaza Strip. But the existential threat that lingers above the heads of Israelis is by no means something new.

In Israel's first war—the War of Independence in 1948—the tiny country went up against a military coalition of its neighboring Arab states (including Egypt, Iraq, Syria, Lebanon, Jordan, Saudi Arabia, and Yemen) and the Arab Liberation Army. Since the country's establishment seventy years ago, it has been involved in five wars, two wars of attrition, innumerable border skirmishes, missile attacks in the north, and two Palestinian uprisings.

Israel is, of course, not the only country that suffers from the continuous threat of war and terror. What is unique about Israel, however, is both the way in which the population deals with this situation and the resilience of its civilians.

WHAT DOES RESILIENCE LOOK LIKE?

One month before the New Year's Day attack in Tel Aviv, the world was caught off guard by the horrible series of terror attacks in Paris. Parisians were instructed to stay home, and the streets of the City of Lights were empty and dark.

Brussels—the capital of Belgium, home of the European Parliament—was practically shut down for five entire days, including the school system, public transportation, and entertainment venues. The uncertainty the Belgian authorities faced—about the location, plans, and next steps of the terrorists—brought them to the conclusion that the price of shutting down the city for five days was a necessary cost to keep their population safe.

On a different corner of the planet, in Israel, people live in a routine of uncertainty. We wake up every morning and continue our day-to-day routine, knowing in the back of our minds that anything can happen at any time.

In mid-December 2015, a bomb threat shut down the Los Angeles School District and 650,000 kids stayed home from school. According to NBC News, America's two largest school districts received similar threatening emails but reacted in opposite ways:

New York shrugged it off, while Los Angeles shut down its system. The different responses reflect starkly different attitudes to stress and threat.

Even during the peak of missile attacks in Israel, Israeli children walked to school every day. The evening following the New Year's Day attack, social media in Israel was full of posts like this one: "The party tonight at the Ouzan Bar will take place as usual, starting at 11:00 p.m. Due to the situation, entrance fee is only 20 Shekels. Hope to see you! Terror will not win!"

For forty-eight hours after that Friday afternoon, the armed terrorist was not found. However, the police forces, the mayor of Tel Aviv, and the prime minister of Israel all had the same message for the residents of Tel Aviv: Stay alert. But keep your life routine, including going out. This is what resilience looks like.

Every child is able to understand this message—that no matter how bad things are, we must continue to operate normally. Uncertainty is not a comfortable situation to manage, but it's different when it is your routine. Dealing with uncertainty is therefore a critical capability when you grow up and live in Israel.

Given all the stress, threat, and uncertainty, you might be surprised to learn that out of fifty countries, Israel was ranked third "Best Place Worldwide to Raise a Family" by the 2018 InterNations Family Life Index. France was ranked twenty-first; the United States, fortieth; Brazil, last.[1]

MAKING THE BEST OF A BAD SITUATION

Israelis have learned to accept an unstable reality and created a culture of adaptability and persistence. Instead of fleeing to safer regions, Israelis developed an infrastructure of security, on both the military and civilian fronts. While the military grew stronger and more efficient, the civilians strengthened the economy and cultivated a technological industry that continues to contribute to both the global and the domestic market.

The wars Israel has fought have not slowed the country down. During the six years following 2000, Israel was hit not only by the bursting of the global tech bubble but also by the most intense period of terrorist attacks in its history and by the second Lebanon War. Yet Israel's share of the global venture capital market did not drop—it doubled, from 15 percent to 31 percent. In fact, the Tel Aviv stock exchange was higher on the last day of the Lebanon War than on the first, as it was after the three-week military operation in the Gaza Strip in 2009. Moreover, immigration to Israel did not stop even during the most intense periods of terrorist attacks and wars. On the contrary, even in times of war, Israel continues to attract Jews from around the world, as well as entrepreneurs and businesspeople. It is striking that in a country that suffers from a daily routine of terror attacks or the fear of terror attacks, industry continues to flourish, immigration flows, and the people conduct their lives normally.

MAKING LEMONS INTO LEMONADE

The challenge of ensuring Israel's security serves as a powerful incentive to come up with innovative and efficient technologies and solutions. Advances in technology are there to meet the constant flow of new threats to Israel's physical safety. Means of protection that once worked are no longer sufficient in the face of cyber threats, for example. As unfortunate as it may be, it is precisely these threats that drive the Israeli economy forward.

Often, out of a need to protect oneself grows a creative idea that can be applied to other situations. For example, if a certain technology protects against a security threat within a military context, why not also apply it to civilian security needs? This is one of the reasons that in Israel the military and civilian industries are so intertwined—they constantly influence one another.

Cybersecurity is perhaps the best example. Out of a pressing need to protect the country, technologies that can overcome any cyber threat were born. These technologies can then be applied to the civilian sector, whether for PayPal, banks, or any other company doing business online.

This was how Check Point, a global market leader in cybersecurity, was created. It was founded in central Israel by Gil Shwed, Marius Nacht, and Shlomo Kramer. Unsurprisingly, Shwed came up with the idea for the world's first VPN (virtual private network) products while serving in the IDF's Intelligence Unit 8200, Israel's counterpart to the NSA. Today, Check Point's software is used in the world's biggest industries; among its customers are most Fortune 100 companies and most national governments. The company is currently worth $18 billion and is publicly traded on Nasdaq.

The idea that Israel's difficult security situation is actually fertile ground for technological and economic development puts things in a different perspective. Seeing threats as a challenge makes them less frightening—something that can be dealt with. Instead of being overcome with a sense of helplessness, Israelis take matters into their own hands and actively participate in protecting themselves, as well as contributing to the country's financial well-being. Equally important, Israelis have turned the difficult experience of living under the threat of war and terrorism into something that makes us stronger in other aspects of our lives.

HARNESSING STRESS

Kelly McGonigal, a health psychologist, has an interesting approach to stress. "Can changing how you think about stress make you healthier?" she asks.[2] Stress is usually something we try to avoid. Often, we choose our career paths based on how much pressure they will put on us. We try to protect our children from feeling stressed about academic achievements or because of events in the news. We perform any number of activities that are meant to relieve our stress, such as yoga and meditation.

But McGonigal advocates a different approach to stress. She believes that if we view stress positively, we can harness it in our favor. Instead of seeing stress as an inhibiting factor in an emergency situation, we need to see stress as a physical and mental mechanism that assists us in difficult times. In a lecture McGonigal gave she explains: "The next time you are going to feel stressed you will remember this talk and you will think, 'This is my body helping me rise to this challenge.' And when you view stress in that way your body believes you and your stress response becomes healthier."

McGonigal's view corresponds to my own ideas about how best to handle stress, learn from failure, and build resilience: to think of every experience as a chance to develop skills, just like you exercise to develop muscle tone. With practice, we can learn how to cope with stress and leverage stressful situations for growth and development.

IT CERTAINLY BRINGS PEOPLE TOGETHER

We don't plan for it, we don't know when the siren will sound, where we will be, and who else will be around. The moment it happens, though, we run to the nearest security room, as we have countless times before, and meet others in the same position. Suddenly, strangers who seemingly have nothing in common find themselves squeezed in a room together. Sometimes all they do is tell jokes, sometimes they chat and realize they served in the same unit in the army, but either way, they connect.

In recent rounds of conflict that involved rocket fire from Gaza or Lebanon, people and institutions from around the country came to the aid of areas within range of the rockets and missiles. In the cities of Ashdod, Ashqelon, and Sderot, for example, a constant barrage meant summer camps needed to be canceled. Many of those kids' families were invited to stay with families in the north of the country, some of whom had themselves been hosted by southern families during the Second Lebanon War (2006). These types of arrangements, while common, are usually spontaneous and organized via social media by citizens who simply want to help one another.

It's widely assumed that in times of crisis people will band together, supporting and coming to each other's aid. McGonigal attributes this kind of togetherness to neurohormones such as oxytocin. She explains that oxytocin "fine-tunes your brain's social instincts. It primes you to do things that strengthen close relationships. Oxytocin makes you crave physical contact with your friends and family, it enhances your empathy, it even makes you more willing to help and support the people you care about."

But what many people tend to miss, she adds, is that oxytocin is in fact a stress hormone that our pituitary gland produces as part of the stress response, making it as much an integral part of our stress coping mechanism as adrenaline. Oxytocin motivates us to seek support. When we are stressed, our biological response is driving us to share how we feel with others, seeking support rather than dealing with it on our own or suppressing it. It is a response designed to ensure that we pay attention to when someone else in our lives is struggling so that we can be there for them. "When life is difficult," says McGonigal, "your stress response wants you to be surrounded by people who care about you."

If we look at the social aspect of stress in the Israeli context, we can see how it encourages the further tightening of the already complex social networks of Israelis. Not only do people come to the aid of those who are currently under attack, whether it is citizens of the north during the Lebanon War, or citizens of the south during the continuous missile attacks, these events also represent a collective national experience. Stress in Israel is part of the culture, of our shared history, of what keeps us together.

It is no wonder that children who grow up in Israel under a constant state of uncertainty—who are given the guidance and tools to deal with this situation—can develop important skills for dealing with uncertainty in all aspects of their lives. No wonder so many Israelis are drawn to the entrepreneurial world, with all its challenges and uncertainty—the uncertainty feels like home.

8

RISKFUL MANAGEMENT

When you think of yourself at the age of fifteen, what is the first thing that comes to your mind? Or even better, if you have a fifteen-year-old at home, like I do, how would you best describe them? I admit that there is an entire range of adjectives I would use, ranging from "crazy" to "inspiring"; from "funny" to "deep"; from "irresponsible" to "committed." Are these contradictory? How can they all apply to the same fifteen-year-old?

Like with most teenagers around the world, Israeli youth find themselves struggling with existential questions, with a growing sense of independence and a need to break free from social conventions and their parents' control. But they have only five or six years to revel in this phase, to experiment, take risks, and make mistakes, all under the care and supervision of their parents.

This period, which will come to an abrupt end for most with their enlistment in the IDF, is seen in Israel as precious and protected. Israeli society affords its youth the opportunity to act stupidly; irresponsible behavior at the age of sixteen or seventeen is not likely to have life-changing consequences. Israeli kids are expected, and even encouraged, to explore aspects of life that will not be available to them once they join the military or after they are released from it.

Indeed, in Hebrew there is a very telling term used to refer to teenagers. They are not called "youth" or "teens." Formally, they are referred to "growing-ups," which is of course suggestive of the process they are undergoing. But, more frequently and casually, you hear the expression "stupid age" (it sounds better in Hebrew— *tipesh esre*) used to refer to those turbulent teenage years.

The Israeli habit of calling teenagers "stupid" might sound insulting. However, the connotations associated with the term are not negative. The Israeli youth in his or her "stupid age" is seen very differently from the American "teenager." Yes, around the world youth between the ages of twelve and eighteen are prone to doing stupid things, but this experimentation is viewed forgivingly and is even welcomed in Israeli society.

Partly, this is because of how delimited this period of youth's lives is. When Israelis turn eighteen, unlike in other societies where youth enjoy what's been termed an "extended adolescence" in which they typically continue their studies, most Israelis are drafted into the military.

The fact that Israelis are required to join the army at the age of eighteen forces young people to engage with pressing ideological and political questions. They must face national issues because, in the very near future, they will inevitably take an active part in national life. This has been the case throughout Israel's history, and has often led youth to play surprisingly daring and instrumental roles on the national stage.

YOUTH ON THE FRONT LINES

In 1936, a revolt started among the Arabs in the British Mandate of Palestine. What begun as civil disobedience became a violent resistance movement of guerrilla groups who attacked British and Jewish targets. The Arabs were protesting the significant influx of Jewish immigrants fleeing Europe in response to growing anti-Semitism.

One Jewish response to the security threats posed by the Arab revolt was the Tower and Stockade movement. Between the years of 1936 and 1939, Zionist settlers established new settlements by building a tower and a stockade practically overnight. Fifty-seven Jewish settlements were founded this way throughout the country, including Kibbutz Sde Eliyahu, where Malka Haas developed the junkyard playground as we saw in chapter 1.

Many of the participants in these clandestine operations were teenage members of Jewish youth movements. The towers were inspired by structures made by scouts in their campsites. The structures were built from raw materials that were prepared in advance, easy to erect but sturdy.

Several aspects of this movement are worth mentioning, not the least of which is the Israeli approach to getting things done efficiently and quickly. But perhaps the most striking aspect of this piece of Israeli history is the great involvement of youth in the building of a future nation.

WHO ARE THE TZOFIM?

The Tower and Stockade operations were not the first time, and certainly not the last, that youth took an active part in shaping and building Israel. Youth movements were active throughout the country before Israel's establishment in 1948. Zionist youth played a critical role in servicing poor, immigrant communities. In the years before and directly after the establishment of the state, Zionist youth built walls around new settlements, took turns guarding from the watchtowers, volunteered in field hospitals, worked in fields and plantations, helped take care of young children while their parents worked, and prepared mentally and physically for a military service in one of the many pre-state paramilitary organizations.

Seventy years later, the majority of Israeli youngsters take part in youth movements, most of which are still involved in one or more of the activities mentioned above. There are over fifty-five youth movements in operation in Israel, with over 246,500 members and 26,800 guides. Their numbers rise each year. While their activities have evolved over time, their mentality remains the same: to build and preserve Israel—its values, safety, and the well-being of its citizens.

The biggest youth movement, with over 85,000 members spread over 205 tribes, is the Tzofim. The Tzofim, while one of many youth organizations in Israel, is so big, so well known, and so industrious that it is taken here as exemplifying the state of mind shared among many others. The tribes are where they meet, the actual location, but also stands for the specific pack—ranging from tribes of one hundred kids to ones larger than a thousand. Each tribe has its own name, colors, songs, and legacy. In our neighborhood, Shevet Aviv, the Aviv Tribe, is the most dominant one.

A BIT OF BACKGROUND

Tzofim means "scouts" in Hebrew. The Scout movement was first conceived in Britain in 1907 by Robert Baden-Powell and was part of a widespread phenomenon of seeking to develop the skills and moral character of young boys and girls through activities in the outdoors.

Today, too, the Scout movement places emphasis on outdoor activities such as camping, woodcraft, hiking, backpacking, and sports. Scouts are encouraged to take part in voluntary work, to learn by doing, and to develop responsibility, self-reliance, collaboration, and leadership skills. A global movement, it includes over 164 national organizations and over thirty-eight million Scouts and Guides. On the surface, Israeli Tzofim seem just like other

Scout groups around the world, but if you take a closer look, you will see some surprising, and significant, differences.

Let's take a quick look at the Scout movement in the UK and United States. The Boy Scouts of America's website describes what can be gained from a Scout membership this way: "Scouting promises you the great outdoors. As a Scout, you can learn how to camp and hike without leaving a trace and how to take care of the land. You'll study wildlife up close and learn about nature all around you. There are plenty of skills for you to master, and you can teach others what you have learned."[1] The "About" page of the British Scout Movement's website says something similar: "Scouts take part in activities as diverse as kayaking, abseiling, expeditions overseas, photography, climbing and zorbing. As a Scout you can learn survival skills, first aid, computer programming, or even how to fly a plane. There's something for every young person. It's a great way to have fun, make friends, get outdoors, express your creativity and experience the wider world."[2]

Participating in such diverse and physically challenging activities is an empowering experience for children. This is why these activities are also embraced by the Tzofim movement. However, if you visit the Tzofim's "About" webpage, you will encounter a different message:

[The Tzofim is] a Zionist and national youth movement, whose mission is to establish and develop frameworks that imbue education and values, in which children and youth from all over Israel will engage in a variety of social activities to guide their personal development and which will provide them with recreation and fun. Tzofim teaches its scouts Jewish values and Zionism, with the goal of building an Israeli society that is Zionist, ethical and activist and that will benefit and satisfy all its citizens. Whether it be emphasizing the integration of unique sectors of the population, empowering and integrating immigrants into society, or strengthening Jewish and Israeli identity in Israel as well as in the Diaspora, Tzofim's main goal is to ensure that we reach as many young people as possible, so as to build a better tomorrow, today.[3]

The differences among the movements' descriptions are compelling. Despite the fact that the Tzofim engage in outdoor activities just as much as any other Scout movement, this is not once mentioned in the "About" page. Instead, what we find is the ideology that stands behind the movement: what it means to be part of something on a larger, social, and educational scale.

The Tzofim were born out of dire necessity. In 1918, the year the movement was established, Jewish communities in Palestine needed workers to develop the country. Youth movements proved highly efficient in such practical spheres as construction (e.g., founding new settlements), security, and agriculture. Equally important, a national framework was necessary to meet pressing social needs: to integrate Diaspora Jews coming to live in Palestine within local Jewish communities and to educate youth at a time when educational institutions weren't yet established. Youth movements were a way to bring together the young people arriving from dozens of different countries into a cohesive nation. They were a way to nurture the values of Zionism, Judaism, work, and social responsibility.

In the absence of an organized bureaucratic system (remember, this was decades before the establishment of the State of Israel), new immigrants were forced to make their own way in a foreign, underdeveloped landscape. Youth movements of the time worked to strengthen and unite weaker populations by appealing to a common goal: building a Zionist state. Today's Tzofim live and breathe these same values.

This is not to say that Scout movements outside of Israel are not involved in social activism or that it isn't one of their goals. However, when we compare the defined goals and activities of the Tzofim with Scout movements elsewhere, we see a much more socially oriented organization. So, while the Tzofim has its roots in the British Scouts and the ideas of Free German Youth movements, once put in an Israeli context, the Tzofim became something uniquely Israeli.

WHERE ARE THE ADULTS?

Madrich: A *madrich* is a guide, an instructor, usually in an educational or instructive framework (excluding schools). The word *madrich* comes from the root word *derech*, which means "way." A *madrich* guides the way.

Chanich: The word *chanich* comes from the root word *chanicha*, which means "initiation." A *chanich* is a person being trained, an apprentice, someone learning by practice.

Every *chanich* has a *madrich* and vice versa; their very existence depends on each other. Substituting these words with a direct translation of "pupil" and "guide" loses their inherent meaning, which hints at the process of education and guidance involved in every activity of learning.

In the first week of June, three weeks before the end of the school year, Yarden brought home a printed message for us:

On Tuesday, June 5, we will hold the first Tzofim gathering for the third graders, as preparation for next year. If your son or daughter is interested in joining, we will pick them up at the school gate at 4:00 p.m. and walk together to the tribe's building. Alternatively, they can meet us there at 4:30 p.m.

We will walk them back to the school gate at 6:30 p.m. We are looking forward to next year and hope to see them on Tuesday.

Thanks,
The new madrichim

That's it. No names of the guides. No phone numbers. Nothing. Would you send your kid to a youth movement meeting with guides you don't know? I'm not sure. But we did.

Twenty-five kids from Yarden's class were waiting at the school gate at 4:00 p.m. They walked together to the Scouts gathering location, the Aviv Tribe, and two hours later they walked back to the school gate, excited to embark on this new chapter in their lives, being part of a youth movement. I still don't know the name of the *madrich* who walked with them, but I know he or she wasn't out of high school. I did, however, get a text message from Daniel, Yarden's thirteen-year-old brother, who saw him at the tribe base: "Mommy, Yarden is with his age group. Super excited!" That's all I needed. Next year, Daniel will be trained as a *madrich* for ten-year-old kids.

One of the guiding principles in the Tzofim is minimal adult intervention. Historically, this came out of necessity. From the beginning, missions and activities were independently conceived, organized, and executed. The young members did not need adults to orient them then, and they hardly need them now. The Tzofim is an organization for youth, run by youth. They are almost entirely self-sufficient, setting their own goals and planning their own activities. As such, the movement is made up of hundreds of personal stories, one of which is Tsahi Ben Yosef's.

Since early childhood, Tsahi has always been surrounded by a community. At an early age he joined and was warmly embraced by the Tzofim, where he took on various roles over the years. He began his route as a cadet, moving up to becoming a guide, then a brigade leader, then a tribe leader. He was on a mission to Europe on behalf of the movement, established the first Scout tribe in the city of Yavne, and initiated a parent-guidance group, all projects that received the full support of the organization and that are still active today, led by others. All before the age of eighteen.

Tsahi served in an IDF intelligence unit for six years. Once he completed his service, he became project manager at the prime minister's office, and later a product manager at AlgoSec. Tsahi was extremely well-equipped to handle both the requirements of his military service and of his later jobs; after all, he was trained to manage projects since he was eight years old.

It was only a matter of time until he would launch his own entrepreneurial venture, and what better field for him to get involved in than education. In 2012, he cofounded LotoCards, a unique platform for educational logical games for children. And in 2013, he cofounded RoadStory, a mobile platform of real-time and interactive maps for kids. In 2015, together with two army pals, Tsahi cofounded and became CEO of Crossense, a digital measurement solution company, which was later acquired by Toluna, where he is now the vice president of digital products.

About the Tzofim, which Tsahi believes had a critical positive influence on him, he explains: "The children occupy almost all of the positions, from the youngest *chanich* to the oldest *madrich*. There is the head of the tribe, usually a parent volunteer, who serves as a safety net and gives a sense of support to the kids, but other than that everything is in the children's hands."[4] The *madrichim* are teens in tenth, eleventh, and twelfth grades. They are responsible for the educational and recreational activities within the tribe: from weekly activities to volunteer work to group discussions to summer camps. Those who are younger (usually starting in fourth grade) are the *chanichim*. This hierarchical structure is unique to Israel. In other Scout movements, guides and counselors are aged eighteen and up.

This hierarchy, which gives adolescents responsibility for educating children not much younger than themselves, demonstrates how youth are perceived in Israel. I cannot emphasize this enough: "stupid" though they may be in their adolescent years, youth in Israel are expected to assume an active role in shaping their future and in developing practical and social skills. We will return to the issue of youth responsibility and independence in later chapters. For now, let's look at just how much freedom of thought and expression this structure encourages.

Unlike in traditional classrooms, learning activities in the Tzofim involve discussions, brainstorming sessions, outdoor activities, volunteering, and so on. Through these skills-based activities, the *chanichim* and their *madrichim* create a community of learners, in which they build knowledge together.

At every stage, the *madrichim* are not following a scripted curriculum. They aren't all given the same training, materials, or detailed instructions. Rather, they are expected to improvise, to utilize what they've learned in their years as a *madrich* to get the most out of the situations they find themselves in with their younger *chanichim*. This kind of adaptive, spontaneous instructing method is, according to Dr. Keith Sawyer, a leading scientific expert on creativity, incredibly effective. The Tzofim offers Israeli youth the type of learning environment Dr. Sawyer recommends, one that "is open-ended, is not structured in advance, and is an interaction among peers, where any participant can contribute equally to the flow of the interaction."[5] It was no surprise when Yair Seroussi, one of Israel's top business executives who served, inter alia, as head of Morgan Stanley Israel and was formerly chairman of Bank Hapoalim, Israel's largest bank, told me, "As chairman of the bank, I used to say that all managers, at all levels of the bank, should possess the mentality of a Scouts leader (Tzofim tribal head), someone who takes responsibility, is accountable and not afraid of making decisions, while leading his team."[6] Yair bases his belief on his personal experience as a young Tel Aviv Tzofim member and from his two older sisters' experiences, who were both also very active in the youth movement and set an example for him. He finds this is true for seventeen-year-old Scouts "managers" and certainly true for managers at Israel's largest bank. "I don't have many memories from high school," he tells me, "All the memories from my adolescence are from the Tzofim." Naturally, he insisted that his two daughters join the Tzofim and saw them flourish in this empowering environment.

CREATIVITY, SPONTANEITY, AND IMPROVISATION

He who cares for a day plants seeds, he who cares for a year plants trees, he who cares for generations educates.[7]

—JANUSZ KORCZAK

Every activity in the Tzofim is structured on the model of creative thought, spontaneity, and improvisation. Tsahi Ben Yosef explains how this approach is applied in daily activities.

Thinking out of the box is encouraged in routine activities just as it is in annual projects like the three- to five-day-long summer camp. Throughout the year, for example, there are set biweekly activities that the *madrichim* do with their groups. The topics and values to be discussed are assigned by the senior level of the entire tribe. But other than assigning those very general topics, like "What Is Justice?," the senior level does very little. It is all in the hands of those sixteen- and seventeen-year-old *madrichim*.

Rather than giving them a minute-by-minute lesson plan, the *madrichim* decide how to convey a certain topic to the kids in their charge. They must adapt the question and tone to their group, be familiar with the abilities and preferences of their *chanichim* as well as their comfort zones, and how to challenge them to overcome their discomfort: in cases where the topics of activity do not interest them; when they're hungry or tired; or just not that cooperative. They are simply left to figure it out for themselves, while keeping in mind that every session has to be new, interesting, and engaging for the children. . . . Add to that the fact that every year the senior *madrichim* (who are now eighteen and are preparing for their military service) graduate and get replaced by seventeen-year-olds who are eager to lead, innovate, and make their mark. Wanting to do something that has never been done before, the new stratum comes up with unbelievably creative and sophisticated structures in summer camp, for example. Instead of being assigned with a specific structure or activity, youth are given a platform on which to express or even prove whatever it is they want to express or prove.

The burst of creativity we see in the Tzofim involves more than just providing youth with a platform; the very structure of the movement is part of what drives its members to innovate. Precisely because the senior *madrichim* keep changing, those who are newly in charge have a great desire to make their mark. Innovation is built into the structure and core of the movement.

AN ENTREPRENEURIAL ENVIRONMENT

Entrepreneurship requires more than creativity. If you ask Narkis Alon, now a serial entrepreneur living in Tel Aviv, she would probably say her most memorable childhood experience is that of being part of a family and a community.

Her father, Professor Noga Alon, a renowned Israeli mathematician and computer scientist, and her mother, an employment lawyer, formed Narkis's first support circle. As a child and teenager, she took part in empowering and educational programs, and was put on the road to self-fulfillment from a very young age.

Outside her family and school, she was a devout Tzofim cadet. The Tzofim youth movement provided her with structure, opportunities for management and creativity, and above all a community. At eighteen, Narkis joined the exclusive Israel Defense Forces' Intelligence Unit 8200 community, where she further nurtured the entrepreneurial mentality she grew up with.

When her discharge came, she was shaken. After spending an entire life in supportive familial and educational networks, being thrown into a non-communal world was rattling. So, like most discharged soldiers, she went traveling overseas, and when she came back, she knew what she had to do.

Narkis now dedicates her life to building communities and support systems to help people grow personally and professionally. In 2011 she cofounded ZeZe, an organization that creates jobs for communities in need by initiating, managing, and growing financially sustainable social enterprises. In 2013 she cofounded and was CCO of Elevation Academy, where she helps integrate weaker communities, including people with disabilities, the ultra-Orthodox, and more, into the start-up industry. She completed a double-major bachelor of arts in psychology and film from Tel Aviv University. And in 2016, she cofounded and is now CEO of Doubleyou.life, an international community of women entrepreneurs.

The communal character of the Tzofim, for Narkis, is what makes it the ideal entrepreneurial environment. "My entire exposure to entrepreneurship really began in the Tzofim," she says.[8] As mentioned, all of the activities in the Tzofim are performed by its members. This means that from the birth of an idea to its final execution, entire projects are in the hands of children and adolescents. A project's success is dependent on their skills and on their ability to learn from their mistakes. In summer camp, for example, *chanichim* learn the relationship between vision and execution; they organize the entire camp and are asked to engineer unique wood structures.

"For a project to work, you have to go through several stages that are almost parallel to those you have to go through in the entrepreneurial world," Alon explains. "You have to make it presentable, recruit people to support you emotionally and financially, recruit people to work on it physically, and finally, you have to become a person who people want to cooperate with, someone who can make people believe in his vision. It is an extremely powerful experience."

As *chanichim* and *madrichim* progress in years and gradually assume more responsibilities, the challenges they face become bigger. This teaches individuals in the movement what it is they are good at (and not only what they like), and what they still have to work on. Alon recalls:

In eleventh grade, there was a lot of emphasis on novelty, on doing things that were never done before. I was appointed head of structure and we were working on a chain-reaction machine. It was the first time something like this was done in my tribe. Our structure was elected the central structure for the whole tribe, and we won second place among all the other tribes that were competing. I learned a lot from this project. I saw how good I was at recruiting people, at embedding a vision in them that would motivate them throughout the project. I also learned that I had exceptional organizational skills, but at the same time that I dislike being in the organizer's shoes.

Alon applied the lessons she learned in the Tzofim to her rich entrepreneurial work. "The challenges children come across in the Tzofim have to do with more than time management or even with dealing and managing other people," she adds. "These can be learned in many different ways. But what I found to be unique in the Tzofim is the opportunity it gives you to get to know yourself."

9

LET THE CHILDREN DO IT

Being a part of the local and national community is a value shared by all Israeli youth movements. Over the years, *chanichim* from the different youth movements take part in various community-based projects, whether through volunteering in existing programs or initiating new ones. Each age group contributes in accordance with their ability. There are countless examples, including visiting with and helping the elderly, in particular Holocaust survivors; food collection and distribution; and tutoring young refugees in Hebrew.

One of the most powerful projects my son took part in was celebrating the birthdays of children of refugees from Africa. Nearly every week a handful of Israeli-born kids would organize a party—complete with cake and candles; activities and games; gifts and songs—to celebrate the birthdays of refugee kids born that week. For most of them, it was the first such celebration of their birthday they'd ever had.

Youth movement members' engagement with the broader community is one of the most significant and potentially life-changing aspects of their experience. Often, the experiences they share with their peers in contributing to and learning about their community can set them, individually or as a group, marching down an unforeseen path.

KREMBO WINGS

Krembo: A chocolate-covered marshmallow cream–topped cookie
treat. The Krembo is considered Israel's winter snack and is
sold between October and February.

The story of Krembo Wings begins with sixteen-year-old Adi
Altschuler. When she was only twelve, Adi started volunteering
with ILAN, which offers programs, services, and facilities to children with physical disabilities. She became close friends with Kobi
Kfir, a three-year-old child with cerebral palsy. Adi soon felt like
part of Kfir's family, developing a unique relationship with Kfir
that went beyond verbal communication.

Throughout the years of their friendship, Adi noticed that what
Kfir most missed out on was time with friends. "I knew how much
he loved social interaction," she told NoCamels in an interview,
"but the only people he interacted with [outside of school] were
his family and me."[1]

In 2002, at the ripe age of sixteen, Adi joined LEAD, a nonprofit
youth leadership organization that gives Israeli teenagers experience in planning, implementing, and managing community projects. Within this framework, Adi was asked to choose an issue that
troubled her and devise a solution. By the end of the year, Adi had
launched Krembo Wings. It started out small, organizing activities for Kfir and his classmates. She managed everything, coordinated with the parents, and arranged for transportation. "Soon
enough," she says, "more parents, friends, and educators heard
about what was going on and wanted me to expand. Everything
took off." But Adi kept the structure of Krembo Wings the same:
like most Israeli youth movements, Krembo Wings is led by its
youth members, working together to enable children living with
any type of motor, cognitive, or sensory disability to take part in
enjoyable social interactions and become part of community life

in Israel. These youth are participants, guides, instructors, managers, and planners. They lead and plan the activities, organize all of the volunteers, coordinate events, and ensure that everything is running smoothly. Not surprisingly, the movement's mission is also to foster the leadership skills of the volunteer counselors.

Years later, as president of what has grown to be a widespread and well-known youth movement, Adi recalls the motivation that drove her to establish Krembo Wings: "So that Kfir and children and youth like him will have a social life, so they won't be lonely. So that they will have the same opportunities as everyone. But actually, it's not just for them, it's for me, it's for us, so that we will not be alone."

Today the movement serves more than four thousand youths aged seven to twenty-one, from forty-seven branches in communities across Israel representing a broad range of cultural, religious, and socioeconomic backgrounds. Adi's efforts to offer children with disabilities a reprieve from social isolation have paid off.

"In the beginning, we were just a bunch of sixteen-year-olds. We didn't have a vision or strategy or business plan," said Adi a few years ago. In 2009, Adi and Krembo Wings were awarded one of Israel's most respected prizes, the Presidential Award for Volunteerism. In 2014, Adi was elected one of the six future world leaders by *Time* magazine, and in the same year she spoke at the UN about social entrepreneurship as a vehicle for growth in developing countries. This is an entire organization built on the idea that youth are capable and should take charge of improving the society they live in. It may seem unbelievable: giving a teenage girl or boy—kids in their "stupid age," after all—responsibility for over seventy volunteers in addition to dozens of special-needs children. But parents and institutions across Israel are doing just that.

"You feel that you're in charge of something important and it makes you grow up fast," says Shir, a former head of the Modi'in branch of Krembo Wings. "You learn about management and how to deal with the difficult situations. Adults tell me they had to get to thirty before being in a position of responsibility over so many people." What's more incredible, no one is "giving" these young people responsibility; they take it on themselves. Adi Altschuler was not assigned this project. She created it from scratch. Today she is a respected social entrepreneur and, luckily, not the only one of her kind.

YOUTH IN THE LEAD

By the time Sharin Fisher was a sixteen-year-old high school student, Intelligence Unit 8200 had already made quite a name for itself as an exclusive technological and business training club that offered lifelong membership to those who passed through it.

Luckily for her, Sharin had all the support she needed to prepare for the screening process. She handpicked courses and extracurricular activities, studied Arabic and computer science, and received the full support of her family and school.

In 2013, when Sharin was ready to start her own venture, it was for the purpose of replicating the invaluable support system she enjoyed growing up and throughout her service, knowing that starting at an early age is key to shaping the future generations of cyber and computer specialists.

So, following her master's degree in diplomacy, strategy, and international relations from the University of Texas and the Interdisciplinary Center Herzliya (Israel's IDC), Sharin moved on to found Techlift. It became the first technological youth movement in Israel, operating on behalf of the 8200 Alumni Association. The program inspires teenagers (in grades 7 through 12) to seek higher levels of achievement and provides them with the necessary skills and conditions they need to become future tech innovators and entrepreneurs.

Like many Israeli innovations, Techlift was also born of necessity. Sharin explains: "For me, it began in the military, where I spent eight years in Unit 8200. . . . The problems the unit has to deal with are often a matter of life and death. To solve them, one has to think outside the box."[2]

The teaching methods in military units like 8200 are focused on how to solve unpredictable, seemingly unsolvable problems. There is no point in applying old methods to new problems, which is why the unit trains its soldiers to think creatively.

When senior staff came to Fisher with the acute problem of lack of human resources, she knew she had to come up with something completely new. "The problem was that, out of six thousand high school students who excel in the fields of science and technology, less than 10 percent try out for the unit, and only two hundred eventually pass the exams. With the growing threats of cybersecurity, the unit needs to recruit at least one thousand people a year. That's a huge shortfall," she said, and it puts the security of the country at risk.

When tasked with solving this problem, Fisher tried to find its source. "At the end of the day, I thought, the military accepts only what the education system manages to produce. The problem, then, begins with the education system. But then, again, how can we expect the Ministry of Education to suddenly train its teachers in a field [cybersecurity] that was only born a few decades ago?" Fisher was right; teaching methodologies used in schools are not relevant for these kinds of twenty-first-century challenges. "We need to teach children to deal with problems that do not exist yet. Youth need to learn how to learn, how to think creatively, not get stuck on patterns and applications. That is the only way in which we will become an autodidactic people who are capable of actively constructing their own future," Fisher explains.

Fisher decided to proactively create a change when she left the army. "I was invited to be a judge in hackathons, and I saw that many children who are passionate about technology do not have the means to pursue their passion. Some prestigious cyber education programs are not accessible to most children in Israel. Although Israel is known as the 'start-up nation,' the percentage of Israelis who work in high-tech or in a start-up is small. This has created socioeconomic gaps among the highest in the developed world. Large populations, including the ultra-Orthodox, new immigrants, and Arabs, are barely involved in the world of start-ups and high-tech."

Recognizing this problem, Fisher founded Techlift, a youth movement that teaches technology to any child who is interested in technology, regardless of his or her background, grades at school, or past accomplishments. "We take an existential problem like water pollution and together work to invent a robot that can filter water and detect what is causing the pollution," Fisher describes. "Another fun thing we are working on is building an escape room that is both physical and virtual. This would be the first escape room of its kind, and will involve, for example, a task of cracking a computer code." *Chanichim* are encouraged to remain and grow within the movement, eventually becoming *madrichim* themselves. "Where the Ministry of Education fails, youth movements will succeed," claims Fisher. "We are building a generation of leaders, a strong infrastructure of quality manpower that will lead the change in technological education."

The structure and ideology of Techlift is founded on the structure and ideals of the Tzofim, of which Fisher was a member since the age of ten. Children are given the ability to acquire skills that they later apply in real life. "What I am interested in," says Fisher, "[is] reaching the weaker population and helping them become active members of society, helping them become people who make a change by actually building something. This idea is what youth movements, the Tzofim in particular, are all about."

MDA

On January 12, 2018, an Israeli ambulance team in the city of Modi'in in central Israel had a remarkable day. In the space of a few hours they helped deliver two babies en route to the nearest hospital. So far, this might not strike you as a particularly unusual ambulance story, right? But what if I told you that the volunteer who helped deliver both babies, Shaked Ron Tal, was barely fifteen years old?

Shaked was on duty along with the ambulance driver, who is a licensed paramedic, and two other young volunteers. The first birth was at around 7:00 a.m., as they were rushing a thirty-seven-year-old woman to the hospital. Still flush with the excitement of that event, they were called at around 10:00 a.m. to take another expectant mother to the hospital. This time, too, a baby girl was born on the way to the hospital. Shaked was extremely moved: "It was very exciting for me. I feel fortunate that I was given the privilege of being part of a team that helped deliver not one but two women in one shift. I wish the mothers and their families a lot of good luck, and may we have many more days like this."[3] Don't forget, Shaked was barely fifteen years old.

Shaked is a volunteer with the Israeli equivalent of the Red Cross, Magen David Adom (MDA). Like Red Cross organizations across the world, MDA trains nurses; coordinates blood donation clinics; helps the disabled, the needy, and the elderly; and provides ambulance and rescue services at sea, in cities, and on the road. In Israel there is one major difference: out of MDA's seventeen thousand volunteers who maintain the organization, eleven thousand are teenagers aged fifteen to eighteen! This is not a typo: over 60 percent of the volunteers in the Israeli Red Cross are in their "stupid age."

Since its establishment in 1930, Israeli youth have been participating in MDA's operational activities: from youth brigades in the

1948 War of Independence; to evacuating casualties during wars and murderous attacks in the '70s; and during the unprecedented terrorism of the 1990s, youth were among the first to answer the call. The hundreds of thousands of Israelis who require MDA services each year see these young angels in action.

Other countries also have youth Red Cross volunteers; however, unlike in other countries, Israeli MDA youth perform advanced-level CPR; rescue people injured in car and work accidents; and care for the injured at critical times. Overall, MDA youth volunteers invest more than 1.5 million hours of volunteering per year. As part of their advanced training, they learn to handle mass-casualty events and are eligible to participate in a summer course (during summer vacation) to be trained as *madrichim*. These kids ultimately take on other responsibilities, such as supervising the training of volunteers, coordinating shifts, and more.

In recent years, questions have surfaced regarding youth's extraordinary involvement in Israel's ambulance service infrastructure. Can they handle it? Should youth be charged with such grave social responsibility? Regardless of the claims on either side of the debate, the fact remains that Israeli youth are highly involved, physically and emotionally, in all medical events in Israeli society. They volunteer in shift work, assist on ambulances that would otherwise go unassisted, and they're eager to learn and help.

Both Israeli society and the kids themselves see Israeli youth as capable and as a contributing part of society. They may be prone to riskier, even "stupid" behavior, but they are capable of rising to very intense and dynamic occasions and are accordingly entrusted with great responsibility. These are no mere adults-in-waiting, not yet ready to take on roles within the community, but rather they are an active part of any major organization, whether political, social, educational, or cultural.

In Israel, youth are expected to take responsibility for how society looks now, as well as in the future. Of course, ambulance service presents challenges, some of which might not be welcomed by a teen's parent. But the fact that teenagers can be found across the country, assisting the population in its time of need, illustrates that in the social sphere, youth are perceived as co-citizens and not as children.

LEAD

With over fifty-five different youth movements that include over 246,500 young members, I can hardly do justice to them all here. But a belief shared by all of them is that youth are contributing members of society. And as such, they have both privileges and responsibilities. These are not foisted on them, but rather enthusiastically taken up by them.

Israeli youth are eager to act. Since they are not treated as children, they have an opportunity to generate real change within our society. Just like adults, they may fail or they may succeed; the point is that they are expected to try. It is no wonder, then, that organizations that encourage youth to take charge and to be social leaders are common in Israel. One such organization is LEAD.

LEAD is an apolitical association dedicated to cultivating youth leadership in Israel. Considered a globally unique project, the program focuses on youth-oriented methods developed and implemented by an interdisciplinary group of experts from the fields of social leadership, psychology, and education. Sixteen-year-olds are eligible to join the program regardless of background, as long as they are found to have the leadership potential the programs look for. The two-year training program for LEAD "ambassadors" guides them through the conception, planning, execution, and management of independent projects that are socially oriented. LEAD facilitates meetings and trainings with leading professionals from fields such as the sciences, social science, business, government, and education, who dedicate some of their time to empowering the future generation of leaders, even if they are only sixteen years old.

Remember Adi Altschuler from Krembo Wings? This is exactly how she got started. At sixteen, Adi was given the opportunity to be an entrepreneur. With encouragement, resources, and support from LEAD, she managed, in just one year, to launch one of the most meaningful youth movements on the scene.

Upon graduation, which coincides with the end of high school, LEAD *chanichim* become part of a community of graduates, still active within the organization. In fact, the alumni program makes LEAD the longest leadership-development program in the world, as the selected participants who started at age sixteen stay part of the organization until the age of thirty-five. LEAD, and other organizations like it, don't believe in waiting. They view youth as a thinking, capable, and motivated force within society that should be harnessed rather than ignored or dismissed.

What's common to all these programs—Krembo Wings, Techlift, LEAD, and MDA—is their extremely practical approach. Youth are leading and involved in the actual doing. Adi, Sharin, and Shaked are not only visionaries but also real doers, applying what we call in Hebrew a *tachles* approach to life. *Tachles* is a dual-meaning phrase that expresses practicality as well as a feeling of having captured the point. It means we are goal oriented, emphasizing or pointing out a bottom line, while acting and doing.

MAGSHIMIM AND CYBER GIRLZ

Finally, we've reached our last stop: the Magshimim (Fulfill) and Cyber GirlZ programs, extracurricular educational programs for gifted children aged twelve to eighteen. Magshimim and Cyber GirlZ were initially founded to provide training in computer sciences and cyber learning, to better prepare Israeli youth for their compulsory military service in intelligence and technological units of the Israel Defense Forces. Year later, though, these programs are now seen as partly responsible for educating Israel's skilled, high-tech workforce. After nine years of operation, there have been more the one thousand graduates as of 2018. Seventy percent of the graduates join the cyber and technological units in the Israel Defense Forces as their military service. The percentage of candidates and actual soldiers from peripherical areas in cyber units such as the 8200 Intelligence Unit has increased from 3 percent to 25 percent. Hence Magshimim proves to be making a clear change in Israel—both from security and economic angles, in addition to the long-term social impact it is creating, by offering a platform that is geared toward closing social gaps.

Sagy Bar, former head of human capital development at the Israeli Cyber Bureau and the founder and CEO of the Cyber Education Center, explains that originally, the programs were founded to address the lack of human resources for the military's cyber branch. "There just weren't enough people who were capable of doing the job," Sagy recalls.[4] "This was 2010, but since then there was also an increasing need coming from the industry itself. Israel was lagging behind simply because of lack of manpower." For over two decades, Sagy, back then a lieutenant colonel in an elite intelligence unit of the Israel Defense Forces, has headed complex integrative technological projects for military intelligence, leading them from concept to solution. He is the recipient of the Israel Defense Prize, a prestigious prize given by the president and minister of defense for excellence in contributing to the defense of the State of Israel. But it takes more than being an accomplished engineer, manager, and military commander to found programs such as Magshimim and Cyber GirlZ. Sagy is a man of vision who cares deeply about the security of the State of Israel and about its social challenges. And through these two ambitious initiatives, he is paving the way of combining both worlds.

The Magshimim, and later on Cyber GirlZ, programs stepped in to begin training Israeli children in the skills they'd need to succeed in the military and in business, as well as in social entrepreneurship. Participants are free to choose their path. They are not obligated to join a specific military branch, nor do they have to do anything with their skills in the future. "We simply provide them with the necessary tools to fulfill their dreams," says Sagy, "whatever they are. We take their potential and we channel it toward something concrete, which they later can work with in whatever way they see fit. It's another opportunity, another key to success, which we give them as early as their school years.

"The obvious relationship between these programs and the world of an entrepreneur," says Sagy, "is this ability to create something that at first no one wants or understands the need, and to then bring it to a place where it creates a significant change, where it becomes an inseparable part of society. These programs today are an integral part of the Israeli culture. This, to me, is the essence of entrepreneurship—to identify a problem, to come up with a solution, and to make that solution not only relevant but vital."

Sagy manages the programs at a strategic and operational level as part of his work with the Rashi Foundation. The IDF has long since been lobbying for their continued expansion, and they have become so successful and substantial that civilian companies are likewise requesting program graduates. Companies even invest funds (through donations) in these programs because they understand they are developing their future workforce in the fields of engineering and cyber.

Although it started out as a government-sponsored program, today Magshimim has also become a kind of youth movement. "It has its own ecosystem," says Sagy. "The graduates and the seventeen-year-olds are training the fourteen- and fifteen-year-olds. They are responsible for a substantial part of the summer activities, for example. We didn't initiate the graduate community that emerged, it was all their own idea."

Sagy sees this as one example of the kind of creativity the Israeli attitude toward youth fosters. "Part of what's unique about Israel is this attitude toward the development of the younger generations." Their experiences contending with the challenges of daily life in Israel, their experiences in youth movements and in the military, mean that by the time they reach twenty-one, "we have a quality, powerful, forged group of people, who are incredibly motivated to go out there and do." And what are your plans for the future? I ask him. "We are evaluating how to bring our know-how and expertise in creating successful frameworks for training kids in what we believe are the skills for the future, to other countries as well."

10

RESOURCEFULNESS

Educators in countries without compulsory military service often ask me, "How can we create a stronger connection between youth and community? How can we teach them responsibility and accountability?" They assume that in Israel it is military service that catalyzes these characteristics. I don't adhere to this assumption. And I definitely do not recommend compulsory military service unless it's really necessary. Actually, I believe other Israeli programs that target positive causes are equally significant.

In the previous chapters, I discussed Israel's youth movements and the ways in which they engage the individual with the community. But Israel offers civic-minded youth further ways to make a contribution, the most sought-after of which come with a price: postponing life for a year. But is it a price, or is it actually a prize?

A YEAR OF SERVICE

In Israel, there are various programs teens can apply to that allow them to dedicate a year, following high school, to community service and personal enrichment. The stated purpose of these programs is to prepare participants (called *chanichim*, as in the youth movements) for a full and significant service in the Israeli army, while instilling the values of social involvement and good citizenship. The most common are *mechina* (preparatory program) and *shnat sherut* (year of service).

What's unique about the *mechina* programs is their emphasis on informal studies, allowing participants to freely explore subjects ranging from philosophy, psychology, and political science to literature and history. *Shnat sherut* programs tend to emphasize community service in peripheral or otherwise disadvantaged areas.

But all these frameworks serve as a bridge between childhood and adulthood, between school and military service, offering youth a new experience of community life and autonomy. Participants leave their family homes for the first time and move in with twenty other people their own age, independently managing every aspect of their lives. They learn to take care of themselves on a budget, get along with their peers, and most of all, discover what they have to offer to their community and of what they might be capable of.

Wendy, a close friend of mine whose two daughters graduated from one of these programs, helped me understand: "I don't feel that Noa and Tamar paid a price by going to a *mechina* before their military service. Rather the opposite. These eighteen-year-olds are given responsibility way beyond their years, and essentially create and govern their own community for a year. Every project they take on is done from scratch, with little or no resources. It is values-based education and leadership training at another level— they didn't get anything close to this in the K through 12 school system."

At Tamar's graduation ceremony from the Ein Prat Mechina, Wendy and her family heard about the volunteer and social change projects the young people did during the year. In Tamar's case, she built a five-day camp for 130 Ethiopian kids, ages six through eighteen, in the southern city of Beersheba. This was done so that the parents of these kids could go to work while the kids were on break from school for the holiday of Chanukah. It involved finding a venue and arranging all the details, large and small: from food, to content, to insurance, to fund-raising (they needed to raise $4,000), and to finding places to sleep for her fellow *mechina* members who would be running the camp.

It may come as a surprise to some, but no one actually told Tamar to take on this project; she was merely encouraged to be *rosh gadol* (literally: big head). This is not meant as an insult—implying that she is arrogant or that we are disapproving of her because she thinks she knows everything. It certainly does not suggest that Tamar, in fact, has a big head. It is used figuratively to express a person who willingly takes on responsibilities and who readily initiates. It's a role model for others. All great entrepreneurs possess the *rosh gadol* mind-set: they can picture a different future, a missing piece of the puzzle, and just pick up the gauntlet. What frameworks like the *mechina* or *shnat sherut* truly enable and encourage is precisely this attitude of being *rosh gadol*. The system provides youth with the resources and tools to act; whether they follow through with it is up to them.

Wendy attests to the degree to which Tamar's sense of responsibility, accountability, and self-reliance flourished during this year. "I don't feel she paid a price by choosing to be part of the gap-year program. Nor does she. Actually, she decided to add on an additional six months at Ein Prat, devoting a total of eighteen months to community service and leadership training before her military service even begins.

"I further saw the power of the *mechina* model when I introduced a visiting friend from London to the Ein Prat Mechina program," Wendy told me. "This woman is now bringing the very same *mechina* model to Zimbabwe, where she is building leadership academies to help high school graduates get ahead."

The phenomenon of volunteering for a service "gap" year is growing and gaining momentum. In 2015, 5 percent of eighteen-year-olds in Israel chose to spend a year in an unpaid civic service framework before beginning their two to three years of compulsory military service. This means that they won't be able to start their "real" lives—college, career, marriage—until they are in their twenties. And yet more and more Israeli youth are volunteering for these types of programs every year, and, with spots limited, competition is fierce. Being admitted to these programs is now considered extremely prestigious.

CHILDREN'S VILLAGE

Megadim is one of two SOS Children's Villages in Israel (one of about five hundred worldwide) that care for children who cannot live with their biological families. Barbara Bamberger, a journalist for *Tablet*, describes the villages as "structured around a philosophy that strives to give every child a supportive and stable home that is part of a larger town or village."[1] She further writes:

> Megadim is a self-contained campus within a neighborhood in the northern Israeli city of Migdal Ha'Emek. The children who live there have been removed from their homes for any number of reasons, ranging from physical and emotional abuse to poverty and neglect. They are placed in Megadim only after the search for other alternatives, such as finding a family member to take them in, has been exhausted. About 80 children, aged 4 and up, are divided into eight "family" homes in Megadim. Each house has a "mother," an adult who makes her home in Megadim, and children of varying ages who adopt the role of siblings.

Megadim is one of the many institutions that simply cannot support enough personnel to give the kids everything they need. But with the help of *shnat sherut* volunteers, the community is thriving. Each family in the village is assigned a *shnat sherut* volunteer to help the mother and act as role model and mentor for the children. The youth volunteers are involved in every activity of the village, from trips to celebrations to projects in the community. As Barbara Bamberger explains, the volunteers basically help run the institute. They do everything from keeping the village in good shape, to doing administrative work in the office, to planning extracurricular activities, to working closely with the children in the vegetable garden or the petting zoo.

As you can see, the responsibilities these youth must take on involve their becoming adults, people whom children can look up to and count on for help. This can be a difficult but meaningful process of growing up, one in which youth become acquainted with the true needs of society and must choose their role within the group.

Within both *mechina* and *shnat sherut*, there is a network of mentors, social workers, and other adults that supports the group throughout the year, placing them within an appropriate transitional framework. So, while they're expected to take on responsibilities and become independent, they're offered as much support as they need—from the web of adult companions to their peers, with whom they share their lives for a year. The platform serves as the perfect balance of freedom to experiment and nurturing supervision.

WHY KIDS SHOULD "POSTPONE LIFE"

Izhar Shay is the general partner at the venture capital firm Canaan Partners Israel; the founder of Start-Up Stadium, a very popular Israeli tech community and podcast; and author of *As Beautiful as You*. He is an influential figure of the Israeli tech ecosystem. But he also happens to be a father of four, three of whom chose to do a *shnat sherut*. "When Shir, my eldest daughter, came to us with the decision to volunteer, we were very happy about it," he says.[2] Shir, now twenty-six, chose to spend that year in a challenging neighborhood in the poor city of Hadera, working with autistic children during school hours and managing the Tzofim (scouts) tribe of the neighborhood.

"Working with children from the autistic spectrum," says Shir, "is something we chose to do together as a commune." Her commune consisted of herself and four other youths, none of whom knew each other before coming to the *shnat sherut*. "We didn't get too much support from the adults who were responsible for us—some kind of bureaucratic failure," she explains, "but in some weird way everything actually worked out for the best. Each member of the commune understood his role in the house and we got along perfectly. We became a family."

After her *shnat sherut*, Shir went on to become an officer in Intelligence Unit 8200, the elite IDF intelligence unit, so that she was in her mid-twenties by the time she completed her military service. "I did care about being older than others when I start studying and working. But age was never really a deciding factor. I wanted to live life to the fullest, to be in the moment. I realized that *shnat sherut* is a once-in-a-lifetime opportunity." Today Shir is studying occupational therapy at Tel Aviv University. In her spare time, she helps children from underprivileged towns with their English studies and volunteers at her grandmother's home for the elderly.

Shir's decision to volunteer was entirely her own, and her group's choice to dedicate their time to working with children on the autistic spectrum was similarly made independently. Shir and all volunteers for these programs, perhaps for the first time in their lives, are making truly autonomous decisions. Up until this point, Israeli youth have been part of educational frameworks that have governed their lives for twelve years, five or six days a week, hours upon hours each day. School is the only institution they have known and lived throughout their childhood.

In most Western countries, turning eighteen simply means joining yet another educational institution. The similarities between
a college and high school are not small, and ultimately they represent yet another framework designed to guide young people's focus
and evaluate their behavior, restricting their freedom to explore
and make mistakes.

Now consider *shnat sherut*, a year where youth live independently, in groups of approximately a dozen members, and volunteer as an individual or a group, in any sector of society they find
important. Fulfilling the roles of responsible adult, supportive
friend, role model, and more, *shnat sherut* youth are given an opportunity to show initiative and social responsibility, under loose
supervision. This means that if they fail, it's their failure, and if
they succeed, it's their success. This is their first real encounter
with ownership.

Experts such as Jeffrey Arnett, a key thinker in the field of
developmental psychology, point out that in countries where this
kind of gap year (or the years spent in the military) does not exist,
youth often exhibit problems integrating into adult society later
on. These difficulties are manifested in a sense of alienation and
rebellion, or alternatively one of indifference and avoiding social
involvement. School does not prepare young people to enter the
workforce and take on social roles. The options that are available
for them when they graduate from high school are to continue
their studies, find a job as an unskilled worker, or not integrate at
all—all of which fail to meet their needs.

Gap years that involve volunteering in informal frameworks
provide young people with a gradual yet efficient transition from
adolescence to adulthood. It requires that they learn a variety of
skills: organizational abilities, social initiatives, development of
meaningful relationships with their peers and those younger and
older, team management and leadership, and an intellectual ability to deal with theoretical and ideological issues.

While the volunteer work youth do is significant and, in some cases, even indispensable, many realize during this year that it is not possible to change society overnight. Often, their work goes unrewarded and the results they've hoped to achieve are barely noticeable. This is a difficult realization. Coming from the clear and defined world of school and the loving embrace of the family, it is difficult to accept that there are things that are out of one's control. Facing disappointments and overcoming despair are two of the greatest challenges youth encounter during their year of service.

So, should we encourage youth to postpone their lives for one or more years? There really is no correct answer. On the one hand, it's true that postponing university and job seeking for four or five years is significant (taking into account the years of compulsory military service). Even one year is a long time to be out of the game. But then again, isn't going to university at eighteen actually postponing life? Is learning a profession at the age of eighteen, before knowing one's society or even oneself, more beneficial than doing so a few years later, after living through a challenging, wonderful, sometimes excruciating experience? These are questions that close to ten thousand Israeli youth have found the answer to in years of service.

SCALE AND SUSTAINABILITY

IF WE CONSIDER Israelis' teenage years as their efficiency stage, in which they test their limits, experiment, and take risks, but also learn to rely on themselves as responsible, accountable, contributing parts of society, then the following years, when most Israelis join the military, can be seen as their scaling-up phase.

A business that reaches efficiency at last has a well-working mechanism. But just when it seems like fewer resources are being wasted and all the company's parts and roles are well defined and integrated, it's time to ramp up toward scale.

At this stage in the life of any business, different elements come together, forming a more robust organization. It becomes clear which specific human capital the business must rely on: who its professionals are and what expertise they need to have, what the values and culture of this specific business organization are. Structures supporting these principles are established in a more formal way: the C-Suite executive leaders, the mid-level management, team leaders, and so on. The business is now ready to scale and hopefully sustain its market share.

In the case of Israel, the military formally acts as such a scaled organization, comprising hundreds of thousands of individuals. You might think there is no connection at all between business organizations and military ones. I assume that what comes to your mind when you think of a military organization is structure. Hierarchy. Orders. Discipline.

Standardization. However, the Israeli military does not conform to this image. Rather the opposite is true.

Try to put aside what you envision when you think of a military organization, what you learned from movies and history books. Let me introduce you to a different type of military organization, whose building blocks and culture are more and more relevant to the future of scaled businesses. Ready?

11

HUMAN CAPITAL

Let's return to the characteristics that come to mind when we think of a military organization: Hierarchy and structure—probably. Formality and orders—for sure. Standardized equipment, a clear chain of command, extended periods away from family and friends, and rigid protocols. In the military, one assumes, members are not encouraged to think outside the box. Do what you're told to do. Not more. Not less.

Let me surprise you: the Israel Defense Forces, or IDF, though a highly professional military organization, is in so many ways the opposite of what you envision. As we'll see in this and the coming chapters, the experience of Israeli soldiers is quite different from that of conscripts to other militaries around the world. The Israeli kindergarten or playground physically resembles the American kindergarten or playground, but with a few key differences influencing its dynamics; and the Israeli teenager's experience largely resembles the European or Asian teenager's, but again with a few meaningful discrepancies. Likewise, the IDF is, in almost every way, uniquely *Israeli*.

Take this snapshot, for starters: once out of training, most soldiers address their superiors by their first names; crucial decisions during fighting are typically made at the level of small command teams; standard equipment is being altered on a daily basis; commanders are very often responsible for soldiers even two decades older than they are; and most Israeli soldiers would not go more than twenty days without returning home to spend time with family and friends.

Now that you've been reading about Israeli society for more than a hundred pages, none of the above is likely to come as a surprise. But while this description may seem a natural extension of what Israelis are used to from before their military service, conscription is nonetheless a seminal event in youth's lives, and their military experience often shapes them in ways nothing previous could really have prepared them for.

CONSCRIPTION AND SORTING

While seventeen-year-olds in other countries are preoccupied with preparing for college or entering the job market, most Israeli high school seniors are readying themselves for compulsory military service of approximately thirty-two months for men, twenty-four months for women. For many, this means jockeying to be chosen by elite units in the IDF. For others, this will be a chance to live independently of their parents for the first time. For all, it means becoming a contributor to Israeli society.

In a sense, their service in the IDF is a culmination of all the experiences they have accumulated throughout their childhood and youth. They always knew they would join the military and, in many ways, have been preparing for recruitment day since the first time they saw the news. Now it's here.

According to public sources, the IDF has, as of 2015, 176,500 conscripts and 445,000 reserves.[1] For every 4 to 20 soldiers there is one noncommissioned officer, for every 20 to 40 soldiers one platoon leader, and a company commander usually oversees anywhere between 40 and 100 soldiers.

The screening and sorting process of all these people is of the most interesting in the world, I dare say. It proves to be highly successful, accurate, and efficient, and it plays a significant role in steering young people toward their future career and life paths.

How does the IDF match teenagers, as young as seventeen, with the position that fits them best? With no CVs to review, no relevant background or accomplishments, the Israeli military relies on an assessment of skills, on one hand, and potential for growth and learning, on the other. Skills and potential rather than knowledge and experience—quite the opposite of what screening processes in most business organizations look like, where past accomplishments and credentials are highly valued.

This is particularly critical in the technological, high-tech, and cyber fields—both within the military and without. These are areas in which needs are constantly changing and are thus highly unpredictable. In today's military environment, as in the current job market, everyone must adapt constantly. Skill sets that many generations have worked so hard to acquire are often made redundant overnight. Recruitment and placement are no longer about what specific skills someone has, but rather about how they can apply those skills in various settings. The focus—across the board—is shifting from expertise to agility, flexibility of mind, speed of learning, and being extremely comfortable with change.

WHAT EVERY SEVENTEEN-YEAR-OLD ISRAELI GOES THROUGH

Formally, the recruitment process begins somewhere around age seventeen, with an official notification calling on the teenagers to present themselves at an army induction facility. During this *tzav rishon*, meaning "first order," the focus is on the basics. All enlistees are interviewed and go through a procedure to assess their ability to read and write Hebrew. They also provide a summary of their latest school reports. The IDF is interested in knowing about any technological background and education that the enlistee might have.

The second notification soon arrives, and that second day is devoted to a thorough medical examination at the end of which the recruit's "medical profile" is determined. The enlistees then go on to an interview with a psycho-technical interviewer, usually a female soldier only a year, or maximum two years, older than the inductee, but who has been specially trained for four months in evaluation techniques, psychology, interpersonal relationships, and the identification of mental problems or stresses. The primary purpose of this interview is to chart the personality traits of the recruit: motivation, ability to withstand stress, social or antisocial behavior patterns, and suitability for specific roles in the IDF.

The scoring system of these psycho-technical interviews was developed by Nobel laureate Daniel Kahneman, a founding father of cognitive heuristics, who, at the age of twenty-one, was tasked with finding a way to evaluate candidates for combat duty in the Israeli military. In practice, armed with the medical profile and the results of the psycho-technical evaluation, the IDF is ready to consider candidates for various volunteer units of the army. These roles include aircrew, seagoing naval duties, and some elite forces functions. Those found suitable are sent written material about the roles and are invited to undergo more complex psycho-technical evaluations, special medical tests, and a series of interviews with psychologists and professionals from the unit concerned.

Candidates with the necessary medical, fitness, and intelligence scores receive an invitation for the Israeli equivalent of the American SFAS—Special Forces Assessment and Selection—which in the IDF is referred to as *gibush*, best translated as "formation." Twice a year, hundreds of qualified aspirants undergo rigorous testing to try to earn a spot in some of the IDF's most exclusive units. They're tested on their strength, their physical and mental endurance, and their skills in teamwork and cooperation. Their tasks include everything from sprints to mind exercises. Commanders monitor the candidates to assure they can handle both the physical and the emotional strain of these units' demanding activities.

The focus of the *gibush* and psycho-technical exams is always to test the candidates' mental and physical suitability for the unit, as opposed to his or her previous knowledge or education. In other words, most units are interested in what the candidate can do—what challenges they can and can't deal with and how quickly they can be taught different skills. While there are specific roles that require an extensive background in science or technical skills (such as some positions in the navy), most elite, combat, combat-support, and noncombat units, and some intelligence units, do not require any prior technical or academic qualification.

NOT SO IN OTHER COUNTRIES

In Israel, the combination of nearly universal conscription, the high turnover rate, and this customized screening process means that any youth, regardless of his or her background, can be selected for the most prestigious and elite units. It also means that a person can become the highest-ranking officer in the army without having completed high school (though, as they move up through the ranks, they will be sent by the military for further academic training).

This is a system that disregards a person's past or lack of practical knowledge and only looks for skills, capabilities, and potential. However, this is not the case in other armies around the Western world, particularly when it comes to routes to becoming a military officer.

In the British Army, only those who have a successful academic record can become officers. In their system, British teenagers can become officers directly out of high school. That is, they need no military background before they are trained to command conscripts. The skills according to which they are selected are unrelated to their achievements in military training, on the battlefield, or in everyday communications and interactions with peers, all of which are qualities that are crucial for an Israeli soldier to be elected for officer training.

This means two important things for people entering the British Army. First, individuals who didn't have the chance to get a good education in their youth are unlikely to become officers. Second, there is a clear distinction between conscripted soldiers, who are physically and mentally familiar with army life, and officers, who spend most of their lives in the classroom and are then expected to command those who have actual battlefield experience. The US Army is similar to the UK's in this respect. In the US military, commissioned officers enter the military with a four-year college degree already in hand, and from the start are on a path toward becoming an officer. Warrant officers are promoted from within the enlisted ranks due to their technical expertise. Similarly, in the French army, the higher the level of education, the higher the level of accessible positions.

Whether or not it is important for an officer to have practical military experience, including life on the battlefield, is debatable. The fact is, however, that there are significant differences between armies whose officers have no practical experience and the IDF, whose officers were all rank-and-file soldiers themselves. Only after a soldier has proven he or she has the set of skills and necessary potential to be a good officer will they be considered for officers' training courses and later move up the ranks. So, in reality, soldiers are selected for command from within the unit, and those who select them are their own officers who have observed them from their initial training to their active service, and the bases for their selection are their qualities and personality traits relevant to the battlefield. But given how short active military service typically is, the process needs to be condensed into only a few months. Within a very short time frame the IDF needs to identify those suitable for officers' training, put them through the six-month course, and get them back to their unit to complete the rest of their military service as a commanding officer.

CASE STUDY: IDF'S INTELLIGENCE UNIT 8200

One of the largest units in the entire IDF is an intelligence unit called 8200, which we've encountered a few times already in this book. It is the Israeli equivalent of the NSA, only in Israel it is part of the military, the consequence of which is that Intelligence Unit 8200 "professionals" are young soldiers. As with many other units, the quality of the recruits and their suitability for the role stand in direct relation to the unit's ability to fulfill its mission. In the case of Intelligence Unit 8200, where the rigor of the screening process means that only a small fraction of all recruits will be accepted, their "background" becomes important.

But what is considered relevant background might surprise you: academic achievements are considered, but so are the social activities the teenagers were involved in, such as participation in youth movements. The unit is also open to youth who were recommended by their principals, either because of extraordinary creative thinking or their out-of-the-box attitude. And every soldier in the unit can recommend one candidate to be admitted to the screening process, even if that nominee does not meet the entry requirements, a means by which many have come to join the unit. Intelligence Unit 8200, like other elite units in the IDF, make a point of reaching out to 100 percent of the relevant cohort about to join the military. Only 1 percent of the most talented 1 percent of the youth will eventually succeed in going through the screening process and joining those units—cherry picking at its best.

The screening process of Intelligence Unit 8200 is an ever-evolving process; from year to year the process is improving and accumulates more gray tones. Three decades ago, for example, there was a clear divide between intelligence and technological positions. With time, the dividing lines have been blurred and new admission criteria have been applied accordingly. Positions in Intelligence Unit 8200 require strengths in various areas, including teamwork, persistence, endurance, computer skills, a talent for languages, and so on. As the job becomes more complex and intricate, so does the screening process, which is why, with time, more subtle tests have been devised that include an analysis of cognitive and interpersonal capabilities, as well as a psychological profile.

Candidates are tested on their cognitive abilities, facility with languages, and programming and mathematical problems. But rather than assessing the candidate's previous knowledge, what is being tested is their ability to deal with an area they haven't encountered before. For example, tests might include teaching some portion of a new language during the exam itself (up to five hours long) to see how the candidate deals with it. Those that show promise will go on to the course, during which, in only six months, the cadets will become highly proficient in that language.

The screening process for another course, for instance, does not look for any actual skills to begin with. Instead, it is screening for people who have a range of qualities including an ability to motivate others, emotional intelligence, broad vision, and an understanding of situations. Much like in the civil market, where a company manager doesn't have to be the best marketing person or the best engineer but does need to know how to manage the experts, military leaders do not necessarily have to be the top cyber experts, but they do need to be able to motivate, manage, and lead others.

Further testing for the unit includes an eight-hour cognitive assessment, a situation exam that looks at candidates' ability to work in a team, to lead, to work under pressure, to express themselves coherently and concisely, and so on. In the final stage they go through an additional interview, after which the list of cadets is finalized.

Throughout the IDF, by the time a cadet begins a course they are already seen as part of the unit, be it intelligence, combat, navy, or any other kind. The purpose of most courses is not to screen but to ready recruits for service. Ideally, the initial screening process will have accurately predicted who can pass the course. By the time the course is complete, there's no question of whether or not they fit but rather where exactly within the unit they fit.

NOT JUST FOR THE IDF

My company, Synthesis, is inspired by and based on these screening methodologies. With limited information about individuals, we are capable of assessing their main personality traits, their drivers, their motivators, and their fit to a specific environment. Equipped with this personal assessment, we can also guide them in training themselves to leverage an agile mind-set to solve problems and achieve goals.

The insights we glean about people are ones Israeli employers are naturally used to considering during hiring processes.

Even outside the elite units, the military experience of Israeli job applicants tells prospective employers what kind of selection process applicants navigated and what skills and relevant experience they may already possess. Army veterans have proved that they possess a certain set of skills not only applicable to, but often crucial for, various jobs in the civil market. Having gone through three years in a combat unit, for instance, might not have given you any programming skills, but it certainly shows that you are capable of adapting, enduring, working in a team, that you are a quick learner, and more.

Employers looking for new employees might do something very similar to what military officers in charge of screening processes do: look at the skills and capabilities that a person has, rather than technical experience or knowledge in a specific field.

12

CULTURE

In my senior year of high school, when I was seventeen and a half, I was summoned for Intelligence Unit 8200's screening process. Back then, we didn't know the name of the unit or its role, which became well known only in recent years. It was a secret unit; we were only told it was part of the Intelligence Corps. I sat for some tests and was interviewed by someone who looked pretty young to me, in his early twenties at most. A few months later I got a letter in the mail congratulating me on passing the tests—I didn't even know for what—and, by the way, if I wanted to take on a meaningful role in the Intelligence Corps, I would have to take a three-month course *before* being drafted. The course would begin in August, right after my high school graduation.

I agreed. I began the course a month after my eighteenth birthday. For three months I lived in a pastoral civil facility in the center of Israel, nothing resembling a military base. The only people wearing uniforms were our instructors—whom we knew by their first names, and assumed they were in their early twenties. From 8:00 a.m. until midnight every day, five days a week, plus an additional five hours on Friday, we learned things that were completely new to us. We were about thirty young men and women.

Although we sat in a classroom, this was a very different type of studying than the one we knew from high school. Yes, there

were hours of formal teaching, when an "expert" (or someone
we *thought* was an expert, only to learn later that these so-called
experts were only a few years older than we were) introduced us
to a specific topic. But most of the hours were dedicated to what
was called "SF," which stands for "self-work," like homework in
school. Only the "self" does not stand for solo work, but rather for
the entire group of thirty, or smaller groups within this group, as
we saw fit. We spent hours upon hours exploring, learning, practicing what was introduced to us earlier that day by the "experts."
Very rapidly, I realized two important things. The first was that
as talented as some of us may have thought we were, we were
now surrounded by even more talented people. In this milieu, we
were no longer above average. The second important lesson was
that there was no way any of us could cope with all the material
on our own. We needed to rely on others to help us and be capable
of helping others. It was incredibly intense, but I remember this
period as one of the most enriching and empowering experiences
of my life.

After three months, we graduated from the course—all of us—
and officially joined the military, where we served for at least the
next three years. Before we took up posts within different teams
in the unit, we spent three more weeks in boot camp. Finally,
we were on a real military base, with all it entailed. Uniform.
Structured timetable. Meeting other soldiers from all around the
country. And only then, once trained in the protocols, methods,
and values of the IDF, were we assigned to our teams within Intelligence Unit 8200.

I can't share much about my responsibilities and duties during my military service. However, I can say that I did not miss
even one day of service in over four years. I woke up every morning feeling that the security of my country was dependent on me
and my team. Funny enough, we all felt the same. After nine
months as a junior intelligence professional, I was elected to join

the officer training program, which meant committing to another year of service. Officer training took six months, including both basic and professional training. And then I returned to my team, now as commander, or, as we called it: team leader.

The math is simple: eighteen months after I joined the military, I had already completed a professional training course; held a junior position in a highly advanced technological environment; and was selected to and completed officer training. Now I was the team leader of the same group I left only six months earlier as a junior member. For the next twenty-four months I held this position, at the forefront of Israel's intelligence efforts in a specific area. As members of my fifteen-person unit completed their military service and left, I trained new members. I was fortunate to have a rare opportunity, for the last six months of my military service, to serve as head of the faculty of Intelligence Unit 8200's officer training school. I was not yet twenty-three at the time. This may sound to you like an incredible journey. For many young Israelis, this is just normal.

AN ARMY OF THE PEOPLE

One of the things that differentiates the IDF from other armies around the world is the fact that there is an extremely high turnover of soldiers. The individuals who constitute each unit are completely replaced every three years, with the exception of a number of officers, who usually continue their service for another year or two.

Replacing the entire force every three to five years is unheard of in other armies. Upon joining the US Army, for instance, people either enlist for a period of four years of active duty followed by four years in the reserves (Individual Ready Reserve, or IRR) or they embark on a professional military career with the intent of remaining in service until they retire.

The turnover rates significantly affect the structure of an army. In Intelligence Unit 8200, 90 percent of the human capital is replaced every five years. Can you imagine the American NSA going through such turnover? Can you imagine any big corporation replacing 90 percent of its human capital every half decade?

Beyond its consequences for the military, the IDF's high turnover rates mean that Israeli society must constantly absorb waves of soldiers who need to be reintegrated into civil life. But, upon discharge, soldiers do not sever their relationship with the military: most go on to serve in the reserves for anywhere from three to thirty years. So, it's no wonder that the army is considered to be "the army of the people." But this, of course, is just the tip of the iceberg.

The IDF is interwoven with Israeli society in many respects. One thing that strengthens the military-civilian relationship is the fact that, as I mentioned in the previous chapter, soldiers serve in Israel no more than a six-hour drive from their families. This enables them to return home every other weekend or every third weekend to spend a couple of days with family and friends. The sight of soldiers swarming bus stops, streets, and other public spaces, particularly on Friday afternoon and Sunday morning, is familiar to all Israelis.

Moreover, what Israeli soldiers defend is literally their own land, often even the actual town in which they grew up. Since Israel is a small country, most citizens have had the chance to explore and become familiar with its hills and valleys. Having to then serve and protect the actual land, soldiers often develop a strong emotional connection with their military role. What is implied here is that there is an emotional bond that is created between Israeli soldiers, the land, and the general population, due to the proximity of the battlefront to the home front.

But by far the most powerful experience that soldiers, particularly combat fighters, have in the IDF is that of forming intense relationships with their peers. The social bond that is created when sharing in an often challenging experience fosters the kind of camaraderie that military organizations are famous for.

In the IDF, strong social bonds are created both naturally and intentionally. Naturally, because whenever you place a group of people in close quarters, requiring them to work closely together under extreme conditions, you can expect them to form a powerful, unbreakable bond. Intentionally, because ideals of brotherhood and mutual care are sought during screening processes, and camaraderie is regarded as one of the most valuable assets of the IDF and is actively encouraged throughout one's service.

During screening, whether it is for intelligence, noncombat troops, or the elite combat units, many tests and trials are geared toward assessing a person's ability to relate to others, to support others, and to be a good team member. Without these skills, the IDF cannot function. Take the example of a screening test done for the Duvdevan unit, a special operations force within the Paratroopers Brigade. After a physically and psychologically grueling day, the group of seventeen-year-olds are ordered to carry one of their teammates on a stretcher up a sandy hill. But they are also told that those who would like to rest can do so. The test is of course not to see whether they can make it to the top, but rather to see which of them choose to sit while their teammates carry the load. Those who sit down are unlikely to continue to the next phase.

Since its initiation, the IDF has made a point of striving for camaraderie. The value of friendship, or what in Hebrew is better known as *reut* or *achvat lochamim*, is perhaps the most important one a soldier will learn throughout his or her service.

Camaraderie is of course critical for morale and motivation. In combat, in particular, each member of the unit relies on the other in order to survive and to carry out successful combat operations. In his book *Combat Motivation: The Behavior of Soldiers in Battle*,

Anthony Kellett, the Canadian military researcher and historian, explains that "Israelis regard fighting as very much a social act based on collective activity, cooperation, and mutual support."[1] In battle, every soldier depends on the other and on the professionalism and leadership capabilities of the unit commander. As Sergio Catignani explains in his article "Motivating Soldiers," the IDF method dictates that company commanders should be characterized by having some specific qualities and values, for example, "face-to-face leadership quality, personal integrity, and *the ability to create mutual trust between the sub-commanders and the soldier and to [instill] trust* in the weapon and fighting systems."[2]

One of the strongest characteristics of Israel's historical military struggles is the asymmetry of Israel's forces and its enemies. In light of this, Catignani, a scholar of security and strategic studies, explains that the way in which Israel has managed to ward off attacks against it, both conventional and nonconventional, even while being significantly outnumbered, "has been due mostly to its superior qualitative edge based on its armed forces' professionalism, superior training methods, and combat morale."

A MELTING POT

So central is the IDF's emphasis on camaraderie and morale that its application is grounded in actual policies that have their roots in the 1950s and '60s. During the first two decades of its independence, Israel's leaders sought to create for the young Israeli society a uniform identity. They therefore adopted a melting-pot policy. With this policy the state hoped to be able to assimilate the overwhelming waves of immigrants who arrived from many different countries, often with extremely different cultural backgrounds. By doing so, the state hoped to carve out a new and differentiated Israeli identity.

The melting-pot policy, however, was problematic. It intentionally ignored the multiculturalism that the newcomers brought with them, often forcing entire communities to forfeit their identity for the sake of unification. In time, this policy was revoked and more tolerant approaches were taken. But regardless of its problems and difficulties, the melting-pot policy has achieved a great deal. The young country managed to absorb thousands upon thousands of immigrants and to harness their abilities and motivations for the sake of a common goal, which has always been to build Israel.

The army, of course, was and continues to be the ultimate melting pot. Not only does it place people from all ethnic and cultural backgrounds together in close quarters, it also strips them of their cultural and social signifiers and provides them with new grounds upon which to form an identity. Being a melting pot is a necessary requirement for any military organization, particularly one that follows a flat-hierarchy model, as does the IDF (we'll get back to this in the next chapter). If you want soldiers to trust their peers and their commanders, you cannot have them feeling superior in any way due to their social, ethnic, or economic background. Soldiers must be secure in their sense of camaraderie, viewing their world as consisting of the friendships, experiences, and skills they have acquired in their service.

In Israel, though, the armed forces' sense of camaraderie goes beyond that of soldiers on active duty. Since they are an integral part of society, both by virtue of their physical presence in the streets and by the fact that soldiers (relatively) quickly return to civilian life and civilians frequently become soldiers again in reserves, it's not hard to imagine how the soldiers' sense of camaraderie extends throughout most of Israeli society. Israeli society as a whole has a shared experience of military service upon which national camaraderie is built.

As the political scientist Ronald Krebs describes, the power of the military to create social cohesion is well documented throughout history. "President Theodore Roosevelt and his fellow Progressives hoped that universal military training would 'Americanize' the mass of newcomers who had recently landed on America's shores, and Leonid Brezhnev, a Soviet politician, similarly believed that widespread service in the Red Army would forge a united Soviet citizenry."[3] As characteristic of great world leaders, Roosevelt and Brezhnev chose to deal with their country's multinationalism situation by turning to the armed forces and applying military draft policies to help instill a sense of national unity and community.

Krebs continues: "This view of the military as a key institution for the labeling and transmission of social values has roots stretching back to ancient Greece." This was extremely common during the early twentieth century, and was an international practice across Europe, as well as Africa and Asia, which, after gaining independence in the decades following World War II, "charged their armies with weaving a national fabric rent by communal rifts." But as with Israel's melting-pot policy, this belief in the military's ability to unite a nation and to blur social and ethnic differences was soon abandoned. What persisted in Israel, however, was a natural consequence of the conditions under which the IDF operates. Where policy failed, natural circumstances succeeded.

SOCIAL BONDS THAT EXTEND THE MILITARY MILIEU

The story of *reut* does not end when one's obligatory service ends. The social bond that was initiated during a soldier's service is then strengthened on an annual-or-more basis for the next twenty years, as soldiers return to the military for service in the reserves. Beyond its practical military function, strengthening social bonds is the greatest power of the reserves.

The experience of the reserves (the fact that every year a person must drop his work, personal life, and other occupations and go back to wearing a uniform) is deeply embedded in the Israeli

experience and it serves as a constant reminder of that initial unifying experience Israelis have in their early twenties.

Like with most policies in Israel, the reserves stem from necessity; Israel, since the initiation of the state, has always suffered
from an imbalance between high commitment and motivation
and low numbers. The country was simply never able to afford a
standing army to meet its defense needs and challenges.

In his book *The Israel Defense Forces: A People's Army*, Louis
Williams explains that "because the army cuts across all segments of the population, and because the reserves are organized
according to each individual's service from before their initial
discharge, the army often turns the pyramid of civilian organization upside down. Thus, a university professor may find himself
under the command of one of his students, or a plant manager
subordinate to one of his workers when they turn out for their pe-
riodic service in the reserve."[4] An army structured so is undoubt-
edly a major contributor to blurring the lines of class and social
strata that are felt in other aspects of Israeli society, as well as to
a national sense of being one family and taking responsibility for
each other's well-being.

But the involvement of the military in civil life goes beyond the
passive (yet powerful) relationships that are created circumstantially. In addition to being a natural bridging platform between
different social sectors, the military also takes on an active role in
promoting social issues it deems significant within the Israeli society. "Following the War of Independence," Williams gives as an
example, "the IDF established a 'minorities unit' (Brigade 300)
consisting mainly of Druze, a few Circassians and some Bedouin.
The unit operates to this day and its members take a crucial role
in border patrol and other functions."

To take another example, the education offered to soldiers by
the IDF during their initial service goes far beyond the professional training required for the effective execution of military

objectives. As soldiers are soon to be civilians, the IDF has a role in preparing them for civil life. Thus, many people who might be considered of smaller marginal military importance, such as new immigrants or Israelis of disadvantaged backgrounds, enjoy the benefits of IDF's education, including Hebrew language courses and support in receiving a high school diploma.

In addition, during their regular service, soldiers participate in weeklong educational seminars that focus on the history, geography, nature, and society of the State of Israel. The army has educational units located at Yad Vashem, the main Holocaust museum in Israel, and the Diaspora Museum. The IDF also takes part in helping youth at risk by combining classroom instruction with work on an army base. Importantly, these programs are designed not for soldiers but for weaker groups within Israeli society; the operational benefits here are marginal or nonexistent.

Indeed, as Moshe Sherer, a professor at Tel Aviv University, states, "The IDF offers a second chance to educationally deprived youth from lower economic backgrounds by means of a program especially designed to educate, train, and equip such young people with civilian skills to facilitate their integration into society."[5]

Finally, not only is the military involved in Israel's social sphere, but the opposite is true as well. That is, civilians participate in nonoperational military activities. For example, many voluntary organizations raise funds and participate actively in programs that are beyond the means of the defense budget. Thus, not only does the Association for the Wellbeing of Israeli Soldiers raise money to provide sports equipment, cultural needs, and presents for soldiers, but its volunteers can also be found on the battle lines, bringing cakes and fruit and, if necessary, taking messages back to families.

It is important to understand that the Israeli army is completely enmeshed in Israeli life and is an integral part of the

Israeli experience in many respects. Israelis are constantly cross-
ing the borders between the military and civilian spheres and
leveraging this fluidity in both realms.

MILITARY CAPITAL, SOCIAL NETWORKS,
AND ALUMNI SOCIETIES

In considering the relationship between the military and the Israeli tech industry, Ori Swed and John Butler of the University
of Texas Sociology Department offer an unusual definition of
"military capital."[6] Instead of the term referring to the assets of
the defense establishment, they describe military capital as the
aggregate of human capital (new skills gained in the military),
social capital (new social networks), and cultural capital (new social norms and codes of behavior). In their study, Swed and Butler
found that military capital is highly valued and utilized in the
Israeli tech sector. Among other things, the data revealed that
90 percent of tech workers are veterans. They found that those
segments of the population that do not go through the IDF service
also do not partake in the industry. A concerning statistic reveals
that "only 3 percent of salaried employees in the tech industry
are Israeli Arabs. For the Haredim, the ultra-religious population
that is exempt from service, the figures are even less significant
and stand on 2.4 percent." These two groups alone compose about
30 percent of the general population. And while they are repre-
sented in most of the economy's divisions, the researchers found,
"they are nearly excluded from the tech industry." Social problems
aside, this data shows that those who do complete military service
have a clear advantage over those who have not served.

This privileged position stems from several factors. One is
the capabilities soldiers gain during their training and perfect
throughout their service. Another, perhaps even more significant

factor is the social connections one acquires during their service. The more connected and the more connecting the individual, Swed and Butler point out, "the more social capital [they] possess."

Social networks built during service in the IDF are commonly maintained and expanded beyond the military context. For example, official societies, forums, and groups founded by veterans act as social hubs, extending the camaraderie formed during military service into civilian life. These networks are critical for the process of helping veterans reintegrate into society. In most countries, veteran reintegration and job placement are challenges managed by the state. A study by Raffaella Di Schiena on the relationship between civilian organizations and deployed military units found that in the United States, the phenomenon of homeless veterans precipitated the assignment of a federal task force whose role is to deal with the challenges of reintegration.

The Israeli case, on the other hand, presents a different model of reintegration wherein military service is perceived as an advantage and the social networks created during and after a soldier's service function as a launching pad. According to Swed and Butler, "over 70 percent of the [Israeli] population believes military service contributes to personal connections, [and] over 68 percent of the population believes that IDF service increases the chances of being hired."

Often these social networks are institutionalized in the form of alumni societies. There are numerous such groups active today, with goals varying from promoting the unit's values and legacy, to helping veterans reintegrate into civilian life and find a job, to encouraging Israelis to volunteer while traveling abroad ("Fighters for Life").

But perhaps the most organized and influential of these alumni groups is the 8200 Alumni Association. The name 8200 came to prominence as its graduates made their names in the local tech and venture capital industry. Compared with other military veterans, graduates of Intelligence Unit 8200 have been the most successful at leveraging their military capital in their civilian careers.

The 8200 Alumni Association was established in 1989 and, as is the case with most military alumni associations, had as its initial purpose nurturing and maintaining the legacy of the unit. Today the association consists of more than sixteen thousand members and operates in numerous sectors of Israeli society.

The story of the 8200 Alumni Association is a story of metamorphosis, and it starts with one of Israel's industry leaders, Nir Lempert, a specialist in change.

Currently the CEO of the Mer Group, Nir is an expert when it comes to leading organizations that need to go through turnaround processes. Before Mer, Nir was CEO of Israeli TV broadcaster Channel 10, which he helped see through numerous crises, and before that he was executive deputy CEO of Yes, Israel's multichannel TV company. He then spent nearly a decade as the CEO of Zap Group, previously known as Israel's Yellow Pages. Nir led the transition of the company from print to digital, essentially saving it from becoming redundant, a transition that took almost seven years. It might seem ironic that as a change expert, Nir should spend nearly a decade in a single organization. But a closer look reveals that the company he first came to work for and the one he left ten years later have very little in common.

Aside from agility, loyalty seems to be Nir's most prominent quality. He gave the IDF twenty-two years of his life, serving in different roles within Intelligence Unit 8200, until he finally retired as a colonel. But his romance with 8200 is far from over. Today, he serves as chairman of the 8200 Alumni Association, where he focuses on encouraging initiatives that promote entrepreneurial skills and mind-sets among Israelis.

Nir recalls that it was in 2006, when he took on the 8200 Alumni group's chairmanship, that the association began to expand its scope. "We started dealing not only with the unit's legacy, but also developing and enriching the alumni network and helping it act within the broader community."[7] The success of the association is evident first of all in its numbers. "Since its establishment," says Nir, "we grew from several hundred to tens of thousands. We have lots of volunteers who take an active role in the different activities and projects.

"As a worldview," says Nir, "we decided to capitalize on the networking power of the 8200 Alumni Association, the alumni knowledge, experience, and even our so-called brand name. We wanted to see how we can introduce this concept, this phenomenon into Israeli society as a whole. As of today, we have five running programs, in addition to numerous other activities and projects. All programs are open to everyone, not only Unit 8200 alumni. They are managed and executed by the members of the association but are not directed exclusively for them. On the contrary, they reach out to as wide an audience as possible. The majority of participants in these programs are, in fact, from outside of the association.

"What we aim to do is give tools for new entrepreneurs who are still in the conceptual phase. We are less interested in the idea itself and focus more on the person. What we do in practice is connect people. We reach out to lecturers, we introduce case studies, and connect the outside community with the alumni network. What happens then is that members of the association who are, as I said, not necessarily 8200 graduates, connect to the graduates of 8200, thus forming a new community of their own."

In 2010, I personally pivoted, leaving behind my career as general counsel (namely, legal counsel) to tech companies, and began an entrepreneurial journey. My first endeavor was the 8200 Entrepreneurship and Innovation Support Program (EISP), which I founded on behalf of the 8200 Alumni Association. Our goal was to leverage the existing network of 8200 alumni for the benefit of first-time entrepreneurs, whatever their background. Building on the core values of the unit, including screening methodologies, we were able to identify the most promising early-stage entrepreneurs and provide them with effective access to the 8200 network, while creating for them a new network of their peers. There are now over one hundred start-ups and tech companies who graduated from the program; together they have launched the 8200 EISP Alumni network. What began as a project of the 8200 Alumni Association has since turned into a separate, independent network.

Throughout Israel you will find examples where the model of association and networking that was formed in the army is being copied and applied to the civilian sphere. One such example was spearheaded by Nir and the 8200 Alumni Association, which created a program targeting Arab and Druze entrepreneurs. "What we find with these populations is that they are facing two major challenges," Nir explained. "First, traditionally, most of them live in peripheral areas and second, they are a minority. Circumstantially, then, they are not part of the general social network, not to mention the 8200 network (as few of them join this unit). We are trying to help them infiltrate the tech ecosystem. Hybrid, the program in discussion, is a kind of accelerator that over several months brings entrepreneurs together with more experienced entrepreneurs and companies to review case studies. We also have another program called 8200 Women2Women, which takes around thirty women, most of whom are 8200 graduates, who systematically act as mentors to other young women (not necessarily 8200 graduates) who are at a significant crossroads in terms of their careers."

The 8200 Alumni Association is a great example of the effectiveness of grassroots efforts, which are so common in Israel. As Nir explains, "The association has no formal mechanism, there is no manager on the payroll who gives orders, there are no offices—

everything is done completely virtually. Even my role as chairman is to facilitate. My role is to synchronize, to be the conductor. We are proud of the fact that one hundred percent of our funds reach their destination. From A to Z, everything is managed and executed by the veterans themselves."

13

MANAGEMENT

WHO'S THE BOSS?

Circumstances often force systems as well as individuals to adapt themselves, resulting in either positive or negative results. Luckily, in the IDF many constraints lead to positive and effective results that in time develop into protocols and finally into whole attitudes, cultures, and philosophies. One of the most difficult challenges the IDF faces is the lack of manpower. As discussed in earlier chapters, military staff is replaced every three to five years, making it extremely difficult to rely on senior commanders, in particular. The recruitment and officer training system that the United States utilizes, for example, would be impossible to replicate in Israel because of the country's limited resources. The Israeli system is a direct result of what is and isn't possible, and, incidentally, it works out extremely well.

Compared with other militaries, there are few senior positions in the IDF populated by career soldiers. So, throughout the ranks, every year new people must be trained to assume diverse roles. This is true of officers, as I explained when I shared the story of my own military career. In the IDF, there is no fast track to becoming an officer. Like me, most officers are promoted from within their units and later return to them, without much seniority over their teams. Each and every Israeli officer was once a simple soldier. This has a clear benefit for the military: it first uses the entire population as soldiers and only then sends them up the ladder.

These conditions contribute to another aspect of the IDF that is unique: its flat-hierarchy model. Because officers typically return to the unit they served in beforehand and are often in a position of commanding soldiers that they were drafted and trained with, it is difficult for both the officer and the soldiers to treat the commander with the kind of deference you'd see in other militaries. They know the (now) officer intimately and as one of them. But instead of hindering discipline, this fosters a culture in which respect for the commanders is earned—the officers had trained and fought with them, and it's because of their performance that they went on to become officers in the first place. Louis Williams argues that because every soldier, whether a private, a sergeant, a platoon leader, or the chief of staff, started the same, and because the IDF is so skilled in unifying people from different backgrounds, rank is seen only as the recognition of competence and command ability. "Officers and other ranks," he adds, "are issued the same uniforms and eat the same food. In line and field units, they will share the same mess halls and live in the same quarters."

Another feature of the IDF's flat, nonhierarchical culture is that it works to drill responsibility down to lower levels. Today, as the military historian Edward Luttwak explains, "The IDF is deliberately understaffed at senior levels. Which means that there are fewer senior officers to issue commands. Fewer senior officials means more individual initiative at the lower ranks."[1]

MARKET ARMY

"Bedouin Love Song," a well-known Israeli ballad, tells the story of a born wanderer who every so often gets swept away along with the desert sands, leaving behind his tent. This beautiful song reminds me of a new version of wanderers, those who flourish as global citizens of the world.

Born in kibbutz Kiryat Anavim in 1970 to two truly sabra parents, Nadav Zafrir started his travels as early as two years old. First, his family moved from the kibbutz to a moshav, both places forms of Israeli settlements marked by a great cultural difference at the time. His father was a dairy farmer, something that was to define Nadav's life on many levels. His childhood memories are a mix of feeding calves and watering the family's orange groves. His first-ever memory is of rushing to the shelter while his father put on his military uniform and his mother grabbed a transistor radio that would be their only source of information in the shelter during the ongoing Yom Kippur War.

When he was seven years of age, his family moved to the Dominican Republic, where his father established a dairy cooperative as part of the Israeli foreign ministry's effort to support developing countries. Nadav was enrolled in an American school, where he spent three formative years. The family returned to Israel for a couple of years, only to move again, this time to Quito, Ecuador, where Nadav's father ran a sausage factory. At age eighteen, Nadav came back to Israel to join the military.

The life of a wanderer is not easy. It is marked by constantly adapting oneself to a changing environment, making what seemed like lifelong friends only to lose them through time, simply due to circumstances. Starting over takes practice, and Nadav had plenty of it. It comes at a price, but the reward is immense as well.

Nadav's military career cannot be fully disclosed. All that is known is that he made a journey from the Paratroopers to Special Operations, through select technology units, and ultimately served in the Intelligence Unit 8200, where he also founded the IDF's Cyber Command and eventually commanded the unit as a brigadier general. Quietly maintaining a rich professional life, a web of relationships, and everything else that is involved in

being a high-ranking officer is not a skill easily learned. Perhaps
learning to metamorphose himself, each time having to adapt to
a different culture, among different people, presented with new
challenges, is what made Nadav a great officer, leader, and unique
entrepreneur.

Nadav's greatest achievement as an entrepreneur is his role
as CEO at Team8, a think tank and venture creation company
that he cofounded in 2013. Team8 focuses on tackling the biggest challenges at the intersection of big data, machine learning,
and cybersecurity. Nadav's attitude to fighting cyber attacks is
to beat the attacker to the punch—build a company, devote all
your resources to accelerate its development, market fit and scale,
and then build another one. Constantly force yourself to reinvent.
Don't take "common knowledge" and "best practices" as guidelines. Don't get attached to your own opinions. Once a year force
yourself to win in the everlasting learning war between attackers
and defenders.

This is the way to stay in the game and ahead of the market. To
date, Team8 has given birth to Illusive Networks, Claroty, Sygnia,
Hysolate, and Portshift, all promising cybersecurity companies.
Team8 is now focusing on enabling secure data-driven transfor-
mation, such as with their latest company launch, Duality Technologies, whose cofounders include MIT professors and world
pioneers in advanced mathematics.

Nadav serves on several cyber-related advisory boards and is
considered a well-established authority on cybersecurity in academic, business, and military contexts.

Nadav explains that complexity coupled with an accelerated
pace of change means that management paradigms must be challenged as well. A classic, hierarchal chain of command is bound
to fail and must be replaced by a more loosely coupled, flat, and
agile model. In a world that is undergoing change at an increasingly rapid pace, it is unreasonable to assume that real progress

can be made under a monolithic management model. Complexity is present not only in technology, but in manufacturing, marketing, and sales. In such a world, you should establish a system that promotes transparent data collection and decision-making processes that are constantly seeking consideration of alternatives and invite criticism. "In practice," he says, "there is no time for hierarchy both in a military context and in today's business world; both require a channel of communication which is not confined by hierarchy."[2]

It is important to emphasize that the IDF is certainly a hierarchical system. What differentiates it from other hierarchical organizations (be it military or civilian) is that, as Nadav suggests, "in the IDF the head is always consulting the body parts. There is a strict chain of command, but the higher levels are not detached from the lower ones. Decision making is thus a flat, spread-out process." As I mentioned earlier, this approach also implies that lower levels must take part in, or at least be aware of, strategic planning. Since there isn't always time to climb the chain of command, every soldier must be aware of the bigger objective and be capable of acting toward its achievement.

"As David Ben-Gurion [Israel's first prime minister] advocated," recalls Nadav, "every soldier must view himself as if carrying the scepter of the chief of staff. Of course, such a structure doesn't come without its problems. First, it generates quite a lot of *balagan*—chaos—and often there is not as much control over situations as you would like. But then again, it's all about balancing the need for order with the need to be agile. Such a balance will never be achieved with the classic hierarchical structure."

Nadav used his military experience as inspiration for his own company structure. "We are a company-building platform," he explains. "On the one hand, we are fueled by the agility of a start-up, on the other, our in-depth research abilities, company-building methodology is highly structured and requires discipline. Thriving in a complex environment requires the ability to constantly move in the spectrum that lies between chaos and order." Sometimes hierarchy is necessary and sometimes it simply stands in the way. Sometimes you want freedom and sometimes you want direction. Chaos invites vulnerability, but order impedes progress. Nadav is determined: "We believe the most creative innovation happens at the edge of chaos, driven by the flexibility of thought that comes with *balagan*."

Indeed, leadership is an art form that implements flexibility and freshness as much as depth and structure. "Between me and my partners, for instance, there is absolutely no hierarchy, but this doesn't contradict the fact that each has his or her own title and specific field of expertise and responsibility," he explains. "What is important is that the managerial responsibilities are completely shared and transparent, and each can be involved and contribute in any field."

Nadav continues to travel around the world, speaking to entrepreneurs, company executives, and audiences of thousands about building resilience in today's complex environment. Only now his wandering is fueled by a focused vision and passion to connect Israel's innovation heartbeat and technological expertise with the world leaders in business, politics, medicine, and academia. When it comes to solving the world's biggest problems, Nadav believes "it takes a village"—and as a global citizen from birth, he is well positioned to lead it.

Yagil Levy, an associate professor at the Open University in Israel, believes that in both military and civil organizations, a flattened hierarchical structure can help reduce the number of management layers, thus reducing costs. More important, it helps speed up "the flow of information from central command to the unit, as well as among units, and creates incentives for using more detailed and timely information. This model allows the lower levels of the hierarchy to exercise initiative, thus enabling units to react more quickly to events, especially those that are unforeseen."[3]

What the IDF has been doing for decades is now beginning to be advocated for by military officials worldwide. Levy believes that network-centric warfare, for example, is an operative manifestation of flat hierarchy.

FLAT HIERARCHY?

In a business context, a flat organizational structure, like the one Nadav implemented for his company, is one in which there are not multiple layers between the company's day-to-day staff members and high-level executives. Individual employees do not have to go through multiple channels to get to the company's president or other executives. By easing the way in which reports are conveyed, flat organizational structures tend to have a higher number of reports compared to other models, and decisions are in fact made more quickly.

Models that follow a flat structure drive individuals to be more actively involved in the decision-making processes of a company, granting them both power and motivation. From the company's perspective, this helps cultivate creative discussions and operational diversity and promotes tolerance toward a wide variety of ideas and opinions. By empowering individual employees and cutting at least some parts of middle management, feedback from both company internal stakeholders, as well as external customers, can be processed and addressed more effectively and quickly.

People who are wary of a flat hierarchy often assume that hierarchy is essential to the success of an operation, be it military or business. They also assume that those who perform the work on the ground—salespeople in retail stores, for example—are lower in status than those who decide what work needs to be done, and how. In other words, those who actually perform, those who make the on-the-spot decisions, meeting the customers and pitching them on a daily basis, are treated as less capable than those who direct the show. But these assumptions are usually misplaced. The fact is that many successful businesses today thrive thanks to their flat hierarchies.

One such example is Automattic, the company behind Word-Press, which hosts about 20 percent of the world's websites. And yet, Automattic only employs a couple hundred people, who all work remotely, with a highly autonomous flat-management struc-ture. Valve, the gaming company that makes Half-Life, Portal, and many other popular games, and whose software is proprie-tary, is famous for not having bosses at all.

Yet another example is W. L. Gore, one of the most successful firms in the world. With more than ten thousand employees and three levels that make up their organizational hierarchy, includ-ing the CEO, the top-ranking heads, and all other employees, all decision making is performed in teams of eight to twelve people that self-manage everything from hiring to pay to which projects to work on. As Terri Kelly, the (democratically elected) CEO, told Tim Kastelle of the *Harvard Business Review*, instead of follow-ing the classic command-and-control way of doing things, "it's far better to rely upon a broad base of individuals and leaders who share a common set of values and feel personal ownership for the overall success of the organization. These responsible and empow-ered individuals will serve as much better watchdogs than any single, dominant leader or bureaucratic structure."[4]

Jason Fried, cofounder and CEO of 37signals, explains in an *Inc.* article, "37signals has always been a flat organization. In fact, flatness is one of our core values. We have eight programmers, but we don't have a chief technical officer. We have five design-ers, but no creative director. We have five people on our customer support team, and no customer-support manager. We do not have room for people who don't do the actual work."[5] Indeed, what is important is the actual work, the actual goal that needs to be achieved, whether it's in the context of a military operation or a marketing campaign.

Particularly when the environment is changing rapidly and constantly, a flat organizational structure can prove beneficial. Firms that are composed of numerous autonomous teams (all working toward a common goal) can be more flexible and adaptable than those who follow a strict hierarchical model. Marketing specialist Christy Rakoczy Bieber adds that a flat organizational structure also has the advantage of increasing coordination and improving communications. Naturally, "since there are fewer departments, information is better relayed. Since the top management is much closer to the middle and lower management, there is more efficiency in communicating messages."[6] Better communication practices mean decision making can be done more quickly, helping smooth out these otherwise bureaucracy-laden processes. Moreover, "with a flat organization, policies are easier to implement since they can be communicated more easily." This requires a lot of transparency, enabling people lower down in the organization to understand the business model and think with a strategic mind-set.

Such an approach can yield huge gains, as in the case of the 1967 Six-Day War. Pascal-Emmanuel Gobry, a well-known culture, politics, economics, business, and technology columnist, described it well: the IDF had no existing battle plan for its invasion of the Sinai Peninsula, but "after taking the crucial gateway city of El Arish, . . . IDF units pushed past all the way to the Suez Canal. This was not done on orders of anyone, but simply by the initiative of local commanders who, having kept their earlier objectives, kept advancing. They did not sit down and wait for word from central command."[7]

14

IMPROVISATION AND OPTIMIZATION

Welcome to the army! You are given standard military equipment: helmet, uniform, compass, first-aid kit, and, of course, your rifle. Would you make any changes to this equipment? Or would you assume it is standard for a good reason and not risk tampering with it? What do you think a typical Israeli would do?

Perhaps unsurprisingly, from the moment they enlist, Israeli soldiers constantly try to customize their equipment, uniform, even weapons, so as to make them not just better, but uniquely their own. In Hebrew we have a special word for this: *shiftzur*, which comes from the root *sh.p.tz* and means "to renovate, refit, recondition, to improve." In practice, *shiftzur* means to take an existing object, a piece of equipment, and alter it so as to meet one's personal needs, preferences, and style.

Shiftzur is one of the most widespread phenomena in the IDF. Those with the best *shiftzurim* (the Hebrew plural of *shiftzur*) are praised and copied, including by their commanders. Among the most common *shiftzurim* are ones that have to do with a soldier's helmet, vest, and weapon. Soldiers often start with their bullet cartridge, attaching it to their weapon with a string and wrapping it with insulating tape, so that it won't fall and will stay dry.

Some of the changes are operational, carried out on officers' orders, while others are simply done for show—for the sake of making one's weapon or uniform look cooler, more unique, more personal. For example, soldiers often embroider their unit's insignia on a patch that they affix to their weapon. In fact, the unit's tag is usually found on every single piece of gear the soldier has, from their helmet to their weapon to the bag that they take home with them on the weekend.

While this phenomenon might exist in other armies, it is much less common and certainly less encouraged. One of the reasons is that, as in the US Army, for instance, equipment is already of very high quality and requires very little adjustments. Another reason is that being unique and creative are simply not standard militaristic values. Not so in the IDF, where soldiers are expected to customize their equipment from day one both because it is necessary and because it enables them to express themselves and their unit's pride.

Some units even go as far as to dedicate an entire role to the purpose of *shiftzur*. This was the case for Noam Sharon, a veteran of a special forces unit where she served in the sewing workshop along with several other soldiers whose mission was to help the combat soldiers of the unit optimize their equipment. "The *shiftzur* was either for the purpose of adapting equipment to a specific operation or to a specific soldier and his needs," she explains.[1]

The need for *shiftzur* would usually arise from the soldiers themselves, who would come to our workshop asking to change something about their vests, for example. Every soldier was welcome to come in, explain his needs and difficulties—what needs to be available to retrieve within two seconds, what needs to fit into what—and according to that we would fix his gear. Of course, it wasn't only individual soldiers we worked with. We would also often sit with the unit officers and discuss upcoming operations and the gear they would need for them. We would either customize existing equipment or simply make it from scratch.

The beauty of this position was the fact that we had complete independence of thought and action. One of us was actually in charge of the entire purchasing procedure, from making the shopping list to negotiating with suppliers. We had supervision and accompaniment, but in general the responsibility was all ours. We could let our creativity and our imagination run wild, and that was one of the most rewarding experiences one can have in a military framework.

Surprising as it may sound, Noam was nineteen years old when she held this position, with limited experience in design, fabrication, or sewing. She learned everything on the job.

Dr. Uri Weinheber, operating partner at Cathay Innovation and former managing partner and CEO at TheTime Investment Group, suggests that *shiftzur* is a manifestation of the strong roots of improvisation inherent in Israeli culture, and specifically in the IDF. It's "an example of the Israeli variance," he says.[2] "The military is in a way a microcosm of Israeli society and culture. *Shiftzur* is one symptom of this culture. In fact, it's a national trend by which people observe an existing situation and constantly seek ways to adapt, change, and improve it. There is something very Israeli rebuffing the status quo and striving for better things. It's not about change for the sake of change, but about actually making things better. In Israel, improvement is most often improvised."

Uri's career is an expression of this philosophy. He points out that his is based on three axes: he started as an infantry combat soldier, later served as an officer, and then was first commander, literally the founder, of an elite combat unit during his reserve service. He led his units and participated in numerous operations and wars, and for the past few years has served as a colonel in a frontline combat unit as part of his reserve duty. As an academic,

Uri researches the intercorrelations of science, technology, and society, and his PhD dissertation focuses on Internet-related conflicts and how they instigate new technologies and innovative products. "Conflicts can also be a trigger for improvement and innovation," Uri says.

In the early '90s, his first position within the Israeli tech ecosystem was as a product manager. Passionate about innovation, creative solutions, and disruptive technologies, he became vice president for products, then business founder and CEO of an innovative start-up, CEO of investment companies, and a venture capitalist, and has led dozens of investments in innovative Israeli start-ups, many of which are successful and well known. "Some professionals approach the investment process from a technological angle—these are mostly engineers by profession. Others take a financial angle, most of whom grew up in financial positions and MBA faculties," says Uri. "However, I look at start-ups from a problem-solving point of view." He reflects, "I did this every day as a combat commander; I still do it as an investor in tech start-ups, and I also take this approach in my academic research." He continues: "I'm used to seeking problems, current or future, and coming up with creative and out-of-the-box ambitious solutions, based on limited resources, looking at challenges from the user's perspective."

Uri feels very comfortable in an environment that is constantly seeking something better, using different means—improvisation being one of the most efficient strategies. "Israel as a whole, and the IDF in particular, started as an improvised platform; our culture has an inherent ability (and necessity) to improvise. It's not a settled methodology or protocol, it's a concept that has emerged from necessity, based on the reality on the field. This is why it's a more cultural than procedural aspect of Israelis. And, as with any [organization], the ability to improvise is a direct consequence of necessity."

As *shiftzur* has surfaced out of a necessity expressed by users, it's considered a grassroots phenomenon. As Uri explains, "Improving equipment as well as systems and protocols is a constant bottom-up process, and that's why it is so efficient and productive. The needs and desires come from the 'market,' i.e., from the users themselves. *Shiftzur* is thus an aspect of the IDF's 'product-market fit' process." As Uri sees it, "military equipment is a product that, after being modified by the users, returns to the 'manufacturer' in order to apply the necessary changes and be shipped out again for its next cycle." The equipment is just the metaphor, reflecting processes of all types of products, services, and methodologies.

CASE STUDY: THE ISRAELI AIR FORCE (IAF)[3]

Another essential component of the IDF's pursuit of the optimal "product-market fit" is its rigorous approach to learning from mistakes, best illustrated in the example of the Israeli Air Force.

As Steven Pressfield quotes in *The Lion's Gate*, his book about the Six-Day War: "[The IAF has] a ruthlessly candid debriefing culture. At the end of each training day, the squadron met in the briefing room. Ran, the squadron leader, stood up front. He went over every mistake we had made that day—not just those of the young pilots, but his own as well. He was fearless in his self-criticism, and he made us speak up with equal candor. If you had screwed up, you admitted it and took your medicine. Ego meant nothing. Improvement was everything."[4]

Debriefings in the US Army usually take place within the week following a military operation, which allows the troops to recuperate and gather their thoughts. Usually it is the military unit leaders who lead the debriefing sessions, although soldiers of all ranks are free to participate in the session given that they were involved in the operation. The debriefing groups are usually made up of ten members per session. "Debriefers," explains Pressfield, as they are called in the United States, are people who "are trained in debriefing, knowledgeable about community resources (in order to make any necessary referrals) and familiar with the stress and coping field." The debriefer or the person supervising the debriefing is considered a specialist and would often be someone from outside the unit, perhaps in order to establish neutrality.

The debriefing culture in the IDF, particularly in the air force, is vastly different from what is found in armies such as the United States'. For one thing, in an IDF debriefing session, those conducting the debriefing are the soldiers who were themselves involved in the drill or operation, sometimes with the unit commanding staff. No outside "expert" is involved but rather all lessons are learned from within the unit. Soldiers, for better or (sometimes) worse, are charged with the responsibility of conducting their own criticism and with detecting, analyzing, and learning from their own mistakes. Another difference is the idea of confidentiality versus openness. One of the leading concepts in the US Army's debriefing protocol, as shown by examples of debriefing documents, is that "what is said in the debriefing session stays there. It will not come back to haunt a soldier later, and . . . the information is not designed to identify a scapegoat. Information discussed in the debriefing will not be relayed to the chain-of-command."

In the IDF, sharing the conclusions of a debriefing session is customary, and not seen as a humiliation or as something that could come back to haunt a soldier. On the contrary, if a significant incident occurred, it is seen as important to share its conclusions and consequences with others so as to give everyone a chance to learn from it.

But there is more to the IDF's debriefing culture than it being an effective way of learning from mistakes. The entire attitude and philosophy that guides this culture is deeply embedded in the idea of improvisation and optimization. To really understand the roots and workings of this culture, it is best to look at it from the inside.

No Hebrew word captures the essence of this culture better than *dugri*. It refers to the quality of saying things as they are, without embellishments. Being *dugri* is a way of expressing oneself that is honest and to the point, even, or especially, when it's unpleasant.

Dugri stands at the heart of every debriefing session. The strategy is to take the facts and present them in a comprehensive and accessible way. Imagine, for example, a day that didn't turn out as well as you wanted. Let's say you were giving an important presentation at work. But it didn't go as planned. Afterward you returned to the office and your business partner asked you, "How was the presentation?" What would your answer be?

Many people would answer "horrible" or "not so good," which is a description of a feeling. But what if you instead ask yourself, "What will I do differently tomorrow, in order to get me to the outcome I wanted?" In that scenario, the answer "It was horrible" has no relevance.

The IAF debriefing process utilizes three questions to analyze the event and its takeaways: "What happened?" "Why did it happen?" and "What should I do differently next time?"

These questions help frame the process in a helpful way: as a learning experience as opposed to an opportunity to beat oneself up. So, instead of getting stuck on an answer like "The presentation was horrible," the reframed response might be something like "I wasn't so sharp and not as coherent as I would have liked to be. I was very tired because I went to sleep at two in the morning. I should never sleep less than seven hours." You might still add, "It was horrible" at the beginning of the sentence. That can help let off steam and move past the bad feeling, but it won't change tomorrow. The greatest benefit of being *dugri* is just that—bypassing emotional aspects and going straight to the lessons that can be learned.

Which is why the IDF debriefing processes force everyone to focus primarily on the facts. Someone new to the debriefing

process might provide the following answers: What happened?—
"It turned out badly." Why?—"I don't know." What should I do
differently next time?—"Do things right." As you see, there are
no facts and no action items that can be gleaned from that process.
Because they were not being *dugri*, the emphasis was on feelings
and not any specific behaviors, so the process produced no action
items.

Another common mistake people make when analyzing events
is to blame someone else or to not take responsibility. Let's say a
pilot landing his plane deviated from the runway in crosswind
conditions. The pilot could state the right facts, but in answer to
"Why did it happen?" might say, "There was crosswind." Such
a response prevents the pilot from taking responsibility. The
full answer should be, "There was crosswind, and I didn't apply
enough correction."

The best way to learn from an event is to ask yourself, given
the same facts, "What should I have done differently?" That is a
simple lesson but might be the most important one listed here.
There will always be someone else to blame.

A final frequent mistake is to learn the wrong lesson. Let's say
I fell off a bicycle. The wrong lesson would be, "I can't ride a bicycle," or "Bicycles always make me fall, so I shouldn't ride them."
These lessons will not help you do better next time and will pre-
maturely halt the learning process.

A good rule of thumb is to always ask yourself: "Will that lesson help me reach my target?" and "Would someone else learn the
same lesson from the same facts?" Let's say that the reason I fell
was because I looked at the front wheel while riding, instead of
ahead of me, farther down the road. Could I share this lesson with
someone else? In this case, absolutely: "Always look ahead, and if
you want to look at your front wheel, do so briefly, and return your
eyes to the road."

The process described above is useful not only in the case of things gone wrong. The same process works for positive feedback. You can ask, "What went well?" and end up with a list of action items to repeat next time. That is important not only for morale, but because doing something right once doesn't guarantee it will happen the same way next time. Having concrete takeaways can help you continue to meet your goals and help others do so as well.

This is why *every* IAF mission ends with a debriefing for the flight crew. Every squadron has an officer responsible for documenting all the lessons learned, and a system to document and publish the findings for the benefit of others: pilots in the squadron, pilots in another squadron flying the same aircraft, or even the entire organization. A common saying in the IAF is: It's better to learn from somebody else's mistakes than make your own.

Learning from not just your own but also others' mistakes is a key strategy for adapting to a rapidly changing environment, such as that the IAF faces. The IAF is a large organization, but like a tech start-up, it must contend with new challenges all the time and cannot afford to learn its lessons on the go. In order to achieve this, every member of the force must be prepared to improvise and solve problems, while constantly learning and sharing the positive and negative lessons.

THINKING AND ACTING ON YOUR FEET

Some might characterize improvisation as an action that is uncoordinated, unplanned, and often executed poorly. This attitude is certainly unjustified. Improvisation is actually an action that requires extremely well-polished skills, quickness and flexibility of thought, an ability to coordinate knowledge and data, and many other complex qualities.

In English, the word *improvise* originates from the Latin verb "to plan" (*provisus*). *Improvised* (Latin: *improvises*) therefore means "unplanned or unprepared for." In Hebrew, the word for *improvise* is *iltur* and comes from the word *le'altar*, meaning "immediate." Unlike in English, then, where the word for *improvisation* has the connotation of being caught off guard, in Hebrew the word conveys the sense of immediacy—simply living the moment. *Iltur* for Israelis is regarded as the ability to adapt and come up with quick and effective solutions to any kind of problem. When you're down on resources, as is often the case in Israel, you simply improvise. Gradually, one learns to depend less and less on those resources, so that the lack thereof is hardly felt anymore. *Iltur*, in the context of an Israeli state of mind, is not about having to suddenly deal with an unexpected situation. It's about not relying on a plan to begin with but instead living in the moment and adapting.

In the arts, particularly in theater and jazz, improvisation is often the key to a coordinated activity that is not and cannot be planned in advance. In their book *Organizational Change and Redesign*, editors George Huber and William Glick write, "In a group of improvisational players . . . agreements are held to a minimum so that people retain the capability to make individual adjustments to local irregularities. . . . As a result, people are able to accomplish collectively what they could not do individually, but also to cope individually with unexpected problems by virtue of their diverse capabilities."[5]

Context, skills, and silent communication are all necessary for the accomplishment of an improvisational act. Without the ability to communicate with each other effectively, actors could not come up with a shared goal, nor could they coordinate the steps necessary to achieve it. Likewise, without skills they cannot be expected to perform in any given situation, and without context they could not read the situation in the first place and thus would not be able to know what the appropriate response should be. Furthermore, Huber and Glick emphasize, improvisation happens *fast*. "The more improvisational an act, the narrower the time gap between composing and performing, designing and producing, or conceptualizing and implementing."

In a sense, each and every person improvises on a daily basis, in nearly every conversation. In his article on improvisation, the twentieth-century British philosopher Gilbert Ryle says that "[t]o be thinking what he is here and now up against, the improviser must both be trying to adjust himself to just this present once-only situation and in doing this to be applying lessons already learned. There must be in his response a union of some Ad Hockery with some know-how. It is the pitting of an acquired competence or skill against un-programmed opportunity, obstacle or hazard."[6]

Karl Weick, an American organizational theorist, helpfully summarizes the characteristics of groups with a high capability for improvisation:

1. Willingness to forgo planning and rehearsing in favor of acting in real time; 2. Well-developed understanding of internal resources and the materials that are at hand; 3. Proficient without blueprints and diagnosis; 4. Able to identify or agree on minimal structures for embellishing; 5. Open to reassembly of and departures from routines; 6. Rich and meaningful set of themes, fragments, or phrases on which to draw for ongoing lines of action; 7. Predisposed to recognize partial relevance of previous experience to present novelty; 8. High confidence in skill to deal with non-routine events; 9. Presence of associates similarly committed to and competent at impromptu [action]; 10. Skillful at paying attention to performance of others and building on it in order to keep the interaction going and to set up interesting possibilities for one another. 11. Able to maintain the pace and tempo at which others are extemporizing. 12. Focused on coordination here and now and not distracted by memo-

ries or anticipation; 13. Preference for and comfort with process rather than structure.[7]

These very same principles, as manifested in the IDF and debriefing methodology of the IAF, as well as in the performing arts, are also applicable to start-ups and business organizations. I would argue that, as a cultural phenomenon, improvisation can benefit any company, of any size. Improvisation is not only a skill that can be applied, but it can also be conceived of as a form of short-term learning. This is based on the well-established view that learning occurs when experience generates a systematic change in behavior or knowledge. In a field study on organizational improvisation, Anne Miner, Paula Bassoff, and Christine Moorman found that improvisation stands in sharp contrast to other forms of learning in which prior experience is the most important factor for behavior or knowledge changes.[8] They also emphasize the fact that improvisation is often most effective at the level of the team or even whole organization, as when, for example, they worked as a group to design a product change that no single individual could take credit for.

One of the most iconic examples of this kind of improvisation comes from NASA, where, in 1970 on their way to the moon, the *Apollo 13* crew had to overcome numerous challenges, one of which was the excessive heat the spaceship was to encounter on its way back into the earth's atmosphere. To solve this, the engineering team developed an aluminum heat shield, designed to handle excessive heat from an outside source by dissipating, reflecting, or simply absorbing the heat.

Interestingly, it wasn't long before this technology was adapted to function as a fundamental tool in private home insulation. NASA's satellites, too, though originally designed in 1962 to enable Americans and Europeans to view each other's broadcasts, are now being used to provide us with weather reports, advanced navigation systems such as GPS, the ability to keep track of the location of cargo and passenger planes, advanced weapon systems that include location components based on satellite input, and much more. Electric charging, the smoke detector, magnetic resonance imaging (MRI), eyeglass lens coating, and prosthetic limbs were all designed for a specific purpose but later adopted by other industries and sectors.

There are many Israeli examples of improvised solutions from one sector (often the military) becoming products for different sectors. Take Given Imaging, for example, an Israeli medical technology company that makes diagnostic products for the visualization and detection of gastrointestinal disorders. Basically, these are tiny pill-like cameras—PillCams—that can be easily swallowed by the patient, filming the length of the gastrointestinal tract. The technology is currently marketed in over sixty countries. But what's striking about this company is not its success but rather its origins. The idea for the pill was developed by Dr. Gabi Iddan while working in the missile division of Rafael Advanced Defense Systems. Rafael is a well-known Israeli defense technology company that is responsible for the development of weapons and military and defense technologies for the Israel Defense Forces and for export abroad. Dr. Iddan was working on missile technology when he envisioned this miniaturized medical product.

Another example is Zeekit, a shopping app that allows consumers to virtually try on fashion items. The company was cofounded by thirty-two-year-old Yael Vizel, the first woman to command the Israeli Air Force telecommunication officers' course and its field and aerial telecommunication crews.

How does it work? Sophisticated deep-image processing enables Zeekit to map the topography of a shopper's body, so that users can see exactly how an item of clothing will look and fit on their bodies. Vizel came up with the idea during her military service. For intelligence missions at the IAF, Vizel and her team developed systems for taking 2-D photographs and transforming them into 3-D graphics for use in military operations.

She was convinced there must be other uses for the algorithm-based technology and had the idea to create a similar "topography" of the human body. This kind of innovation is so common in the Israeli landscape that organizations have been set up to support it. As early as 1993, Rafael joined forces with Elron Electronic Industries, one of the cornerstones of the high-tech industry in Israel, to establish Rafael Development Corporation, a technology transfer company. The joint venture proved highly advantageous, giving birth to numerous new technologies in industries as varied as medicine, sanitation, aeronautics, communication, and more.

Today, there are seventeen different technology-transfer companies active in Israel, affiliated with the country's world-renowned universities, research institutions, and hospitals. But the wedding of civilian, academic, and military forces goes far beyond technical inventions. What we find in cases such as Given Imaging is a transfer of methods, theories, and ways of thinking and communicating from one field to another. The fact that missile technology can be thought of in a medical context, or any other context for that matter, is remarkable. Israel's interdisciplinary state of mind lends its entrepreneurs, civilian and military, the ability to imagine one thing being used in a different context in a totally different way.

RENEWAL

WE BEGAN OUR journey with toddlers playing in the junkyard. We've "watched" Israelis growing up, charting their course through childhood, adolescence, and military service. We've looked at these stages to help us better understand the ways a young business moves from discovery and exploration of an idea, through finding a solution and a market, to building an efficient, scaled business organization.

Both young adults being released from military service and businesses that are now well established can find that they need more room to grow, new territory to explore. As they master various skills, only to find circumstances around them changing, they are compelled to reinvent themselves. They now have many resources at their disposal—existing networks they are part of and the know-how and expertise they mastered in their domain (which, with some imagination, could probably be applicable to other domains). They possess the right resources, soft and hard, to broaden their horizons and expand their presence.

It's never simple to reinvent yourself. However, you must stay optimistic and have faith in your capabilities, as individuals or business organizations. Doing so will allow you to take on new challenges, stepping out of your routine and comfort zone to explore new horizons. It's this continual attitude of searching, challenging, and risk taking that might be what separates long-term high performers from others whose time at the top is short.

15

LEVERAGING SKILLS AND NETWORKS

When I interview a potential new hire or assess a start-up's founding team for investment purposes, I always surprise them. They are used to being asked very specific questions: about their professional experience, prior positions, specific accomplishments, related data and metrics. I, though, choose to spend our hour together talking about completely different things: their soft skills. Now, it's not easy to get a genuine answer when you ask someone to describe their soft skills. So I have to be more sophisticated. I focus on something relevant that they were part of and get them to talk about the process rather than the actual facts. Instead of asking them what "positions" they held in the past, I ask: "What role did you play in your last job?" A description of their role within the company can provide insight into how they handle themselves.

So, instead of hearing "I was the CFO," I might get "I was the gatekeeper." Then I ask "Why?" just like a kid would. And that's when the more profound answers begin to surface. "Because the CEO is a risk taker, and I needed to balance him." Hmmm, that tells me that this person views these types of dynamics as an essential part of his role. Or she might say: "Because a CFO must be THE gatekeeper of any company, it's an essential part of their responsibility." Okay, that tells me that this is an assumption they have. Do they have the flexibility of mind to free themselves from unnecessary assumptions? The answers to these kinds of questions are much more predictive of an individual's future success in an organization than the usual metrics.

Companies and institutions across the board are recognizing exactly this. Unlike in past decades, soft skills are in higher demand with each passing year. According to the World Economic Forum's report *The Future of Jobs*, "today's job markets and in-demand skills are vastly different than the ones of 10 or even five years ago, and the pace of change is only set to accelerate."[1] In fact, "by 2020, more than a third of the desired core skill sets of most occupations will be comprised of skills that are not yet considered crucial to the job today. Overall, social skills—such as persuasion, emotional intelligence and teaching others—will be in higher demand across industries than narrow technical skills, such as programming or equipment operation and control." This is now becoming the present. It is not futuristic anymore.

This is not to say that those who apply for a job in the tech industry, for example, are not expected to have mathematical knowledge and programming experience. But possessing only very specific skills or being limited to applying them in very specific environments just doesn't cut it anymore. It's better not to have the one skill necessary to perform a certain job, than not to have the cognitive abilities that allow you to acquire different skills quickly and efficiently, and to be able to use them creatively. In a sense, we might say that we have evolved from performing robot-like jobs to being highly skilled computing systems, capable of various things.

NETWORKED

Remember Modu, the Israeli start-up I worked for that had huge promise but abruptly failed? Modu was established by the suc-

cessful serial entrepreneur Dov Moran. His experience and network were primarily in the flash memory industry, while his new
venture, Modu, was in telecommunications. Moran was formerly
an engineer in the Israeli Navy. His first two critical hires were
a chief technology officer and a vice president of R&D. Recognizing that his talent network in the telecommunications space
was small, he very deliberately hired executives with more extensive relevant networks. Incidentally, they were both alumni of
Intelligence Unit 8200, the source of most of the country's R&D
telecommunications talent. His strategy paid off. Within a few
months, Modu hired almost one hundred software and hardware
engineers and experts, and because many of them already knew
one another and had worked together previously in the military,
their onboarding was smooth and extremely effective. They knew
how to work together. The combination of Moran's network, and
those of the CTO and VP of R&D, formed one of the best teams in
Israeli industry history.

It's true that Modu eventually failed as a business. But it gave
birth to a new network, whose members are still active nine years
after the company closed, both in Israel and abroad, where some
of them live today. They have founded dozens of start-ups and
business ventures, often together, and generated hundreds of millions of dollars of value. My most recent meeting with Dov was
on a Friday morning, the start of the weekend in Israel. Over the
past thirty years, Dov has customarily held at least five meetings
on average every Friday morning—meetings that are not directly
related to his businesses. Simple math: thirty years, five meetings
on average per Friday morning, at least thirty weeks per year. Dov
has met almost five thousand people, and these Friday-morning
meetings have systematically grown their own network. He's also
had the opportunity to meet interesting people. "I look forward
to these Friday mornings," he tells me.[2] "I enjoy meeting people

in different stages; involved in various projects and initiatives; sharing their ideas with me or coming to get some advice." Dov conducted these meetings, consulting and helping many, while never taking one penny or share, even when money or equity was offered to him. "Doing these meetings," he says, "was actually very beneficial to me. Taking consideration would put in a different, lesser attractive, and more committed status. Without consideration—they win. I win. That's the formula for a good life." He smiles.

I can testify, as someone who's worked closely with Dov, his belief of "people first," a core value at Modu, is, for him, a life principle.

What we find repeatedly in stories such as this one, and others in this book, is that cooperation breeds inventiveness. Israelis hardly work alone. From childhood they nurture broad networks, instrumental when coming up with innovative ideas. But equally important is the value these networks have when trying to turn a new idea into a successful company. A network can determine how easily and quickly one can reach investors, gain business partners, attract employees, acquire needed resources, and so on. Networks can also offset the fact of not having a proven track record and therefore no endorsed legitimacy, as is commonly the case with new businesses. Luckily for Israelis, private, governmental, educational, and business institutions all work toward building these networks and helping young as well as experienced entrepreneurs to further deepen and broaden their connections and relationships within the entrepreneurial world.

Earlier in the book, I wrote about IDF alumni communities. These networks gave birth to programs like 8200 EISP, which promotes and empowers early-stage, first-time entrepreneurs from all industries. Other specific networks require unique solutions, such as KamaTech, a program facilitating the integration of ultra-

Orthodox Jews into the Israeli high-tech workforce; and Hybrid, a program for early-stage ventures led by Arab, Druze, and Bedouin entrepreneurs in Israel, both accelerators and networking groups for minority entrepreneurs. There are others, which grow out of academic networks, like the Weizmann Institute Students Entrepreneurship Club (WISe), which utilizes alumni to provide students with the relevant knowledge and skills necessary to launch and grow a start-up venture.

But for the most part, networking in Israel follows a natural pattern. Israelis are brought together in school, in youth movements, in military service, while traveling abroad, and more. Their capacity for social contacts is bottomless, and they have a tendency to readily share their connections to benefit others. There is no need to establish an intense emotional relationship with someone before asking him for contact details of someone he might know, to be invited into his own community and network, or another favor; Israelis are more than happy to "hook you up" with whomever they know.

Because everyone is so dependent on networks, Israelis actively participate in and seek to expand them. Social circles are not necessarily about maintaining close friendships (these are formed regardless), but rather about knowing as many people as possible and being able to reach anyone, whether you know them personally or not (most likely you'll soon meet them anyway).

Finally, Israelis' networks are more often than not based on a powerful shared experience. Think of the military, for instance. The friendships that are formed in the unit are so intense that they are extremely durable and meaningful, even if they are not maintained frequently. In Israel, every person you meet is somehow relatable. Total strangers might find out that they've slept in the same hostel in Bangkok, endured a freezing winter in uniform on Mount Hermon, belonged to the same youth movement,

or grew up on the same street. Based on these common denomina-
tors, powerful connections are formed that cut through the need
for etiquette and rigid social mores. This is not to suggest that Israelis are above networking events or other tools that are utilized
by entrepreneurs throughout the world. The point is rather that,
among themselves, Israelis have a unique method of forming and
employing their networks.

PERSONAL SPACE?

Another component to the accessibility of Israelis to one another
has do with the fact that people are strongly connected not only
virtually (which may be true of many other areas in the world)
but also physically. Whenever I set up meetings in the area of
Rothschild Boulevard in Tel Aviv, I allow for double the time I
actually need for the meetings. Just a short walk through the
boulevard is sure to result in numerous stops to greet familiar
faces—be it investors, start-up entrepreneurs, business executives,
or childhood friends.

Israelis standing in line—which usually looks more like a
clump than a neat row—are likely to strike up a conversation; or
to butt in on each other's conversations in a cramped restaurant;
or to ask personal and (by some people's measure) inappropriate
questions while waiting to see the doctor; or, when brushing by
you on the street, to stop to tell you that your child should be wearing another layer and by the way—their grandson is the same age
and why don't they meet at the park tomorrow? On any elevator
you take to a business meeting in one of the tall buildings where
most investors, multinationals, and tech companies are housed,
you will most probably be asked: "Who are you here to meet?"
And after you tell them, they might propose: "So I suggest you
also meet this other person; I think he could be a better fit as an
investor."

The intimacy of physical life in Israel necessarily fulfills the human need for interaction, a need that might be overlooked in countries with vast territories where there are fewer physical interactions. This is so much a part of the Israeli way of life that often Israelis seek out and maintain similar interactions, even when abroad, in myriad ways.

16

GLOBAL OPENNESS

Israel, a tiny country in the conflict-ridden Middle East, is walking among giants. A small state, Israel is isolated politically and geographically from the Western world and is denied forming fruitful economic and political relationships with its neighboring countries. Nevertheless, in the mere seventy years of its existence, it has managed to grow into one of the most significant players in today's international business world. A big part of how this was achieved has to do with Israelis' voracious appetite for experiencing other places.

Israelis travel abroad frequently, often for long periods. In 2015 alone, 285,000 Israelis left the country for anywhere between one and three months, 254,000 for between three and twelve months. A total of 3.1 million Israeli citizens traveled outside the country that year, 1.2 million of whom went abroad repeatedly. In total, 5.9 million departures were registered, a national record. And it's not just young people. The median age of travelers is forty, suggesting that both the young and the old are infected with the travel bug. As of 2015, the population of Israel was 8.38 million, which means that 37 percent of Israelis spend time abroad every year. Just for comparison's sake, the population of the United States is 321.4 million, out of which 73 million traveled abroad in 2015. That's less than 23 percent.

According to the United Nations Statistics Division, an international long-term immigrant is "a person who moves to a country other than that of his or her usual residence for a period of at least a year."[1] According to the Israeli Central Population Registry, the number of Israelis who emigrated as of 2009 was between 542,000 and 572,000. And it's safe to assume that these numbers have continued to increase.

Migration has become a charged political topic in many countries, and Israelis are not unique in having to confront this issue. The number of Israeli emigrants does not compare to that of Syrian refugees or French emigrants (nearly seventy thousand French citizens are registered in Montreal, for example). But of course, Israel cannot compare in numbers to other countries. The point, then, is that, relative to its size, and despite the fact that there is societal pressure in Israel to not emigrate, Israelis show a distinct pattern of seeking out experiences of life abroad.

THE BIG TRIP

A familiar sight at Israel's international airport is dozens of young backpackers, with their huge bags and dreamy eyes, waiting in the check-in line for flights to South America, India, or China. They are too excited to be napping on their bags while waiting to board the plane, but they'll soon have plenty of opportunities for that. Before long they'll be spending hours waiting in bus stations, maybe after an exhausting trek in the mountains of Nepal, hungry but happy, tanned, and free.

Following their military service, young Israeli men and women typically take an extended trip, usually to the Far East or South America, where they spend their days traveling and exploring the culture and landscapes, and meeting with other travelers. This is the Big Trip, also known as the Great Journey. Dr. Shmuel Shulman, from the Department of Psychology at Bar Ilan University,

gathered data on these journeys, which he found could last anywhere from two months to one year. "Although there is a 'must'
list of destinations that these young people tend to visit," he con-
cludes, "their itineraries are usually flexible, and they may stay
in one place for an extended period of time, for weeks or even
months. Experiences during the trip may include not only visiting
exotic destinations but also engagement in reckless behaviors such
as taking dangerous treks or bungee jumping."[2] Fifty-two percent
of backpackers venture to Asia, 15 percent to South America, 12
percent to Central America, 11 percent to Africa, 8 percent to Australia or New Zealand, and only 2 percent to the United States or
Europe.

The cost of the trip varies between 30,000 and 50,000 NIS on
average (approximately $8,500 to $14,000). The young people
fund it by taking at least a full year to work and save money, usually in the service industry (waiting tables being by far the most
common occupation). Then they blow it all on a backpacking trip.
Some may find this insane, but the fact is that these young people
choose exploration over financial stability.

Shulman goes on to argue that the Big Trip offers Israeli youth
something they didn't have access to at home: a truly "unfamiliar
context, away from their families and culture." In this new setting, young Israelis are free to gauge their capabilities, strengths,
weaknesses, and interests, as well as weaknesses and limitations.
"From this perspective the journey can be understood to serve as
an arena for examining, practicing, and experiencing individual
growth. In addition, the distancing may allow the young person
to gain a different or broader understanding of his or her society,
thus enabling the individual to return to their society but on different and more 'personal' terms."

The nomad is a well-known trope in many cultures, but while
you might envision the nomad as a solo traveler, the Israeli nomad
is more likely to travel in a pack, or to otherwise drift toward the

pack at various resting points along their route. There are even destinations known to be targeted by Israelis for these purposes. Most Israelis won't boast of "backpacking alone across a remote island" but rather of "backpacking with a few other Israelis I met at the port."

The Big Trip is a special kind of rite of passage. Unlike traditional rites, the rules of which are set by the elders of a society, Israelis' extended journeys are initiated and supported by their peers. And yet, the trip in many ways does resemble other established rites: extended separation from family and society, intense personal experiences including hardships, and increased self-awareness.

Upon returning from the trip, most of these young people move on to new challenges including academic studies, moving out of the parental home, or starting a serious relationship. According to research conducted by the Shalem Center, more than half of participants define the Big Trip as an experience that significantly contributed to or affected their choice of academic studies. Among five hundred participants aged twenty-one to thirty-five, 63.2 percent went on to get a master's degree, and some a doctorate. Forty-six percent made a decision regarding their choice of studies during the Big Trip or shortly after it, and 13 percent significantly changed their previously planned academic direction. One study participant, for example, named Moran Dekel, is currently studying business management and eastern Asia studies at Hebrew University. She claims that her interest in this field has everything to do with her Big Trip to China, where she got to experience the language and culture.

Beyond the personal benefit to the traveler, some have found in this tradition the potential for contributing to the greater good. Gili Cohen, after finishing an eight-year service in a combat special forces unit, decided, like so many of his contemporaries, to explore Thailand with his wife (their one-and-a-half-year-old

daughter stayed with his mother-in-law). Upon his return, Cohen
noted that what left a lasting impression on him was the night
in Thailand when some 1,350 Israelis clamored to take part in a
Friday-evening service at a local Chabad house.

Cohen realized that he had to tap into this force, that this
might be an opportunity to show the world the real Israel. In an
interview with Herb Keinon of the *Jerusalem Post*, Cohen recalls
telling his wife that just "as there are organizations such as Doctors Without Borders which sends doctors abroad to assist others,
the reservoir of IDF vets going abroad after their service could be
parlayed into something similar that could benefit Israel, while
doing good for the local population. So, when Cohen returned to
Israel, he set to work."[3]

Together with two fellow IDF officers, Yair Atias and Boaz
Malkieli, Cohen decided to put the immense flock of Israelis,
who travel to poverty-stricken areas around the world as part of
their Big Trip, to good use. They would "use the backpackers as
the infrastructure for people to do 'blue-and-white' humanitar-
ian work," he said in an interview. "We wanted to do something
different—a different kind of Israeli start-up." The Facebook
page the three friends opened is called Lochamim L'lo Gvulot
(modified to Fighters for Life, or FFL, in its English translation).
Instead of trekking directly to popular destinations such as Lima
or Kathmandu, the group decided to spend a few weeks volunteering in one of the countries they would be touring. They wrote
a post saying they are working on putting together a delegation
to India and inviting others to join them. It only took three days
for fifteen people to join in, and within one week forty-five had
already signed up.

Today, the FFL Facebook page has over 11,000 followers, and
550 applicants applied for one of thirty-five slots on the delegation
currently volunteering in India. Once they reach their destination city—be it Mumbai, Buenos Aires, Gondar, or Mexico City—

the group mostly volunteers in the schools of the more neglected neighborhoods, where they give English, math, and science lessons, as well as dance, personal hygiene, and Krav Maga.

One of the unique aspects of the program is that it is so cost-efficient for FFL, since the youth are already paying for their own tickets to travel abroad. FFL only has to provide room and board for two and a half weeks. This means that the cost of sending a delegation of thirty-five highly motivated Israeli youth to work in the run-down neighborhoods of Mumbai can add up to as little as $11,000. Today, ten humanitarian delegations are sent each year to help more than four thousand children across the world, including in Argentina, Guatemala, Peru, Kathmandu, Mumbai, Uganda, and elsewhere.

When asked about the purpose and expectations of the Big Trip, young Israelis usually answer along the lines of wanting to have a total sense of freedom, with no commitments to anyone other than themselves. The most they'll typically plan is the actual act of leaving the country, but otherwise specific plans or routes are intentionally left blank. Coming out of a decade in the educational system followed by years in the military, young Israelis have the opportunity to experience such freedom for the first time in their early or mid-twenties.

A big part of the trip, however, is often about overcoming physical strain and challenges. Specifically, the trek is considered a "must do" for any traveler. The treks can last anywhere from a few days to several weeks. They usually involve strenuous and often dangerous hiking on high-altitude mountain routes and narrow trails. Well-known examples include the Annapurna Circuit trek and the Langtang Gosaikunda regions in Nepal, or the famous Inka trail at Machu Picchu in Peru, and the Torres del Paine trek in Chile—along the most dangerous routes, or renting a motorcycle, often without a license, and traveling across unknown countries. Typically, these endeavors are pursued while

undergoing extreme experiences and engaging in high-risk behavior.

Why on earth would these young travelers, just recently released from active duty where they experienced tremendous
physical and mental hardship, put themselves through such an
experience? To understand their motives, we must clarify first
the Hebrew concept of *davka*. Typical of the Hebrew language,
davka is a double-meaning word. One use of *davka* is to describe
an action that is intentionally rude, inconsiderate, or simply an-
noying. One could, for example, keep the car windows closed
while driving through a quiet neighborhood on Shabbat playing
music on the radio. Driving with their windows down and the
music blasting is an act of *davka*. The other side of *davka* is more
personal and not at all offensive or harmful. It is when someone
does something for reasons that are unclear to anyone other than
the person himself. It is why one might climb Mount Everest
despite the risks involved or run a marathon despite having a
heart condition. It is when we do things because we want to experience, to feel, and to be able to say, "We did it."

When young Israeli travelers put themselves in these types of
situations, it is often an act of *davka*, related by them with a sense
of pride at overcoming and prevailing over immense difficulties.
Think about the physical daring we saw in the toddlers' junkyard
playground and amplify it to the scale of a thrill-seeking adult.
The situations Israelis put themselves in, whether intentionally or
not, demand ultimate resourcefulness, and as such are a source of
pride. It may not be clear to an outsider, but for the person going
through with a risky or silly action, the motives for doing it are
crystal clear.

Some Israelis who have completed the Big Trip report having
experienced feelings of enlightenment. Often, they come back
with a different perspective on life, on their aspirations and abilities, on the lifestyle they want to lead, on the conduct of their own

culture and country, and so on. In the words of a returned traveler: "The Big Trip opens your eyes."

IT'S A SMALL WORLD AFTER ALL

After finishing my military service, I had three months before starting university. A female friend from 8200, Einat, and I decided to travel to Mexico for six weeks. Just the two of us. We planned only a few stops along the way—some of which we eventually changed on the go—and took off on an exciting adventure. Like many other Israelis who have traveled internationally, we also have stories about walking into a tiny hostel in a distant Mexican village only to hear "Hi, there," in Hebrew, from others who arrived there before us.

Einat and I, like most Israelis on the Big Trip, told ourselves before we left that we wanted to get as far away from the familiar as possible, but that "Hi, there" we'd get in some of the most unlikely locations was always a welcome one. We were drawn to other Israelis, whom we felt we could rely on. It gave us a sense of home away from home. One of my least pleasant memories from our trip was a bad stomach virus I caught while staying on an isolated beach called Playa Zipolite. For three days, I couldn't eat anything, lying on a mattress with a high fever and stomach pains. Einat took care of me. But she was not the only one. A group of Israelis who were also on the beach, whom we did not know but who heard Einat speaking to the guesthouse owner about me, immediately offered their help. They took turns sitting with me for the next seventy-two hours, not leaving me alone for a second.

Despite the fact that Israeli backpackers constantly demonstrate a tendency to distance themselves from fellow Israelis, they also tend to take a very similar route to one another. Their itineraries are very much alike, they often find themselves in, or sometimes actively seek out, the company of other Israelis, and they spend a good deal of their time in Israeli cliques. They sleep in the same dorms where thousands of other Israelis have slept; they dine in restaurants that are either run by Israelis or that cater predominantly to Israeli backpackers and feature typical Israeli food and even menus in Hebrew. Finally, they visit Israeli embassies and consulates so as to keep in close touch with their families, even receiving letters, packages, and newspapers from Israel.

Once home, Israelis urge each other to take on this adventure, to do what others have done before them as well as conquer new territory. Having seen the world, particularly the Developing World, is considered social capital in Israel. It groups a person together with others who have had similar experiences. When meeting new people and upon sharing stories about each other's lives and future plans, Israelis ask whether the other person has gone to such and such a place and on such and such a trek.

THE ISRAELI BUSINESSPERSON ABROAD

Israelis venture abroad not just for the Big Trip (or a "short trip" if that's all they can manage), but to pursue studies and advance their careers. And as with the Big Trip, those seeking professional growth outside their homeland rely on networks of Israelis. Leaving the country's borders does not entail losing the community or social networks that Israeli citizens spent their entire life building. On the contrary, when abroad, Israelis further strengthen their relationships and expand their networks, putting both to great use.

Take ICON, for example. ICON (Israel Collaboration Network) is a Silicon Valley–based nonprofit that brings together Israeli entrepreneurs and American investors, executives, and industry influencers. Basically, they target Israelis who are interested in fund-raising or doing business in Silicon Valley and connect them to the local community. They provide information, support, and advice, in the form of guides, group meetings, or platforms that encourage interaction and collaboration among ICON members— Israeli tech founders, the Silicon Valley tech community and leaders.

The person behind the wheel of ICON is Yasmin Lukatz, a born businesswoman and the executive director of the organization. After her military service as an air force operations officer, Yasmin's career took off. She started as an event organizer at the Tel Aviv Port. Later she earned an accounting, economics, and law degree from Tel Aviv University, and then an MBA from Stanford. She worked for Ernst & Young and then founded one of Israel's most popular newspapers, *Israel Hayom*, and chaired its board of directors.

Yasmin now lives in Silicon Valley with her family, but often returns to Israel to screen for one of ICON's most prestigious programs—the SV101. This unique boot camp is an entrepreneur training program that equips a select group of founders of ten start-ups with the most crucial tools necessary to make it in the Valley, with three goals in mind: getting actual feedback from a Silicon Valley perspective; getting a better understanding of how things work in the Silicon Valley; and lastly but not surprisingly, creating and leveraging a professional network in Silicon Valley. Out of hundreds of applicants, Yasmin helps, through ICON and SV101, the yearly group of ten start-ups become a part of the entrepreneurial society of Silicon Valley.

Venturing alone, especially in Silicon Valley, is a mistake no entrepreneur should make, she says. "In Israel, an entrepreneur looking for an investment or some good advice will leverage every connection he can—a friend from the military he hadn't talked to in years, his brother's university roommate, or his ex-girlfriend's uncle. But arriving in Silicon Valley, there are no army buddies or former roommates—and no second chances to make a first impression. That's where ICON's value stands out: the relationships and connections we've built over the years, and the experience that we have gained, are the support network and the safety net every entrepreneur wishes for. Israelis feel they have a home away from home here, a place to get an honest, 'no sugarcoat' advice, and the help they need with no strings attached."[4]

The most powerful networks and companies usually originate from one frustrated person who decides to do something about a problem, and such was the case of Darya Henig Shaked, founder of WeAct (Women Entrepreneurs Act).

When Darya moved to Silicon Valley in 2015, she was alone and going into the unknown, but she was only a stranger briefly. It wasn't long before she made friends with over two hundred Israelis, all part of the start-up community, and realized the entrepreneurial treasure she had stumbled upon.

Before she became an entrepreneur, Darya served as an officer at the IDF Spokesperson unit, where she happened to meet Ehud Barak, Israel's former prime minister. Later she became his and other prime ministers' consultant. After a short political career and a bachelor of law degree from Bar Ilan University, Darya moved on to working at Vital Capital, an international private equity firm focused on sub-Saharan Africa. In 2015, she and her husband, Eyal Shaked, also a tech investor, decided to move to Silicon Valley.

Darya herself became an entrepreneur not so much out of an inherent drive but out of the desire to solve a problem. She kept meeting Israeli entrepreneurs, particularly women, who said they were worried about making the move to the other side of the Atlantic. Darya sympathized; she knew that exiting Israel's all-embracing network and entering the Valley's disparate collection of people was hard, and that it was especially hard for women, for whom relocation meant becoming even more of a minority, as gender inequality remains a problem.

To help, she founded WeAct in 2016, a Silicon Valley home for female entrepreneurs, a place for them to interact and form a community. In 2018 she founded another venture to help women enter the investment industry and create the needed change, this time from the top down. Now with three children, Darya continues to break all norms and gender boundaries simply by being one of the most prominent woman-entrepreneurs in the Valley.

The first WeAct mission to Silicon Valley, in November 2016, brought twenty leading Israeli female founders together. For them, WeAct and their group became a powerful network: there to recommend new software and to widen international networks and experience, but also there to help with cultural and gender-bias issues, career advice, and investment-related questions. Darya believes this network is the most powerful by-product of WeAct, which she did not foresee.

Darya adds: "I think the Israeli side of WeAct is extremely powerful, although I believe every country should have one. Most of the Israeli female founders were raised by working mothers (as this is the reality in Israel). Feminist in my opinion, they served in a variety of roles in the IDF, most of them as officers. With or without technical training, they chose unorthodox majors for their education, and even in their professional careers they were usually 'the only women in the room.' I believe we were all brought up to speak our minds, with no regard to hierarchy, and learned how to do it in a difficult environment and with perseverance. All of these factors in the Israeli culture, of always challenging the hypothesis and striving to make everything better for everyone, is a very entrepreneurial way to look at life. And as a network it has a multiplying effect."[5]

Darya's efforts focusing on women entrepreneurs are strengthened by several other initiatives, private or governmental, relating to Israeli women in tech. According to recent research,[6] only 8 percent of Israeli start-ups are led by women—similar to much of the Western world. This number might look, rightfully, low to you, especially given the fact that Israeli women serve in the military like their male peers.

In February 2019, the board of the governmental Israel Innovation Authority approved the launch of a designated incentive program for increased support of women-led initiatives during their start-up stage. This decision presents a significant step toward narrowing gender bias and increasing the number of female entrepreneurs in the Israeli innovation ecosystem and within two years aims to double the number of women entrepreneurs the Innovation Authority supports.

Another fascinating example for powerful networks is the case of Israeli start-ups in New York and the community built around them. A reflective project that first identified this as a phenomenon is Israeli Mapped in NY, the brainchild of Guy Franklin.

As a teenager, already picturing his military service, Guy wanted to be a radio broadcaster at Army Radio, a.k.a. Galatz, but that wasn't meant to be. He switched to wanting to be an architect, but when that fell through as well, he ended up studying law and accounting at Tel Aviv University, and then taking up a job at Ernst & Young as an accountant-consultant to start-up companies. It wasn't until 2012, when he was offered the opportunity to relocate to the Ernst & Young head office in New York, that he realized he was meant to be an entrepreneur all along.

Guy continued his work as a consultant to start-up companies, and the more involved he became with the New York start-up scene, the more Israelis he met. He noticed that the Israeli presence in New York was oddly abundant, and out of curiosity, mostly, he started mapping the Israeli start-ups in the city.

Just as he suspected, Israelis were flooding the market. In 2013 Guy found that there were over 100 Israeli start-ups operating in New York, and the number kept growing, reaching over 350

start-ups within a couple of years, making Israel the greatest exporter of start-up companies to the city. Seeing the spread of companies on a map created a physical visualization that brought the
importance of this phenomenon to light. But one thing was still
missing—connectivity.

Soon, Guy's map received attention not only from start-ups but
also from investors, government officials, talents, corporations,
media, service providers, and event organizers. As soon as they
were aware of one another, the New York Israelis naturally started
connecting. Not long after, a whole ecosystem started forming
around the platform.

Guy is now the general manager of SOSA NYC, an innovation
hub where corporations, entrepreneurs, investors, and interested
parties can simply connect. We're all here, he says, now we just
need to leverage it.

ICON, WeAct, and Israeli Mapped in NY are just a few examples. There are many other similar networks spread across the
world. The common thread among them all is an interest in Israeli
technology and innovation and the desire to "pass it forward"—to
help other community members thrive. But the pattern of forming Israeli communities is not exclusive to the tech and entrepreneurial world. There are dozens, if not hundreds, of other
organizations, platforms, online communities, physical communities, hubs, and more that offer Israelis abroad a chance to meet
each other for information, networking, and support, as well as to
smooth their transition to the international world.

Israelis traveling or relocating abroad can easily and quickly
find tourist information, as well as information about work regulations, where to find a job, how to get connected with other Israelis
and non-Israelis of the business world, and much, much more. Just
as on the Big Trip, Israelis doing business outside their homeland
maintain the Israeli way of life: seeking out and creating close-
knit communities, even seven thousand miles away from home.

17

YIHEYE BESEDER

Israel's tech sector has gone from strength to strength in the past three decades, to some extent carrying the rest of Israel's economy with it. In roughly the last two decades, the share of exports in GDP has reached an average of about 36 percent; in the same period the share of imports in GDP reached an average of about 35 percent. Israel is third (after the United States and China) in terms of the number of companies listed for trading on Nasdaq. Foreign direct investments in Israel (in all sectors) reached about USD 19 billion in 2017, an all-time peak. That's a staggering increase from 2014, when USD 6.7 billion was invested from overseas.

Indeed, the conditions for foreign investment and international trade in Israel are extremely convenient. Low tariffs and an improved domestic regulatory environment have helped make international trade possible. Reforms to enhance the market openness of Israel's regulatory framework for trade are regularly put forward. The adoption of international standards (or basing new standards on international ones) is encouraged by law, and a recent resolution seeks to further harmonize existing Israeli standards with those held internationally. In addition, Israel took it upon itself to follow a certain standard set by the international economic community. By setting up its fiscal and monetary macroeconomy to adhere to the guidelines of the Maastricht Treaty and the Washington Consensus and instituting important foreign currency reforms, it managed to make the shekel, its domestic currency, a tradable one.

Besides building the infrastructure needed to attract foreign investors, the government also encourages internationals to invest or operate in Israel by offering grants, advantageous tax structures, and exemptions to help companies offset expenses in capital, R&D, and wages. All these efforts brought on very positive results.

Between 1998 and 2012, Israel's tech industry grew at more than double the rate of the nation's GDP, expanding by an average of 9 percent annually. In 2015, 2,355 start-up companies were active, employing just over 20,600 people (35 percent more as compared to 2014). Of the 2,775 companies that opened between 2010 and 2015, 420 (15 percent) had closed by 2015. This is significantly less than the world average.

According to the US Bureau of Labor Statistics and to the Small Business Administration, 33 percent of businesses fail within the first two crucial years. While the number of surviving businesses is consistently 50 to 60 percent, having a 33 percent chance of failure is still extremely high and demands high risk tolerance. Despite the gloomy chances start-ups display in the United States, the start-up capital of the world, the number of Israeli start-ups that open each year exceeds the number of those that close.

Between 2010 and 2014, the number of start-ups in Israel grew on average 4.4 percent annually. However, since 2014, the number of new start-ups launched has dropped by 6 percent on average annually. While the numbers recorded by the statistics bureau represent a possible downturn, 2016 saw more people join the sector—a 7 percent increase compared to 2015, and an increase of 6 percent on average in wages for those employed in the Israeli tech economy.

In 2017, Israeli start-ups collectively raised $5.5 billion in venture capital funding, 50 percent higher than three years before. In

2018, Israeli high-tech companies raised $6.4 billion in 623 deals, marking a record following six years of consecutive growth. The total capital raised in 2018 was 17 percent higher compared to 2017, but a remarkable 120 percent higher compared to 2013.

Thanks to years of thriving tech sector activity, Israel still has more start-ups per capita to show for than anywhere else in the world outside of Silicon Valley.

Relative to its size, Israeli start-ups received nearly two times the funding of American start-ups and have long ago surpassed Europe and China. Again, an all-time record. Finally, in recent years, Israel has seen a significant increase in the number of foreign investors, and the establishment of multiple venture capital firms looking to invest in innovative start-ups. Some of the more impressive examples include Disruptive VC, TLV Partners, 83North, and Aleph. Israel is also leading the world in investment in R&D, most of which is private, not governmental.

Eugene Kandel, former head of the National Economic Council, the former economic adviser to the prime minister, and the current CEO of Start-Up Nation Central, a nonprofit organization connecting governments, corporations, and investors from around the world with the innovation ecosystem in Israel, believes that the main comparative advantage of the Israeli economy is its ability to provide innovative technological solutions to a variety of problems increasingly facing the world. Kandel says that these are problems Israel has been dealing with for one hundred years, and by force of circumstances, traditional ways of addressing them were insufficient. Israelis came up with innovative solutions only by way of trial and error, and gradually managed to prosper and provide water, food, energy, and health care to Israeli citizens.

The role Start-Up Nation Central is playing—providing accessible information about the Israeli ecosystem as well as personal access to its players—isn't exclusive to it; the government and other organizations are working tirelessly to make connections, provide data, and help navigate the country's regulations. I myself am asked on a nearly daily basis to present and talk to foreign delegations visiting Israel, including heads of states and executives from the world's largest corporations, investors in emerging economies and tech entrepreneurs, as well as business students. They are all interested in understanding the nature of the Israeli tech ecosystem, but, more important, what they can learn from it.

NOTHING IS PERFECT

Indeed, the Israeli tech ecosystem is a successful one that sets examples in so many ways to rising hubs of entrepreneurship around the globe. However, it is far from being perfect. One of its most critical challenges, and some might say opportunities, is its current lack of diversity in human capital.

Imad Telhami was born to a Christian family, which forms a minority group in the Druze village of Isfiya, which forms a minority group within Israel, which in turn forms a minority within the Middle East. Thanks to his father's worldview, Imad came to see the fact of being a minority as a strength. His father took up teaching rather by chance; he went to Lebanon to study medicine, but when the War of Independence broke out in 1948 he came back to the village. Seeing the state of education, or rather lack thereof, of the village's children, he made it his life mission to educate the village's youth and help put them on the right path. His teachings were marked by love, and money was not important. If a child's family could not afford books or school trips, Imad's father would cover the cost. He would not let a child out of his grasp until he had learned, and not having money never factored into his decision to help. What he taught Imad was the invaluable lesson that with love and absolute faith one can move mountains. Money will come, he would say, but making money should never be one's life's goal.

If we were to choose one word to describe Imad's upbringing, it would be *shalom*. Perhaps the most well-known and highest-frequency word in Hebrew (used both as "hello" and "good-bye"), *shalom* literally means "peace." It is one of the most charged words in the language, denoting a state of harmony and acceptance between enemies—what many would describe as a utopia. But for Imad, *shalom* is simply a way of life.

This might be baffling to some. How could a minority love the decision-making majority without feeling bitterness, as those who are oppressed are so often inclined to feel? To Imad, following the example set by his father, the secret to living in shalom is to foster respect for and acceptance of the other. In Imad's village, it was not respectful of the Druze customs and traditions for men to wear short trousers or sit cross-legged. To respect these norms, although Imad and his family did not follow the same traditions, meant to accept the other's worldview, to play by their rules not out of indigence, but out of adapting oneself to an environment so as to enable life to exist side by side. Imad's childhood centered on acceptance, consideration for the other, and adapting not as sacrifice but out of love and respect. It was thanks to this childhood, difficult or not, that Imad became the industry leader he is today, and an example of how shalom can truly be realized.

At eighteen, Imad was planning on becoming a doctor, but with the advice of his father he went on to study industrial engineering and design at Shenkar College in Ramat Gan, a central city in Israel. Once a week he would return from the bustling center of Israel to his home in the village. Although he never officially graduated, he excelled in his studies and was remarkable enough to be spotted by Amos Ben-Gurion, who invited Imad to work for him in his textile factory company, ATA. In ATA his talents were again noted, this time by Yossi Ron, who owned Beged-Or company, and who invited Imad to be his plant manager in 1981. Imad did not receive a warm welcome at his new job. The

Jewish workers went on strike in the hopes of avoiding having
to work with an Arab. But Yossi was adamant, and with persistence, love, and respect, a skill set that Imad perfected as a child,
within one year he became one of the most beloved managers in
the company, so much so that after three years, when he left the
job, they went on strike again, this time to prevent him from going. They failed both times. The harsh experience of having to
bulldoze his way into the business world taught Imad a valuable
lesson. The Jewish-Arab conflict is not a fact but rather a result of
circumstances. People are similar, he thought. "We all breathe,
eat, laugh, cry, and behave the same way," he told me.[1] "We share
the same fears, difficulties, and joys of life. But when we do not
come into contact with one another it makes it too easy for us to
categorize each other, put everyone into black boxes and eventually drift apart, to the extent of hating each other. Once we do get
to know each other, we realize we're all just people, and things
usually fall into place," Imad explained.

His next stop was Delta Galil, an Israeli manufacturer and
marketer of private-label apparel products for men, women, and
children, employing today more than ten thousand employees
worldwide. When Imad arrived at Delta, he saw Dov Lautman apply this doctrine in every aspect of his company. Dov made Imad
the first Arab plant manager, after which Imad's career soared.
What defined Imad's great leadership were the same principles
he learned as a boy—love and acceptance. Throughout his career
in Delta he would find simple ways of reaching out to people.
Whether it was in Europe, the United States, the Middle East, or
anywhere else where he supervised a plant, he would look for a
language that everyone could understand. He calls this language
"motivation," and he certainly does not mean money. To promote
cooperation and inclusion, Imad came up with the slogan *"love
working with you."* "Love is something everyone understands,"
he says, "which makes it an intercultural language. This does

not mean a manager should declare his love for an employee, an approach that is likely to end in an expensive lawsuit. It means that both employees and managers should manifest compassion, as in the Arab word *hanan*, 'to include, to contain.'" The secret to Imad's success in Delta lies in the thought of how to find the balance between what motivates the employee and what's important to them, on the one hand, and the needs and wishes of the company, on the other.

In 2007, after spending twenty-five years in Delta, Imad and Dov decided to retire from the company. As he was considering his options, Imad came across disturbing statistics—82 percent of Arab women in Israel were unemployed. He decided to take responsibility and soon he built Babcom Centers, which was meant to be a door to employment, success, coexistence, and excellent service. Babcom's business model was to be the leading company in the country when it came to quality of service. To achieve this, Imad realized, Babcom must first achieve true diversity. Imad testified that he "structured Babcom like a bundle of colorful and diverse flowers, all brought together to make one gorgeous bouquet." By bringing out the best of every culture and religion, Imad managed to create a company that served everyone. It has become such a powerful business model that it is now being taught as a case study at Harvard Business School, called "Babcom: Opening Doors."

Although the success of Babcom is undeniable, Imad still felt his dream of driving true coexistence and inclusion was not being fully achieved. "I've been doing this for five years," he said in 2013, "and what new businesses have sprung up thanks to my efforts? Who has followed my example the way I have my father's? Why are Israeli Arabs not part of the start-up nation, despite comprising 20 percent of the population?" What he was doing was terrific, but it was nowhere near what he had in mind.

To solve the problem, he first sat down to define it. "Arabs have five significant fears that prevent them from becoming great entrepreneurs" was his conclusion. While Israeli Jews learn to combat these fears at an early age, Arab Israelis are taught to yield to them, and this prevents them from dreaming big. In Imad's eyes, the first fear is fear of failure. Growing up in a small and confined community and being a minority in a country that is often prejudiced against them has developed an inherent sense of shame among the Arab population. *What would people say if I fail? Who would laugh at me?* They would rather not take risks than have to go through the humiliation of failure. The second fear is fear of government. The Israeli government is at fault more often than not when it comes to the Arab sector, which understandably makes Arabs believe they would not receive the support any entrepreneur needs. The third fear is of the banks. Like the government, they offer little support to Arabs in the form of interests, loans, and credit, often requiring people to take out a mortgage on their land or house, something many, Arabs in particular, find very difficult to do.

The fourth fear stems from lack of success stories. "We could count the number of Israeli Arab entrepreneurial role models on one hand," Imad included. The lack of experienced mentors and inspirational figures is only exacerbated by the success rate seen in the Jewish sector. Finally, there's the fear of networking. The importance of having a strong network to support an entrepreneur along the way cannot be stressed enough. The business and professional network Arabs have comprises, in most cases, the village's head of council and school principal. It may be a valuable relationship, but it is a drop in the ocean compared to the 8200 alumni network, Silicon Valley connections, universities, and other relationships Israeli Jews have lined up.

With the problem well defined, Imad was now able to turn to solutions. He founded Takwin Labs together with Chemi Peres and Erel Margalit, and together they help combat the five inhibiting fears that are plaguing Israeli Arabs. Beyond financial support, they offer Arab entrepreneurs networking opportunities, professional support, access to technology, mentors, and strategic consultants. Above all, they help them expand their dreams tenfold. "Dream big," Imad would say. "It's where it all starts."

The challenge in diversity in human capital in the Israeli tech ecosystem is not limited to the Arab population. There are other groups underrepresented, such as the ultra-Orthodox, women, and people over the age of forty-five—each group for a different reason and root cause.

However, given the constant growth of the Israeli tech industry, creating demand for recruitment of skilled personnel at an accelerated rate while competing for these resources with various players, a notable shortage in talented, skilled personnel is felt. This important challenge is now turning into an opportunity. It has become urgent to fully realize the innovation potential of all segments of Israeli society, in order to generate inclusive and sustainable economic growth. Hence, both governmental initiatives and many private ones are put in place to support the growth by tapping into these underrepresented groups of potential talent.

OPTIMISM AND ENTREPRENEURSHIP

Business journalists and industry experts alike are looking to understand the factors behind Israel's remarkably successful tech ecosystem. This has also been the purpose of this book: to break down exactly what in Israeli culture breeds so many powerful entrepreneurial minds. There is a thriving entrepreneurial culture that underpins Israeli society, not only the business sector. From infancy to adulthood, Israelis are driven toward experimentation, failure, and learning; mental and physical risk taking; and a positive, some would say blind, belief that things will be all right, or in Hebrew: *yiheye beseder.*

The ideas that stand behind this phrase are complex and meaningful. In a sense, they comprise the core from which every other quality we've attributed to the typical Israeli springs from. To understand it, we need to tap into the heart of Israel—its language, history, community, and practices.

Chemi Peres, one of Israel's true sabras, is here to help. Chemi is the son of Sonia and Shimon Peres, former prime minister and president of Israel. Peres served as a fighter pilot in the Israeli Air Force and went on to establish one of the first venture capital firms in Israel, Mofet, which led to his becoming one of the most prominent venture capital personas in Israel. Peres served as the chairman of Israel's venture capital association and later founded Pitango, the biggest venture capital firm in Israel today.

Peres has much to say about optimism and Israel's success in high-tech. "At its core," says Peres, "optimism is a matter of faith. You must believe that things will happen in a certain way. Beyond faith, optimism is also a tool, a mind-set. It can be used to motivate and drive you forward, and there can be no entrepreneurship without an ounce of optimism."[2]

But optimism goes beyond entrepreneurship. Peres continues. "Many people, I believe, use optimism simply because being pessimistic won't get you far; there's not much to do with it, but with optimism you can do anything. My father used to say that he has never heard of a pessimist who discovered a new star. Before he passed away he told me that history paints a much more optimistic picture than we're used to thinking." We tend to overlook signs of change, for better or worse. We use current standards to measure our well-being and quality of life, while failing to notice that, compared to just a few decades ago, things were much worse.

This is why, when looking back, we can suddenly see progress. "Things are becoming more available, more affordable, and people have more opportunities today to enjoy everything the world has to offer. It's not just commodities; it's also education, mobility, and access to medical care." Peres uses the Ebola virus as an example: "The fact that we overcame it relatively quickly and effectively calls for celebration. But since we are so accustomed to the fact that the medical world manages to overcome the most complex of diseases, we take it for granted. Perhaps if we were less optimistic, for example had less faith in medicine, then curing Ebola might have gone down as one of the greatest medical breakthroughs of our time. But because we're optimistic, we assumed that eventually, *yiheye beseder*, so we treat it as just another disease that came and went.

"With entrepreneurs, some of their optimism is pure faith, which one could also call naïve, and some of it relies on their ability to familiarize themselves with the needs of the market, to be objective and critical of their product, services, resources, and abilities, and to assess the risk factors." An entrepreneur must have both faith and practicality, and that faith is often a quality of young, inexperienced people. "It's not for nothing that the greatest entrepreneurs of our time were young people when they first started. The best examples include Bill Gates starting Microsoft, Steve Jobs starting Apple, or Mark Zuckerberg starting Facebook. These specific examples are also good in showing how much of their own well-being young people are willing to sacrifice to get to where they believe they can get," Peres sums up.

There are three kinds of optimism. One is the kind of optimism that is intrinsic. It is faith in yourself that if things were up to you, you would be able to pull it off. The second one is the kind of optimism that places trust in another. Peres explained, "My optimism as an investor, for example, rests on other people. I work with the most excellent people out there, and I have full faith in their capabilities. What you find often in the entrepreneurial world, specifically in Israel, is a combination of these two aspects of optimism. The most successful entrepreneurs are those who know how to recognize what they need in others, as well as to have self-awareness and a true belief that together you can do anything."

Yiheye beseder, like all complex cultural phenomena, contains a potential downfall. *Yiheye beseder* can also be used to diffuse criticism, dodge difficult questions, and avoid hard work. Dr. Etay Shilony, in his book *Israelism,* has noted and criticized the tendency of Israel's organizational culture to treat things carelessly, without consideration or much thought. *Yiheye beseder,* for Shilony, represents the culture of disregard and even negligence that can be found throughout Israel's businesses and government.

"This side of *yiheye beseder,*" said Peres, "comes from an unsubstantiated position. It's not enough to say that things will be all right. One has to make sure they are. It is naïve to believe that things will somehow resolve themselves without hard work. The purpose of the phrase, when used in this way, is simply to appease the mind of the listener and to pass on the responsibility. It can be a dangerous thing, to diffuse responsibility, it can lead to terrible consequences." Nevertheless, the fact that *yiheye beseder* has a negative aspect confirms its complexity. When it's used to reassure one's faith, though, it can be a powerful tool for an entrepreneur, or even a nation, to possess.

The third type of optimism is a mixture of determination and persistence. Take Rafi Yoeli, for example, the CEO of Urban Aeronautics. He has been working on developing internal rotor aircrafts for use in urban areas for almost two decades. Against all odds, he persists. His is a project that does not easily attract investors and partners; the technology always seems on the verge of breaking through, of making it. It's hard to fathom where people like Yoeli get their bottomless optimism. It has a lot to do with being determined, and even more to do with a belief that you are serving a greater purpose. As Peres explained, "In my father's

case, his optimism drew on his faith in Man and from his conviction that he is doing something greater than himself, greater than
his entire generation." Optimism is a way of life.

Israeli optimism is inexplicable. Given the political conditions,
it would have been much more reasonable if Israelis were pessimistic. Peres suggests that the optimistic attitude inherent in
Israel actually stems from the conditions of life in Israel.

"Parents raise their children in high-risk locations. They settle
in the north where they are just a couple of hundred feet away
from Syria, Lebanon, and Hezbollah; they build towns around the
Gaza Strip where they are exposed to missile attacks; they walk
the streets of Jerusalem that have a long history of suicide bomb-
ers. Still, they stay. On the one hand, home is safe, stable, and associated with family warmth and love. On the other hand, there
is the reality that enwraps us, one that for the outside observer
might seem unbearable." The point that Peres is making is that
despite the apparent dangers, children feel safe in their home because it was built by their parents not on fear but on optimism, on
the hope and belief that things will get better or, alternatively, we
can survive anything.

"WE SURVIVED PHARAOH, WE'LL SURVIVE THIS, TOO"

Israeli optimism has strong roots in the history of the Jewish
people. The Jewish narrative is one of survival in the face of attacks, the Holocaust being the most recent and gruesome example.
Yiheye beseder exemplifies the narrative so strongly embedded in
Israeli culture and the Jewish story—that Jews are survivors. As
Meir Ariel, a famous Israeli singer, says: "We survived Pharaoh,
we'll survive this, too." Or take the humorous summation of every
Jewish holiday: "They tried to kill us. We won. Let's eat!" Peres
explains: "This idea that we can get through the most difficult
and dangerous situations instills resilience as well as optimism."

Another aspect of this narrative, as Peres explains, is "the belief that [Jews] are the chosen people. We are unique, strong, and as such we have a responsibility to improve the world around us, to engage in *tikkun olam*, which literally translates as 'repair of the world.' It is a religious concept used today to refer to the need for social justice. These values are passed on from a very young age. Unlike the blind optimism one sometimes comes across, this is a conscious, educated optimism, based on generations of experience and the nurturing of a strong narrative of survival."

In January 2010, Israeli president Shimon Peres said in his speech to the German Bundestag that *tikkun olam* is the Jewish people's answer to the Holocaust. It's the attempt to correct a wrong, to improve oneself and one's environment. "*Tikkun olam*," says Peres's son, "also stands at the heart of the entrepreneurial activity. To be an entrepreneur entails identifying something that does not work as it should, or that can be made better. *Yiheye beseder*, then, also comes as a response to the fact that things are not all right. It's an acknowledgment that even though things are looking bad at the moment, they will pick up soon enough."

Since the 1950s, out of necessity, Israelis have been finding miraculous ways to solve domestic needs, but have been capable, at the same time, of sharing these solutions with the world. The need to make the most of the desert in Israel's south has led to innovative breakthroughs in agriculture, influencing not only Israeli society, but those of many developing countries, providing them with food security solutions for better agriculture and safer food storage. One of the most famous examples is Netafim's drip and micro-irrigation solutions, which rapidly spread worldwide. Their newest models are self-cleaning and maintain uniform flow rate regardless of water quality and pressure.

The concept of *tikkun olam* also applies to health-care innovation, with disruptive inventions that improve medical care around the world: the development of Given Imaging's PillCam, the first capsule endoscopy solution for the digestive tract, might nearly eliminate the need for risky, invasive procedures. Or the development of the immunomodulator drug Copaxone for treating multiple sclerosis. It was developed at the Weizmann Institute of Science in Israel and revolutionized its space. Other inventions sound like something out of science fiction, such as ReWalk, a bionic system to enable paraplegics to stand upright, walk, and climb stairs. It has already been approved by the FDA.

Israeli innovation has also changed the way the world consumes technology: the Intel 8088—the first PC CPU from IBM—was designed in Israel; most of the Windows NT operating system was developed by Microsoft-Israel; the Pentium MMX chip technology was designed in Israel at Intel; the first USB flash drives available in North America were developed by M-Systems, an Israeli company.

Tikkun olam also exists when bringing technology from one space to the benefit of another: Waze, a GPS-based geographical navigation application program for smartphones, provides turn-by-turn information and user-submitted travel times and route details, and has changed the way we all use maps. Mobileye, a vision-based advanced driver-assistance system providing warnings for collision prevention and mitigation, is an Israeli company. Out of their technology for autonomous cars, they came up with OrCam MyEye, a compact, artificial vision device that enables people with vision impairments to understand text and identify objects through audio feedback describing what they are unable to see—literally helping blind people to see.

And the list goes on and on . . .

Yiheye beseder, then, is a layered concept, originating in the heart of an entire people, passed on from generation to generation. It's an idea deeply embedded in history but also with a future outlook: by saying *yiheye beseder,* we're reassuring ourselves and others that even though it's hard to see right now, things will be better in the future. It's an ability to look at the present from different perspectives, to instill hope and security, and to plan one's actions accordingly.

As Peres says, "*Yiheye beseder* is the wind in our sails, it is what gives us the power to move forward, but we must choose the direction ourselves. No sailor, like no entrepreneur, can do without wind or a compass. Many entrepreneurs, Israelis included, have one without the other, but the best ones have both."

Yiheye beseder lies at the heart of Israeli culture and is the driving force behind its entrepreneurial spirit and attitude. For Israelis, now is never our final stop; there is room for change and growth, and the future, against all odds, can be surprisingly positive.

And for you?

ACKNOWLEDGMENTS

I kept my favorite Hebrew word, *firgun*, for this part of the book.

Firgun is used to describe a concept or a behavior of taking part in another person's joyful experience, just for the sake of it, without expecting something in return—a pure sentiment of sympathy. It describes the state of feeling and expressing joy and sympathy at someone else's well-being or achievements without jealousy or selfishness. It is a genuine attempt at making someone else feel good, not to be confused with simply complimenting someone. It is so much stronger than a compliment.

For me, writing this book was not a simple task. And I would have never completed it without the *firgun* I felt from so many people along the journey.

Most important, my three loved boys, Yonatan, Daniel, and Yarden: I started writing this book a few years ago, and you grew up, each in your own special way, as the chapters of the book filled up. Your childhood journeys inspired me to write this book and share its story with the entire world. I wish you a colorful, creative, vivid, impactful life, one of self-fulfillment among friends and colleagues who are important and meaningful to you. Keep using just the right amount of your own chutzpah!

My precious partner, best friend, and husband, Nir: *Chutzpah* is coming out exactly as we are celebrating twenty years of marriage! You taught me, through the years, to dream big. You inspired me to unveil entrepreneurial skills I did not know I had. You always supported and encouraged me in the choices I made. You are my second half and the love of my life, today even more than twenty-five years ago when we first met. I love you so much.

My loved parents, Mira and Motty: Thank you for having given me freedom and space to become the person I am. For showing the direction, without forcing me to walk through a specific path. For setting an example, without expecting me to copy it. For providing a rich childhood environment. Dad, may you rest in peace. You are still guiding me every single day.

My colleagues and friends from the Israeli tech ecosystem, thank you for your *firgun* along the past years, as I was writing *Chutzpah*. Your interest in my work, your support and criticism, made *Chutzpah* more than just my story. It's the story of all of us.

Specifically, I wish to thank:

Adi Altschuler, Adi Sharabani, Benny Levin, Chemi Peres, Darya Henig Shaked, Dov Moran, Eugene Kandel, Guy Franklin, Guy Ruvio, Imad Telhami, Izhar Shay and Shir Shay, Kira Radinsky, Matan Edvy, Micha Kaufman, Nadav Zafrir, Narkis Alon, Nir Lempert, Noam Sharon, Ran Balicer, Sagy Bar, Sharin Fisher, Tsahi Ben Yosef, Uri Weinheber, Yair Seroussi, Yasmin Lukatz, Yonatan Adiri—for finding the time to share your stories with me and accepting to share them with the readers.

Adi Janowitz, Amy Friedkin, Anna Philips, Ariana Kamran, Brian Abrahams, Chaya Glasner, Dan Senor, Wendy Singer, Terry Kassel and the entire PSE Foundation, Daniel Alfon, Efrat Duvdevani and the entire team at the Peres Center for Peace and Innovation, Gabby Czertok, Gadi Zeder, Gonie Aram, Guy Hilton and the entire Start-Up Nation Central team, Mor and Guy Peled, Itay Shhigger, Judy Heiblum, Neta Eshet and Levi Afuta, Rick Allen, Rose Kahn, Saar Friedman, Shirley Schlafka, Saul Singer, Sharon Blatt, Shuky Kappon, Sigi Naggiar, Sujata Thomas, Wendy Revel and the backStorygroup, Yonatan Ido—for supporting my writing journey; reading, editing, serving as a sounding board; suggesting ideas; and sharing your valuable feedback.

Special thanks to Shira Rivelis, who assisted me with the research and spent hours and hours reviewing my writing, helping me turn this dream into an actual book.

Thanks to my precious team and partners at Synthesis and true, for sharing the excitement with me! Shirley—I could not have asked for a better friend and business partner!

And lastly, to my newest family: the HarperCollins team led by Hollis Heimbouch, my publisher, and the Dupree Miller team led by Jan Miller, my agent—Thanks for believing in me. Thanks for believing in *Chutzpah*. I am so happy we chose each other!

GLOSSARY

Balagan [Chapter 2: *Balagan*]: Imagine a busy street: old ladies yelling at bus drivers, merchants arguing about politics, high-tech executives in jeans and baggy T-shirts, children playing in junkyards, soldiers buying falafel on their way to the base. Chaos is at the heart of this place where everything is extremely high strung. But looks can be deceiving. Nothing has pre-coordinated order, and yet everything is functioning very efficiently. It's a state of chaos with the promise of opportunity.

Noun: A modern Hebrew loan word (from Russian) for chaos. adj. *mevulgan* v. *levalgen*.

Example: "The way they're managing that company is complete *balagan.*"

Chanich [Chapter 8: Riskful Management]: The word *chanich* comes from the root word *chanicha*, which means "initiation." A *chanich* is a person being trained, an apprentice, someone learning by practice.

Chutzpah [Introduction]: Rude and opinionated; for example, a stranger at the mall telling a young mother how she should dress, feed, and educate her children. More positively, preferring directness to political correctness for the sake of achieving one's goals. From Aramaic through Yiddish, the word entered modern Hebrew as well as English. Used negatively to describe a person or an action that is rude or offensive; but also used to describe a person or an action that is courageous or daring, particularly in a business context.

Jack Ma, Alibaba's founder, said on October 25, 2018, at the opening of the Israeli Innovation Center, that in his former visit to Israel, he learned two things: "Innovation and chutzpah: the courage to challenge."

Example: "It takes a lot of chutzpah to sign such a deal."

Combina [Chapter 3: Playing with Fire]: From the English word *combination*, *combina* is about advancing one's interests or solving one's problems in unconventional or unofficial ways. *Combina* can be falsely perceived as a mild form of corruption as it requires undermining the usual channels of bureaucracy or command, but the key difference is that *combina* is harmless in the direct sense of the word, and therefore provides a welcome solution.

Noun: Derived from "combination," a way of getting around the system that is beneficial to the actor; a nonofficial solution to a problem. v. *lecamben*.

Example: "They managed to save 5 percent of the fees, what a *combina*."

Davka [Chapter 16: Global Openness]: Doing something counterintuitive or intentionally undesirable for reasons that are not clear to anyone other than the agent. For example, listening to loud music on a Saturday while passing through a religious neighborhood. Also, to express opposition on a certain idea or suggestion. For example, going for a run in the rain is *davka* nice.

From Aramaic, often used with contrarian or ironic connotations, expresses an opposition or annoyance at something that should have happened in a certain way but happened to happen in the opposite, more inconvenient way.

Example: "Did you have to schedule this meeting *davka* on my busiest day?"

Dugri [Chapter 14: Improvisation and Optimization]: Being straightforward and not beating around the bush. It is a speech marker that indicates that what the speaker is about to say next is the takeaway from the entire conversation, so the listener best pay attention. A modern Hebrew loan word (from Turkish and Arabic). Used to describe a speech that is straightforward and candid, often in the context of making blunt or uncomfortable but truthful statements.

Example: "*Dugri*, I don't understand the purpose of this meeting."

Firgun [Acknowledgments]: Used to describe a concept or a behavior of taking part in another person's joyful experience. Imagine your best friend just landed that new job he's been so keen on. Imagine that moment when he calls you up to tell you the good news and you're genuinely happy for and proud of him. You'd probably take a second to rejoice and congratulate your friend, knowing how much he deserves it. The favorite Hebrew word among Israeli tech entrepreneurs.

Noun: The state of feeling and expressing joy and sympathy at someone else's well-being or achievements without jealousy or selfishness. v. *lefargen*, a genuine attempt at making someone else feel good, not to be confused with simply complimenting someone.

Example: "Daniel really *firgen* me yesterday when I told him about my promotion."

Iltur [Chapter 14: Improvisation and Optimization]: Literally in English, "improvisation"; literally in Hebrew, "immediate" (*le'altar*); in practice, a quick and effective fix for any kind of problem. *Iltur* is a quality Israelis learn to perfect from early childhood. Lack of resources requires improvisation, which, if practiced, can become an essential life skill; rather than depending on resources, one becomes resourceful himself.

Noun: Originally from the Mishna and brought into modern Hebrew via military slang. Literally, "to improvise"; "immediately." The practice of coming up with solutions or improvements on the go. v. *le'alter.* adj. *me'ultar.*

Example: "Don't worry about your broken strap, I will *le'alter* a new one in no time."

Katan alay [Chapter 3: Playing with Fire]: Literally, "it's small on me." The closest translation is somewhere along the lines of "no sweat." More profoundly, it is a linguistic tactic to create the sense of being able to do anything. When you say about a task that it's *baktana,* you are not approaching the task from an objective perspective, considering its complexity or the resources it would require; rather, you're considering it from your own perspective, saying to yourself, *"Walla,* it's *katan alay,"* no matter what it is.

Example: "Are you nervous about quitting your job?" "Nah, *katan alay.*"

Leezrom [Chapter 5: Free to Be]: Literally and figuratively, "to go with the flow." It's not enough to allow things to take their natural course; *leezrom* requires making room for the unexpected in our lives, being willing to take part in something that was not part of a plan and seeing where it takes us.

Verb: Literally, "to flow." A person who is *zorem* is one who is easygoing, often spontaneous, participates willingly and enthusiastically in non-preplanned activities.

Example: "Are you *zorem* with trying this tactic?"

Madrich [Chapter 8: Riskful Management]: A *madrich* is a guide, an instructor, usually in an educational or instructive framework (excluding schools). The word *madrich* comes from the root word *derech,* which means "way." A *madrich* guides the way.

Rosh gadol [Chapter 10: Resourcefulness]: Literally, "big head." In everyday Hebrew, doing more than the bare minimum. *Rosh gadol* is an attitude, a mind-set. It is something you are. Being *rosh gadol* means to think about more and to do more than what you were told to think or do. It's about seeing the bigger picture and striving to bring it to fruition. Surprisingly, originated from the military, where Israeli soldiers are encouraged to think big and not just follow orders. Those who are *rosh gadol* are role models. Entrepreneurs are by definition *rosh gadol.*

Noun: Colloquially used to describe a person who takes initiative and assumes responsibilities beyond what is expected of him. Antonym: *rosh katan.* Literally, "small head." Colloquially used to describe a person who does only what is required of him and nothing more.

Example: "Don't just do what you are told, be *rosh gadol.*"

Shalom [Chapter 17: *Yiheye Beseder*]: Literally, "peace." Also, a form of greeting and saying good-bye. Probably the most well-known word in the Hebrew language. It has both everyday and political meaning, which makes it both banal and extremely loaded. Sometimes used as a blessing (e.g., *shalom alecha*—peace be onto you), sometimes as a calling (worldwide peace), and sometimes simply to say *shalom* (hi).

Noun: The Hebrew word for peace, more broadly denoting a state of harmony and safety between two opposing parties. In idiomatic Hebrew, commonly used as a greeting (both hello and good-bye).

Shiftzur [Chapter 14: Improvisation and Optimization]: *Shiftzur* is about identifying a problem, picturing a solution, and breaking it down into doable tasks. Originating in a culture that is economical, the idea is that just because it's not broken doesn't mean you shouldn't fix it. A common military practice, where soldiers self-upgrade their equipment by, for example, hand-sewing a holster for their cartridges.

Noun: Originating in Israeli military slang, *shiftzur* is the act of improving one's equipment by making improvised adjustments to it. v. *leshafzer.*

Tachles [Chapter 9: Let the Children Do It]: A dual-meaning word that expresses practicality as well as a feeling of having captured the point. Can be applied to various topics, from politics to the weather to the quality of a certain product. A modern Hebrew loan word (from Yiddish). Literally, "end, purpose, goal." It means we are goal oriented, emphasizing or pointing out a bottom line, while acting and doing.

Example: "*Tachles*, I don't know why you kept that job for so long. It's good you finally quit."

Yalla [Introduction]: Literally, "let's go!" An expression of eagerness to get down to brass tacks. Can also express haste, impatience, enthusiasm, or simple practicality. Less commonly, a dismissive form of speech; as in "*yalla*, you can take your business elsewhere," or "*yalla*, you don't know what you're talking about." Originally from Egyptian, popularized through vernacular use in Egyptian, Persian, Turkish, and Hebrew film, television, and slang. Most commonly used as "let's go" or "hurry up." In Hebrew, also used to express enthusiasm about an upcoming event or activity.

Example: "*Yalla*, let's do it!"

Yiheye beseder [Chapter 17: *Yiheye Beseder*]: Possibly the key to the Israeli state of mind. No matter what, everything will be fine. From losing your key to getting divorced, this catchphrase expresses the idea that life goes on and that things have a tendency of resolving themselves. It can be naïve and annoyingly indifferent, but it's an approach to life that says: granted, things might not be great now, but we should keep on going because eventually everything will be fine. Used to comfort or appease concerns.

A critical mind-set for innovators and entrepreneurs.

Example: "Don't worry about losing your job; *yiheye beseder.*"

NOTES

INTRODUCTION

1. Warren Buffett, quoted in Israel Ministry of Foreign Affairs, https://mfa .gov.il/MFA/Quotes/Pages/Quote-27.aspx.
2. Yonatan Adiri, interviewed by Arieli Inbal, December 2018.
3. Jack Ma, Opening of the Israeli Innovation Center and the prime minister's Israeli Innovation Summit, Tel Aviv, October 25, 2018.

1: PLAYING WITH JUNK

1. Malka Haas, "Children in the Junkyard," *Association for Childhood Education International* 73, no. 1 (1966).
2. Isobel Van der Kuip and Ingrid Verheul, *Early Development of Entrepreneurial Qualities: The Role of Initial Education* (Zoetermeer: EIM, Small Business Research and Consultancy, 1998).
3. Amnon Zilber and Michal Korman, "The Junkyard as Parable," *Magazine of the Design Museum*, Holon, 2014.

2: BALAGAN

1. Albert Einstein, quoted in David Burkus, "When to Say Yes to the Messy Desk," *Forbes*, May 2014, https://www.forbes.com/sites/davidburkus/2014 /05/23/when-to-say-yes-to-the-messy-desk/#54b681781fdc.
2. Penelope Green, "Saying Yes to Mess," *New York Times*, December 21, 2006, http://www.nytimes.com/2006/12/21/garden/21mess.html?page wanted=print&_r=1.
3. Eric Abrahamson and David H. Freedman, *A Perfect Mess: The Hidden Benefits of Disorder—How Crammed Closets, Cluttered Offices, and On-the-Fly Planning Make the World a Better Place* (New York: Little, Brown, 2006).
4. Janice Denegri-Knott and Elizabeth Parsons, "Disordering Things," *Journal of Consumer Behavior* 13 (2014): 89–98.

3: PLAYING WITH FIRE

1. Kim Kovelle, "Tips to Teach Kids How to Build a Campfire," *Metro-Parent*, July 27, 2018, http://www.metroparent.com/daily/family-activities/camping/build-campfire-tips-teach-kids/.
2. Ke'Tara Wells, "Recess Time in Europe vs America," *Click2Houston*, March 10, 2016, http://www.click2houston.com/news/recess-time-in-europe-vs-america.
3. Lawrence E. Williams and John A. Bargh, "Experiencing Physical Warmth Promotes Interpersonal Warmth," *Science* 322, no. 5901 (2008): 606–7, http://www.ncbi.nlm.nih.gov/pmc/articles/PMC2737341/.
4. Micha Kaufman, interviewed by Inbal Arieli, Tel Aviv, September 20, 2018.
5. Ruth Umoh, "Jeff Bezos' Wife Would Rather Have a Child with 9 Fingers than One That Can't Do This," CNBC, November 21, 2017, https://www.cnbc.com/2017/11/20/how-jeff-bezos-teaches-his-kids-resourcefulness.html.

4: IN HEBREW, THERE IS AN "I" IN "WE"

1. Datia Ben Dor, "My Land of Israel," https://ulpan.com/israeli-music/%D7%90%D7%A8%D7%A5-%D7%99%D7%A9%D7%A8%D7%90%D7%9C-%D7%A9%D7%9C%D7%99-my-land-of-israel/.
2. Matthew J. Hornsey and Jolanda Jetten, "The Individual within the Group: Balancing the Need to Belong with the Need to Be Different," *Personality and Social Psychology Review* 8, no. 3 (2004): 248–64.
3. Stuart Anderson, "40 Percent of Fortune 500 Companies Founded by Immigrants or Their Children," *Forbes*, June 19, 2011, http://www.forbes.com/sites/stuartanderson/2011/06/19/40-percent-of-fortune-500-companies-founded-by-immigrants-or-their-children/#13f9c6827a22.
4. Kira Radinsky, interviewed by Arieli Inbal, Tel Aviv, September 2018.
5. Paul Graham, "What It Takes," *Forbes*, October 20, 2010, https://www.forbes.com/forbes/2010/1108/best-small-companies-10-y-combinator-paul-graham-ask-an-expert.html#22e0cc71acad.

5: FREE TO BE

1. Roger Hart, "Environmental Psychology or Behavioral Geography? Either Way It Was a Good Start," *Journal of Environmental Psychology* 7, no. 4 (December 1987): 321–29, https://www.sciencedirect.com/science/article/abs/pii/S0272494487800051.
2. Kathryn Tyler, "The Tethered Generation," Holy Cross Energy Leadership Academy, *HR Magazine*, May 1, 2007, https://www.shrm.org/hr-today/news/hr-magazine/pages/0507cover.aspx.
3. John Mark Froiland, "Parents' Weekly Descriptions of Autonomy Supportive Communication: Promoting Children's Motivation to Learn and

Positive Emotions," *Journal of Child and Family Studies* 24, no. 1 (January 2013): 117–26.

4. Richard A. Fabes, Jim Fultz, Nancy Eisenberg, et al., "Effects of Rewards on Children's Prosocial Motivation: A Socialization Study," *Developmental Psychology* 25, no. 4 (July 1989): 509–15.

5. World Economic Forum, *The Global Competitiveness Report: 2015–2016*, ed. Klaus Schwab (Geneva: World Economic Forum, 2016).

6. Guy Ruvio, interviewed by Arieli Inbal, Tel Aviv, May 2015.

7. Adi Sharabani, interviewed by Arieli Inbal, Tel Aviv, July 2016.

8. Erika Landau Institute, "The Erika Landau Institute Home Page," http://ypipce.org.il/?page_id=11.

9. Professor Ran Balicer, interviewed by Arieli Inbal, Tel Aviv, November 2018.

6: FAILURE IS AN OPTION

1. Jerry Useem, "Failure: The Secret of My Success," *Inc.*, May 1, 1998.

2. Jerry Useem, "The Secret of My Success," *United Marine Publications* 20, no. 6 (1979).

3. Michael Jordan, *Wikiquote*, https://en.wikiquote.org/wiki/Michael_Jordan.

4. Laura M. Miele, "The Importance of Failure: A Culture of False Successes," *Psychology Today*, March 12, 2015, https://www.psychologytoday .com/blog/the-whole-athlete/201503/the-importance-failure-culture-false -success.

5. Kathryn Tyler, "The Tethered Generation," Holy Cross Energy Leadership Academy, *HR Magazine*, May 1, 2007, https://www.shrm.org/hr-today /news/hr-magazine/pages/0507cover.aspx.

6. Adam Dachis, "The Psychology Behind the Importance of Failure," *Life-Hacker*, January 22, 2013, http://lifehacker.com/5978096/the-psychology -behind-the-importance-of-failure.

7. Vince Lombardi, *Good Reads*, https://www.goodreads.com/quotes/31295 -it-s-not-whether-you-got-knocked-down-it-s-whether-you.

7: CERTAIN UNCERTAINTY

1. InterNations, "Expat Insider." Family Life Index 2018, https://www.inter nations.org/expat-insider/2018/family-life-index-39591.

2. Kelly McGonigal, "How to Make Stress Your Friend," *TED Ideas Worth Spreading*, video file, June 2013, https://www.ted.com/talks/kelly_mcgonigal _how_to_make_stress_your_friend/transcript?language=en#t-530180.

8: RISKFUL MANAGEMENT

1. Boy Scouts of America, "Youth," https://www.scouting.org/.

2. Scouts, "Scouts Be Prepared," http://scouts.org.uk/home/.

3. Tzofim, "Who We Are," http://www.zofim.org.il/magazin_item.asp?item_id =696909405721&troop_id=103684.

4. Tsahi Ben Yosef, interviewed by Shira Rivelis, Tel Aviv, September/ October 2016.

5. Keith Sawyer, "Improvisational Creativity as a Model for Effective Learning," in *Improvisation: Between Technique and Spontaneity*, ed. Marina Santi (Newcastle upon Tyne: Cambridge Scholars Publishing, 2010), 135–53.

6. Yair Seroussi, interviewed by Arieli Inbal, Tel Aviv, November 2018.

7. Janusz Korczak, "9 tzitutim meorerey hashra'a shel Janusz Korczak, ha'mechanech haultimativy" [9 inspirational quotes by Janusz Korczak, the ultimate educator], https://www.eol.co.il/articles/323#, accessed February 2019.

8. Narkis Alon, interviewed by Shira Rivelis, Tel Aviv, September 2016.

9: LET THE CHILDREN DO IT

1. Tara Lifland, "Krembo Wings: A Youth Movement Led by Children for Disabled Children," NoCamels, December 12, 2012, http://nocamels.com /2012/12/krembo-wings-a-social-movement-led-by-children-for-disabled -children/.

2. Sharin Fisher, interviewed by Shira Rivelis, Tel Aviv, October 2016.

3. Darya Henig Shaked, interviewed by Arieli Inbal, June 2017.

4. Sagy Bar, interviewed by Arieli Inbal, Tel Aviv, July 2016.

10: RESOURCEFULNESS

1. Barbara Bamberger, "Volunteer Service Draws Israeli Teens Before They Start Stints in Military," *Tablet*, June 7, 2013, http://www.tabletmag.com /jewish-life-and-religion/133955/volunteer-service-israeli-teens.

2. Izhar and Shir Shay, interviewed by Rivelis Shira, Tel Aviv, July 2016.

11: HUMAN CAPITAL

1. Wikipedia, "Israel Defense Forces," https://en.wikipedia.org/wiki/Israel _Defense_Forces.

12: CULTURE

1. Anthony Kellett, *Combat Motivation: The Behavior of Soldiers in Battle*, ed. James P. Ignizio (Dordrecht: Springer Netherlands, 1982).

2. Sergio Catignani, "Motivating Soldiers: The Example of the Israeli Defense Forces," *Parameters* (Autumn 2004): 108–21, http://strategicstudies institute.army.mil/pubs/parameters/articles/04autumn/catignan.pdf.

3. Ronald Krebs, "A School for the Nation? How Military Service Does Not Build Nations, and How It Might," *International Security* 28, no. 4 (2004): 85–124.
4. Louis D. Williams, *The Israel Defense Forces: A People's Army* (New York: Authors Choice Press, 2000).
5. Moshe Sherer, "Rehabilitation of Youth in Distress through Army Service: Full, Partial, or Non-Service in the Israel Defense Forces—Problems and Consequences," *Child & Youth Care Forum* 27, no. 1 (1998): 39–58.
6. Ori Swed and John Sibley Butler, "Military Capital in the Israeli Hi-tech Industry," *Armed Forces & Society* 41, no. 1 (2015): 123–41.
7. Nir Lempert, interviewed by Shira Rivelis, Tel Aviv, February 12, 2017.

13: MANAGEMENT

1. Edward Luttwak, quoted in *Start-up Nation: The Story of Israel's Economic Miracle*, ed. Dan Senor and Saul Singer (New York: Hachette Book Group, 2009), 53–58.
2. Nadav Zafrir, interviewed by Arieli Inbal by phone, October 2018.
3. Yagil Levy, "The Essence of the Market Army," *Public Administration Review* 70, no. 3 (2010): 378–89.
4. Tim Kastelle, "Hierarchy Is Overrated," *Harvard Business Review*, November 20, 2013, https://hbr.org/2013/11/hierarchy-is-overrated.
5. Jason Fried, "Why I Run a Flat Hierarchy," *Inc.*, April 2011, http://www.inc.com/magazine/20110401/jason-fried-why-i-run-a-flat-company.html.
6. Christy Rakoczy, "Advantages of a Flat Organizational Structure," *Love to Know*, August 2010, http://business.lovetoknow.com/wiki/Advantages_of_a_Flat_Organizational_Structure.
7. Pascal-Emmanuel Gobry, "7 Steps the US Military Should Take to Be More Like the IDF," *Forbes*, August 25, 2014, http://www.forbes.com/sites/pascalemmanuelgobry/2014/08/25/7-steps-the-us-military-should-take-to-be-more-like-the-idf/#741acd8ef834.

14: IMPROVISATION AND OPTIMIZATION

1. Noam Sharon, interviewed by Rivelis Shira by phone, October 2016.
2. Uri Weinheber, interviewed by Arieli Inbal, Tel Aviv, August 2017.
3. Written in collaboration with Matan Edvy, cofounder and CEO of Verstill, Israeli Air Force major (reserve).
4. Steven Pressfield, *The Lion's Gate: On the Front Lines of the Six Day War* (New York: Penguin Publishing Group, 2015).
5. George P. Huber and William H. Glick, eds., *Organizational Change and Redesign* (Oxford: Oxford University Press, 1995).
6. Gilbert Ryle, "Improvisation," *Mind* 85, no. 337 (1976): 69–83.
7. Karl E. Weick, "Introductory Essay—Improvisation as a Mindset for Organizational Analysis," *Organization Science* 9, no. 5 (1998): 543–55.

8. Christine Moorman and Anne S. Miner, "Organizational Improvisation and Organizational Memory," *Academy of Management Review* 23, no. 4 (October 1998): 698–723.

15: LEVERAGING SKILLS AND NETWORKS

1. World Economic Forum, *The Future of Jobs: Employment, Skills and Workforce Strategy for the Fourth Industrial Revolution*, Global Challenge Insight Report, January 2016.
2. Dov Moran, interviewed by Arieli Inbal, Tel Aviv, September 2016.

16: GLOBAL OPENNESS

1. United Nations Statistics Division, "International Migration," United Nations, 2017, https://unstats.un.org/unsd/demographic/sconcerns/migration/migrmethods.htm.
2. Shmuel Shulman, "The Extended Journey and Transition to Adulthood: The Case of Israeli Backpackers," *Journal of Youth Studies* 9, no. 2 (May 2006): 231–46.
3. Herb Keinon, "Using the Power of Israeli Backpackers to Help the World," *Jerusalem Post*, October 17, 2016, http://www.jpost.com/Israel-News/Using-the-power-of-Israeli-backpackers-to-help-the-world-470232.
4. Yasmin Lukatz, interviewed by Arieli Inbal, Tel Aviv, June 2017.
5. Darya Henig Shaked, interviewed by Arieli Inbal, Tel Aviv, June 2017.
6. *Human Capital Survey Report 2018*, Israel Innovation Authority, https://www.dropbox.com/s/2cesfwevfpddgem/2018%20Human%20Capital%20Report.pdf?dl=0.

17: YIHEYE BESEDER

1. Imad Telhami, interviewed by Arieli Inbal, Tel Aviv, November 2018.
2. Chemi Peres, interviewed by Arieli Inbal, Tel Aviv, November 2017.

BIBLIOGRAPHY

Abrahamson, Eric, and David H. Freedman. *A Perfect Mess: The Hidden Benefits of Disorder—How Crammed Closets, Cluttered Offices, and On-the-Fly Planning Make the World a Better Place.* New York: Little, Brown, 2006.

Aderet, Ofer. "Erika Landau, Educator Who Stressed Learning through Emotion, Dies." *Haaretz*, August 6, 2013. http://www.haaretz.com/israel-news /1.540088.

Alon, Narkis. Interview by Shira Rivelis. September 2016.

Altshuler, Yaniv. "Complex Networks." *Social Physics*, January 15, 2014. http:// socialphysics.media.mit.edu/blog/2015/8/4/complex-networks.

———. "Hubs and Centers of Information." *Social Physics*, January 19, 2014. http://socialphysics.media.mit.edu/blog/2015/8/4/hubs-and-centers-of -information.

———. "Networks." *Social Physics*, January 14, 2014. http://socialphysics .media.mit.edu/blog/2015/8/4/networks.

———. "Six Degrees of Separation." *Social Physics*, January 18, 2014. http:// socialphysics.media.mit.edu/blog/2015/8/4/six-degrees-of-separation-1.

———. "Small World Networks." *Social Physics*, January 17, 2014. http:// socialphysics.media.mit.edu/blog/2015/8/4/small-world-networks.

Amplifier. "Krembo Wings: A Youth Movement for Children with and without Disabilities." https://www.krembo.org.il/.

Anderson, Stuart. "40 Percent of Fortune 500 Companies Founded by Immigrants or Their Children." *Forbes*, June 19, 2011. http://www.forbes.com /sites/stuartanderson/2011/06/19/40-percent-of-fortune-500-companies -founded-by-immigrants-or-their-children/#13f9c6827a22.

Arieli, Inbal. Interviewing Yonatan Adiri. Tel Aviv, December 2018.

———. Interviewing Professor Ran Balicer. Tel Aviv, November 2018.

———. Interviewing Guy Franklin. June 2017.

———. Interviewing Micha Kaufman. Tel Aviv, September 2018.

———. Interviewing Chemi Peres. Tel Aviv, November 2017.

———. Interviewing Kira Radinsky. Tel Aviv, September 2018.

———. Interviewing Guy Ruvio. Tel Aviv, May 2015.

———. Interviewing Yair Seroussi. Tel Aviv, November 2018.

———. Interviewing Darya Henig Shaked. June 2017.

————. Interviewing Adi Sharabani. Tel Aviv, July 2016.

————. Interviewing Wendy Singer. Jerusalem, June 2018.

————. Interviewing Uri Weinheber. Tel Aviv, August 2017.

————. Interviewing Nadav Zafrir, phone. October 2018.

Armée de Terre. "Quelle carrière à l'armée de Terre." https://www.sengager
.fr/decouvrez-larmee-de-terre/nos-parcours.

Arnett, J. Jensen. *Debating Emerging Adulthood: Stage or Process?* New York:
Oxford University Press, 2011.

————. *Emerging Adulthood: The Winding Road from the Late Teens through
the Twenties.* Oxford: Oxford University Press, 2014.

————. "A Theory of Development from Late Teens through the Twenties."
American Psychologist 55, no. 5 (2000): 469–80.

Arnett, J. Jensen, ed. *The Oxford Handbook of Emerging Adulthood.* Oxford:
Oxford University Press, 2016.

Avitan, Sivan, et al. "Junkyard: Part A+B." *YouTube.* Video File. Edited by
Nati Struhl. https://www.youtube.com/watch?v=nk2C5Y6DcrE, https://
www.youtube.com/watch?v=hOLxgMAwwas.

Bamberger, Barbara. "Volunteer Service Draws Israeli Teens Before They
Start Stints in Military." *Tablet,* June 2013. http://www.tabletmag.com
/jewish-life-and-religion/133955/volunteer-service-israeli-teens.

Barber, Brian K. *Adolescence and War: How Youth Deal with Political Violence.*
Oxford: Oxford University Press, 2009.

Bar-On, Naama. "Mechanisms of Chaotic Disorder: Order and Disorder as
They Are Created and Alternated by Members of System." *Atidnet.* http://
www.amalnet.k12.il/MADATEC/articles/B7_00003.asp.

Bartone, Paul T., and Amy B. Adler. "Event-Oriented Debriefing Following
Military Operations: What Every Leader Should Know." In *Research for
the Soldier.* Washington, DC: USAMRU-E US Army Medical Research
Unit-Europe, 2015.

Becker, Ada, and Lizi Davidi. "Organizing the Educational Environment."
http://www.gilrach.co.il, July 2000.

Ben-Haim, Gitit. "Junkyard." http://web.macam.ac.il/~tamarli/gitit/index
.htm.

Ben Yosef, Tashi. Interview by Shira Rivelis. Tel Aviv, September/October 2016.

Berkowitz, David. "1.6 Degrees of Separation." *Social Media Insider,* June 5,
2012. https://www.mediapost.com/publications/article/176182/16-degrees
-of-separation.html.

Bertele, Aviv. "*Mechaker: Tiyul acharei ha-tzvah machria b'bchirat to'ar*"
["Research: post army trip is a decisive factor in choosing an academic
degree"]. *Ynet,* February 26, 2014. http://www.ynet.co.il/articles/0,7340
,L-4492098,00.html.

Bhagat, Smriti, et al. "Three and a Half Degrees of Separation." *Facebook,*
February 4, 2016. https://research.fb.com/three-and-a-half-degrees-of
-separation/.

Boroditsky, Lera. "How Does Our Language Shape the Way We Think?" *Edge*, November 6, 2009. https://www.edge.org/conversation/lera_boroditsky -how-does-our-language-shape-the-way-we-think.

Boundless Management. "Flattening Hierarchies." May 2016. http://oer2go .org/mods/en-boundless/www.boundless.com/business/textbooks /boundless-business-textbook/organizational-structure-9/trends-in -organization-68/flattening-hierarchies-321-3983/index.html/.

Boy Scouts of America. "The Adventure Plan (TAP)." https://bsatap.org/.

British Army. Army Be The Best. "Officer Recruitment Steps." https://apply .army.mod.uk/how-to-join/joining-process/officer-recruitment-steps.

Brodet, David. "Israel 2028 Vision Strategy for Economy and Society in a Global World." *Israel Science and Technology Commission and Foundation*, March 2008.

Brown, Benson Bradford, and T. S. Saraswati, eds. *The World's Youth: Adolescence in Eight Regions of the World*. Cambridge: Cambridge University Press, 2002.

Brown, Erika. "Swallow This." *Forbes*, June 10, 2002. https://www.forbes .com/forbes/2002/0610/139.html.

Brzezińska, Anna Izabela. "Becoming an Adult—Contexts of Identity Development." *Polish Psychological Bulletin* 44, no. 3 (2013): 239–44.

Buber, Martin, and Ronald Gregor Smith. *Between Man and Man*. London: Routledge, 2002.

Buell, Ryan W., Joshua D. Margolis, and Margot Eiran. "Babcom: Opening Doors." Harvard Business School Case 418-026, June 2018.

Bureau of Labor Statistics. *Entrepreneurship and the U.S. Economy*. Business Employment Dynamics, April 28, 2016. https://www.bls.gov/bdm /entrepreneurship/entrepreneurship.htm.

Catignani, Sergio. "Motivating Soldiers: The Example of the Israeli Defense Forces." *Parameters* (US Army War College Quarterly) 34, no. 3 (Autumn 2004): 108–21. https://ssi.armywarcollege.edu/pubs/parameters /articles/04autumn/catignan.pdf.

CBS Database. *Start-Up Companies in Israel 2011–2016. Findings from the CBS Database on Start-Up Companies in Israel*. May 21, 2018.

Central Bureau of Statistics. *"Se'i b'mispar ha-yetziot l'kh ul: 9.5 milion yetziot"* ["A record in the number of outbound flights: 9.5 million registered exits"]. http://www.cbs.gov.il/reader/newhodaot/hodaa_template .html?hodaa=201628007.

Chai, Shahar. "Shnat Sherut in Jeopardy: 18-Year-Olds Will Not Volunteer before the Army?" *Ynet*, August 2015. http://www.ynet.co.il/articles /0,7340,L-4691482,00.html.

Chaim, Noy. "This Trip Really Changed Me: Backpackers' Narratives of Self-Change." *Annals of Tourism Research* 31, no. 1 (2004): 78–102.

———. "'You Must Go Trek There': The Persuasive Genre of Narration among Israeli Backpackers." *Narrative Inquiry* 12, no. 2 (2002): 261–90.

Churchman, Arza, and Avraham Wachman. "Kibbutz-Children Who Volunteer for a Shnat-Sherut in the Youth-Movement in the City: The Characteristics of the Experience and Its Influence on the Process of Maturation." In *Kibbutz Education in Its Environment*, edited by Yuval Dror. Ramot: Tel Aviv University, 1997.

Colleoni, E., and A. Arvidsson. "Knowledge Sharing and Social Capital Building. The Role of Co-Working Spaces in the Knowledge Economy in Milan." Unpublished report. Municipality of Milan: Office for Youth, 2014.

Corijn, Martine, and Erik Klijzing. *Transitions to Adulthood in Europe*. Dordrecht: Springer Science & Business Media, 2001.

Dachis, Adam. "The Psychology behind the Importance of Failure." *LifeHacker*, January 22, 2013. http://lifehacker.com/5978096/the-psychology-behind-the-importance-of-failure.

Dannen, Chris. "Inside GitHub's Super-Lean Management Strategy—and How It Drives Innovation." *Fast Company*, October 18, 2013. https://www.fastcompany.com/3020181/open-company/inside-githubs-super-lean-management-strategy-and-how-it-drives-innovation.

Dar, Yechezkel, and Shaul Kimhi. "Military Service and Self-Perceived Maturation among Israeli Youth." *Journal of Youth and Adolescence* 30, no. 4 (2001): 427–48.

Debriefing. "A Quick Overview of Various Debriefing Techniques." 2017. http://www.debriefing.com/debriefing-techniques/.

Deloitte Development. *2015 Global Venture Capital Confidence Survey Results: How Confident Are Investors?* New York: Deloitte, 2015.

Denegri-Knott, Janice, and Elizabeth Parsons. "Disordering Things." *Journal of Consumer Behavior* 13 (2014): 89–98.

Di Schiena, Raffaella, Geert Letens, Eileen van Aken, and Jennifer Farris. "Relationship between Leadership and Characteristics of Learning Organizations in Deployed Military Units: An Exploratory Study." *Administrative Sciences* 3 (2013): 143–65.

Doffman-Gour, Nadav. *"Matana mi-shomayim: pituchei ha-chalal shekvasu et kadur ha-aretz"* ["A gift from above: the space developments that swept earth"]. Geektime, September 2011. http://www.geektime.co.il/nasa-tech-on-earth/.

Dvorkin-Pogelman, Mor. "Children's Books: The Gangs Are Back on the Shelves." *City Mouse*, June 30, 2014. http://www.mouse.co.il/CM.articles_item,608,209,76376,.aspx.

Dweck, Tzafra. "Comparative Study of American and Israeli Teenagers' Attitudes toward Death." Master's thesis, North Texas State University, 1975.

Dyck, Noel, and Amit Vered. *Young Men in Uncertain Times*. New York: Berghahn Books, 2012.

Ecclestone, Kathryn, Gert Biesta, and Martin Hughes. *Transitions and Learning through the Life Course*. New York: Routledge, 2010.

Economist Staff. "Culture Shock for French Immigrants—in French Can-

ada." *Economist*, May 4, 2017. http://www.economist.com/news/americas
/21721675-mutual-incomprehension-takes-newcomers-surprise-culture
-shock-french-immigrantsin-french.

EISP. "8200 EISP 2017." http://www.eisp.org.il/en/home.

Empson, Rip. "Startup Genome." *TechCrunch*, Startup Ecosystem Report 2012.
Accessed March 26, 2019. https://techcrunch.com/2012/11/20/startup
-genome-ranks-the-worlds-top-startup-ecosystems-silicon-valley-tel-aviv-l
-a-lead-the-way/.

Erika Landau Institute. "The Erika Landau Institute Home Page." http://
ypipce.org.il/?page_id=11.

Fabes, Richard A. "Effects of Rewards on Children's Prosocial Motivation:
A Socialization Study." *Developmental Psychology* 25, no. 4 (July 1989):
509–15.

Fernhaber, Stephanie, and Patricia P. Mcdougall. "New Venture Growth in
International Markets: The Role of Strategic Adaptation and Network-
ing Capabilities." In *International Entrepreneurship*, edited by Dean A.
Shepard, 111–15. New York: Emerald Insight Publishing, 2015.

Fischer, Stanley. "Stanley Fischer: The Openness of Israel's Economy to the
Global Economy and the Importance of Israel's Joining the OECD." Globes
Business Conference, December 11, 2006.

Fisher, Sharin. Interview by Shira Rivelis. Tel Aviv, October 2016.

Fjørtoft, Ingunn. "The Natural Environment as a Playground for Children:
The Impact of Outdoor Play Activities in Pre-Primary School Children."
Early Childhood Education Journal 29, no. 2 (2001): 111–17.

Fried, Jason. "Why I Run a Flat Hierarchy." *Inc.*, April 2011. http://www.inc
.com/magazine/20110401/jason-fried-why-i-run-a-flat-company.html.

Friedman, Ron. "Buffet: 'Israel Has a Disproportionate Amount of Brains.'"
Jerusalem Post, October 13, 2010. https://www.jpost.com/Business/
Business-News/Buffett-Israel-has-a-disproportionate-amount-of-brains.

Froiland, John Mark. "Parents' Weekly Descriptions of Autonomy Supportive
Communication: Promoting Children's Motivation to Learn and Positive
Emotions." *Journal of Child and Family Studies* 24, no. 1 (January 2013):
117–26.

Gaaton, Yael. "Children Do Grow on Trees: Children in Mitzpe Ramon and
the 'Forest Kindergarten.'" *Walla News*, April 19, 2016. http://news.walla
.co.il/item/2954044.

Gal, Reuven. *A Portrait of the Israeli Soldier.* New York: Greenwood Press,
1986.

Geektime and Zirra. *Annual Report 2015: Startups and Venture Capital in Israel.*
Geektime, January 2016. http://www.geektime.com/2016/01/11/annual
-report-2015-startups-and-venture-capital-in-israel/.

Giang, Vivian. "What Kind of Leadership Is Needed in Flat Hierarchies."
Fast Company, May 2015. https://www.fastcompany.com/3046371/the
-new-rules-of-work/what-kind-of-leadership-is-needed-in-flat-hierarchies.

Gibbs, Nancy. "The Growing Backlash against Overparenting." *Time*, November 2009. http://content.time.com/time/magazine/article/0,9171,194 0697,00.html.

Globes Staff. "How Israeli High-Tech Happened." *Globes*, August 28, 2003. http://www.globes.co.il/en/article-258771.

Gobry, Pascal-Emmanuel. "7 Steps the US Military Should Take to Be More Like the IDF." *Forbes*, August 25, 2014. http://www.forbes.com/sites /pascalemmanuelgobry/2014/08/25/7-steps-the-us-military-should-take -to-be-more-like-the-idf/#741acd8ef834.

Godesiabois, Joy. "Network Analysis in an International Entrepreneurial Environment." In *International Entrepreneurship*, edited by Dean A. Shepard, 137–64. New York: Emerald Group Publishing, 2015.

Goldberg, Andrew. "Democratizing Corporate Innovation: Why Top Down Rarely Works." *IndustryWeek*, March 27, 2012. http://www.industry week.com/global-economy/democratizing-corporate-innovation-why-top -down-rarely-works.

Graham, Paul. "What It Takes." *Forbes*, October 20, 2010. https://www .forbes.com/forbes/2010/1108/best-small-companies-10-y-combinator -paul-graham-ask-an-expert.html#22e0cc71acad.

Gray, Peter. *Free to Learn: Why Unleashing the Instinct to Play Will Make Our Children Happier, More Self-Reliant, and Better Students for Life*. New York: Better Books, 2013.

Green, Penelope. "Saying Yes to Mess." *New York Times*, December 21, 2006. http://www.nytimes.com/2006/12/21/garden/21mess.html?page wanted=print&_r=1.

Grey, Miri. "War Room." *Mako*, October 29, 2011. http://www.mako.co.il /home-family-kids/education/Article-2ddf7ac34f05811004.htm.

Haas, Malka. "Children in the Junkyard." *Association for Childhood Education International* 73, no. 1 (1996): 345–51.

Hart, Roger. "Environmental Psychology or Behavioral Geography? Either Way It Was a Good Start." *Journal of Environmental Psychology* 7, no. 4 (December 1987): 321–29. https://www.sciencedirect.com/science/article /abs/pii/S0272494487800051.

Hay, Dale F. "Peer Relations in Childhood." *Journal of Child Psychology and Psychiatry* 45, no. 1 (2004): 84–108.

Hofstede, Geert. "Individualism." *Clearly Cultural: Making Sense of Cross Cultural Communication*, n.d. http://www.clearlycultural.com/geert-hofstede -cultural-dimensions/individualism/.

———. "What about Israel?" *Hofstede Insights International*. Accessed March 26, 2019. https://www.hofstede-insights.com/country/israel/.

Holzapfel, Olaf, and Galia Bar-Or. "Interview with Malka Haas and Kloni Haas." *Vimeo*. https://vimeo.com/156767854.

Hon, Shaul. "Let the Kid Search for Himself." *Historical Jewish Press*, July 8, 1970. http://jpress.org.il/Olive/APA/NLI_Heb/SharedView.Article.aspx

?parm=W8f1VbCHvN1uSmXtkCP8KMqD7PhWKQy88Y1Fh6j%2BCCg
DSkTk%2FQ4AZWJQgR1457%2B2Yw%3D%3D&mode=image&href=
MAR%2f1970%2f07%2f08&page=13&rtl=true Maariv.

Hornsey, Matthew J., and Jolanda Jetten. "The Individual within the Group: Balancing the Need to Belong with the Need to Be Different." *Personality and Social Psychology Review* 8, no. 3 (2004): 248–64.

Howard-Jones, Paul, Jayne Taylor, and Lesley Sutton. "The Effect of Play on the Creativity of Young Children during Subsequent Activity." *Early Child Development and Care* 172, no. 4 (2002): 323–28.

Huber, George P., and William H. Glick, eds. *Organizational Change and Redesign*. Oxford: Oxford University Press, 1995.

Hurvitz, Eli. "LinkedIn Profile for Eli Hurvitz." *LinkedIn*, 2018. https://www.linkedin.com/pulse/talent-chutzpah-hard-truth-eli-hurvitz.

ICoN. "Bridging the Israeli and Silicon Valley Tech Ecosystems." 2017. http://www.iconsv.org/.

Institution of Society and Youth, Ministry of Education. Accessed March 26, 2019. http://cms.education.gov.il/EducationCMS/Units/Noar/Techumei Haminhal/ChinuchChevrathi/TenuothNoar.htm.

InterNations. "The Best Destinations for Expat Families." *Expat Insider*, 2018. https://www.internations.org/expat-insider/2018/family-life-index-39591.

———. "Family Life Index." Family Life Index 2016. https://inassets1-inter nationsgmbh.netdna-ssl.com/static/bundles/internationsexpatinsider /images/2016/reports/family_life_index_full.jpg.

Israel Innovation Authority. https://innovationisrael.org.il/en/.

———. "Israel Innovation Authority Launches Incentive Program for Female-Led Startups." https://innovationisrael.org.il/en/news/israel-innovation -authority-launches-incentive-program-female-led-startups. Accessed February 2019.

IVC Research Center and ZAG S&W Zysman, Aharoni, Gayer & Co. Quarterly report, Q1 2018.

———. "Summary of Israeli High-Tech Company Capital Raising—2018." https://www.ivc-online.com/Portals/0/RC/Survey/IVC_Q4-18%20Capital %20Raising_Survey_Final.pdf.

Jeronen, Eila, and Juha Jeronen. "Outdoor Education in Finnish Schools and Universities." *Studies of Socio-Economic and Humanities* 2 (2012): 152–60.

Joint Council of Pre-Military Academies (Mechinot). "Home—The Joint Council of Mechinot." http://mechinot.org.il.

Kaplan, Jonathan. "The Role of the Military in Israel." Jewish Agency for Israel, 2015. http://www.jewishagency.org/society-and-politics/content/36591.

Kastelle, Tim. "Hierarchy Is Overrated." *Harvard Business Review*, November 20, 2013. https://hbr.org/2013/11/hierarchy-is-overrated.

Keinon, Herb. "Using the Power of Israeli Backpackers to Help the World." *Jerusalem Post*, October 17, 2016. http://www.jpost.com/Israel-News /Using-the-power-of-Israeli-backpackers-to-help-the-world-470232.

Kellett, Anthony. *Combat Motivation: The Behavior of Soldiers in Battle*, edited by James P. Ignizio. Dordrecht: Springer Netherlands,1982.

Kelty, Ryan, M. Kleykamp, and D. R. Segal. "The Military and the Transition to Adulthood." *The Future of Children* 20, no. 1 (2010): 181–201.

Kirshberg, Evyatar and Tal Enselman. *"Khevrot ha-zanek (start-up) b'yisrael 2010–2015: mi-motza'im rishonim mitokh basis ha-netunim al khevrot ha-zanek b'yisrael"* ["Start-up companies in Israel 2010-2015: first findings from the database on Israel's start-up companies"]. Central Bureau of Statistics, Press release, September 11, 2016: 1–12. http://www.finance-inst.co.il/image/users/171540/ftp/my_files/xx/29_16_278b.pdf?id=28551085.

Korvet, Rinat, Yaniv Feldman, and Anar Ravon. *"Temunat matzav: sichum shnat 2015 b'stzinat ha-startupim v'ha-hon b'yisrael"* ["Status report: a summary of 2015's start-up and venture capital scene in Israel"]. *Geektime*, January 6, 2016. http://www.geektime.co.il/geektime-zirra-2015-startups-report/.

Kovelle, Kim. "Tips to Teach Kids How to Build a Campfire." *MetroParent*, July 27, 2018. http://www.metroparent.com/daily/family-activities/camping/build-campfire-tips-teach-kids/.

Krebs, Ronald. "A School for the Nation? How Military Service Does Not Build Nations, and How It Might." *International Security* 28, no. 4 (2004): 85–124.

Kunda, Ziva, and Shalom H. Schwartz. "Undermining Intrinsic Moral Motivation: External Reward and Self-Presentation." *Journal of Personality and Social Psychology* 45, no. 4 (1983): 763–71. http://psycnet.apa.org/doi Landing?doi=10.1037%2F0022-3514.45.4.763.

Kutner, Lawrence. "Neatness Has Its Price: Experts: Messy Rooms No Cause for Alarm." *Gadsden Times*, March 17, 1992. https://news.google.com/newspapers?nid=1891&dat=19920317&id=HrZGAAAAIBAJ&sjid=8f0 MAAAAIBAJ&pg=5859,1888167&hl=en.

Lakhani, Jahan, Alix Hayden, and Karen Benzies. "Attributes of Interdisciplinary Research Teams: A Comprehensive Review of the Literature." *Clinical and Investigative Medicine* 35, no. 5 (2012): E260–E265.

LEAD. "The Art of Human Diamond Polishing." http://lead.org.il/en/.

Lefkovitz, Daniel. *Words and Stones: The Politics of Language and Identity in Israel.* Oxford: Oxford Scholarship Online, 2011. http://www.oxford scholarship.com/view/10.1093/acprof:oso/9780195121902.001.0001/acprof-9780195121902.

Leichman, A. Klein. "From the Airforce to the Fitting Room." *Israel 21st Century*, November 30, 2015. https://www.israel21c.org/from-the-air-force-to-the-fitting-room/.

Lempert, Nir. Interview by Shira Rivelis. Tel Aviv, February 12, 2017.

Levin, Dana S. "'You're Always First a Girl': Emerging Adult Women, Gender, and Sexuality in the Israeli Army." *Journal of Adolescent Research* 26, no. 1 (2011): 3–29.

Levy, Yagil. "The Essence of the Market Army." *Public Administration Review* 70, no. 3 (2010): 378–89.

Lieblich, Amia. *Transition to Adulthood during Military Service: The Israeli Case*. New York: State University of New York Press, 1989.

Lifland, Tara. "Krembo Wings: A Youth Movement Led by Children for Disabled Children." NoCamels, December 2012. http://nocamels.com /2012/12/krembo-wings-a-social-movement-led-by-children-for-disabled -children/.

Light of Education. "A Light of Education—A Springboard for Excellence." http://www.ore.ngo/.

Limor, Samimian-Darash. "Practicing Uncertainty: Scenario-Based Preparedness Exercises in Israel." *Cultural Anthropology* 31, no. 3 (2016). https://journal.culanth.org/index.php/ca/article/view/ca31.3.06.

Lukatz, Yasmin. Interview by Shira Rivelis. June 2017.

Luttwak, Edward. Quoted in *Start-up Nation: The Story of Israel's Economic Miracle*, edited by Dan Senor and Saul Singer, 53–58. New York: Hachette Book Group, 2009.

Majer, Oren. "Erika Landau—The Woman Who Taught Us All to Ask Questions." *Marker*, December 22, 2011. http://www.themarker.com/marker week/markeryear/1.1596242.

Markoff, John, and Somini Sengupta. "Separating You and Me? 4.74 Degrees." *New York Times*, November 21, 2011. http://www.nytimes.com /2011/11/22/technology/between-you-and-me-4-74-degrees.html?_r=0.

Martin, Ruef. *The Entrepreneurial Group: Social Identities, Relations, and Collective Action*. Princeton, NJ: Princeton University Press. 2010.

Matt, Susan J. *Homesickness: An American History*. Oxford: Oxford University Press, 2011.

Maxwell, John C. *Developing the Leader within You 2.0*. New York: Harper-Collins Leadership, 2018.

Mayseless, Ofra. "Growing Up in Israel: Positions and Values of Israeli Youth in the Last Decade." *Educational Consult* 5 (1998): 87–102.

Mayseless, Ofra, and Ilan Hai. "Leaving Home Transition in Israel: Changes in Parent-Adolescent Relationships and Adolescents' Adaptation to Military Service." *International Journal of Behavioral Development* 22, no. 3 (1988): 589–609.

Mayseless, Ofra, and Miri Scharf. "What Does It Mean to Be an Adult? The Israeli Experience." In *Exploring Cultural Conceptions of the Transitions to Adulthood: New Directions for Child and Adolescent Development*, edited by Jeffrey Jensen Arnett and Nancy L. Galambos, 5–21. New York: Jossey-Bass, 2003.

McGonigal, Kelly. "How to Make Stress Your Friend." *TED Ideas Worth Spreading*. Video File. June 2013. https://www.ted.com/talks/kelly _mcgonigal_how_to_make_stress_your_friend/transcript?language=e n#t-530180.

Meehan, Colette L. "Flat vs. Hierarchical Organizational Structures." *Small Business Chronicle*, February 12, 2019. http://smallbusiness.chron.com /flat-vs-hierarchical-organizational-structure-724.html.

Merkovitch-Sloker, Gali. "The Cyber Trend Takes Over Youth: Israel Is Leading in the Cyber Field." *Maariv*, December 29, 2015. http://m.maariv .co.il/news/military/Article-519580.

Mestechkina, Tatyana. "Parenting in Vietnam." In *Parenting across Cultures: Childrearing, Motherhood and Fatherhood in Non-Western Cultures*, edited by Helaine Selin, 45–57. Dordrecht: Springer Netherlands, 2014.

Miele, Laura M. "The Importance of Failure: A Culture of False Successes." *Psychology Today*, March 12, 2015. https://www.psychologytoday.com /blog/the-whole-athlete/201503/the-importance-failure-culture-false -success.

Ministry of Defense. *Ha-keren v'ha-yichidia lle'hachavanat chayalim meshucharerim* ["The fund and unit for supporting discharged soldiers"]. https://www.hachvana.mod.gov.il/Pages/default.aspx.

Moorman, Christine, and Anne S. Miner. "Organizational Improvisation and Organizational Memory." *Academy of Management Review* 23, no. 4 (October 1998): 698–723.

Mosko, Yigal. "Meet the Woman Who Invented the Junkyard: An Interview with Malka Haas." *Mako News*, September 12, 2014. http://www.mako .co.il/news-channel2/Friday-Newscast-q3_2014/Article-1c57a4e4cca684 1004.htm.

Moti, Bsuk. "Over 8 Million Residents in Israel; 70% Tzabars." *Marker*, April 2014. http://www.themarker.com/news/1.1993939.

Nachat. "Noar Hovev Tanach" ("Nahat: Bible-loving youth"). Accessed March 26, 2019. http://nachatsite.wixsite.com/nachat.

Naor, Mordechai, ed. *The Youth Movements 1920–1960*. Jerusalem: Yad Yitzhak Ben-Tzvi, 1989.

Nathanson, Roby, and Itamar Gazala. "Israeli Adolescents in Their Transition to Adulthood: The Influence of the Military Service." *Educational Insights* 5, no. 1 (2002).

National Authority of Evaluation and Measurement in Education. *Youth Movements in Israel: The Results of Relative Size Measurements of 2015*. Ministry of Education, February 29, 2016.

Nelson, Larry J. "An Examination of Emerging Adulthood in Romanian College Students." *International Journal of Behavioral Development* 33, no. 5 (2009): 402–11.

Nestmann, Frank. *Social Networks and Social Support in Childhood and Adolescence*. New York: Mouton de Gruyter, 1994.

Newsweek Staff. "Soldiers of Fortune." *Newsweek*, November 13, 2009. http:// europe.newsweek.com/soldiers-fortune-77025?rm=eu.

Novellino, Teresa. "Zeekit Intros Virtual Fitting Room with Rebecca Minkoff for Fashion Week." *New York Business Journal*, September 15, 2016. http://

www.bizjournals.com/newyork/news/2016/09/15/zeekit-virtual-fitting-room-rebecca-minkoff-and-9k.html.

Nurmi, Jari-Erik. "Tracks and Transitions—A Comparison of Adolescent Future-Oriented Goals, Explorations, and Commitments in Australia, Israel, and Finland." *International Journal of Psychology* 30, no. 3 (1995): 355–75.

Ofek, Uriel. *Give Them Books: On Children's Literature & Juvenile Reading.* Tel Aviv: Sfirat Poalim, 1978.

Omniglot: The Online Encyclopedia of Writing Systems & Languages. "Hebrew." http://www.omniglot.com/writing/hebrew.htm.

Organisation for Economic Cooperation and Development. *Enhancing Market Openness, Intellectual Property Rights, and Compliance through Regulatory Reform in Israel.* 2011.

———. *Gross Domestic Spending on R&D.* https://data.oecd.org/rd/gross-domestic-spending-on-r-d.htm.

Park, Hyunjaoon. "Becoming an Adult in East Asia: Multidisciplinary and Comparative Approaches." *Asian Journal of Social Science* 44 (2016): 307–15.

Partnership for a New American Economy. *"The 'New American' Fortune 500." A Report by the Partnership for a New American Economy.* June 2011. http://www.renewoureconomy.org/sites/all/themes/pnae/img/new-american-fortune-500-june-2011.pdf.

Pima, Leora. "Managing Schools under Continuous Terror and Trauma Conditions: Maintaining Sanity in an Insane Reality." *ShefiNet* (October 2008). http://cms.education.gov.il/EducationCMS/Units/Shefi/HerumLachatz Mashber/herum/Nihul-TerorTrauma-Pima.htm.

Pirola-Merlo, Andrew, and Leon Mann. "The Relationship between Individual Creativity and Team Creativity: Aggregating across People and Time." *Journal of Organizational Behavior* 25, no. 2 (2004): 235–57.

Pressfield, Steven. *The Lion's Gate: On the Front Lines of the Six Day War.* New York: Penguin, 2015.

Promovendum. "Heitje voor karweitje: 10 tips voor kinderen!" June 3, 2015. https://www.promovendum.nl/blog/heitje-voor-karweitje-10-tips-voor-kinderen.

Prusher, Ilene. "Building Communities of Kindness." *Time,* September 13, 2014. http://time.com/3270757/adi-altschuler-next-generation-leaders/.

Rakoczy, Christy. "Advantages of a Flat Organizational Structure." *Love to Know,* August 2010. http://business.lovetoknow.com/wiki/Advantages_of_a_Flat_Organizational_Structure.

Raveaud, Maroussia. "Becoming an Adult in Europe: A Socially Determined Experience." *European Educational Research Journal* 9, no. 3 (2010): 431–42.

Rejskind, F. G. "Autonomy and Creativity in Children." *Journal of Creative Behavior* 16, no. 1 (1982): 58–67.

Rittscher, Susan. "Six Keys to Successful Networking for Entrepreneurs." *Forbes*, May 31, 2012. https://www.forbes.com/sites/susanrittscher/2012/05/31/six-keys-to-successful-networking-for-entrepreneurs/#40e3d82 c580b.

Roberts, Amos, and Alex de Jong. "Kids Gone Wild." *SBS*, February 23, 2016. http://www.sbs.com.au/news/dateline/story/kids-gone-wild.

Robinson, Ken. "Do Schools Kill Creativity?" *TED Ideas Worth Spreading.* Video File. February 2006. https://www.ted.com/talks/ken_robinson _says_schools_kill_creativity?language=en.

Roche, Jennifer. "What a Calligrapher Priest Taught Steve Jobs." *National Catholic Register*, January 1, 2012. http://www.ncregister.com/daily-news /what-a-calligrapher-priest-taught-steve-jobs.

Rosin, Hanna. "The Overprotected Kid." *Atlantic*, April 2014. http://www .theatlantic.com/magazine/archive/2014/04/hey-parents-leave-those-kids -alone/358631/.

Ryle, Gilbert. "Improvisation." *Mind* 85, no. 337 (1976): 69–83.

Sagi-Alfasa, Einat. "Key Children: Starting from Which Age Can He Return Independently from School." *Ynet Parents*, September 19, 2014. http:// www.ynet.co.il/articles/0,7340,L-4571833,00.html.

Salomon, Gavriel, and Ofra Mayseless. "Dialectic Contradictions in the Experience of Israeli Jewish Adolescents." In *International Perspective on Adolescence*, edited by Timothy C. Urdan and Frank Pajares, chapter 7, 149–71. Greenwich, CT: Information Age Publishing, 2003.

Santi, Marina, ed. *Improvisation: Between Technique and Spontaneity.* Newcastle upon Tyne: Cambridge Scholars Publishing, 2010.

Sawyer, Keith. "Improvisational Creativity as a Model for Effective Learning." In *Improvisation: Between Technique and Spontaneity*, edited by Marina Santi, 135–52. Newcastle upon Tyne: Cambridge Scholars Publishing, 2010.

Sawyer, Taylor, and Shad Deering. "Adaptation of the US Army's After-Action Review for Simulation Debriefing in Healthcare." *Society for Simulation in Healthcare* 8, no. 6 (2013): 388–97.

Schneider, Elaine F., and Phillip P. Patterson. "You've Got That Magic Touch: Integrating the Sense of Touch into Early Childhood Services." *Young Exceptional Children* 13, no. 5 (2010): 17–27.

Schoon, Ingrid. *Transitions from School to Work: Globalization, Individualization, and Patterns of Diversity.* Cambridge: Cambridge University Press, 2009.

Schoon, Ingrid, and Mark Lyons-Amos. "Diverse Pathways in Becoming an Adult: The Role of Structure, Agency and Context." *London School of Economics and Political Science* (2016): 1–34.

Schwartz, Seth J., James E. Côté, and Jeffrey Jensen Arnett. "Identity and Agency in Emerging Adulthood: Two Developmental Routes in the Individualization Process." *Youth & Society* 37, no. 2 (2005): 201–29.

Scouts. "Scouts Be Prepared." http://scouts.org.uk/home/.

Selin, Helaine. *Science across Cultures: The History of Non-Western Science*, vol. 7. Dordrecht: Springer Netherlands, 2014.

Senor, Dan, and Saul Singer, eds. *Start-up Nation: The Story of Israel's Economic Miracle*. New York: Hachette Book Group, 2009.

Shahar, Golan, Esther Kalnitzki, Shmuel Shulman, and Sidney J. Blatt. "Personality, Motivation, and the Construction of Goals during the Transition to Adulthood." *Personality and Individual Differences* 40 (2006): 53–63.

Shamai, Michal, and Shaul Kimhi. "Exposure to Threat of War and Terror, Political Attitudes, Stress, and Life Satisfaction among Teenagers in Israel." *Journal of Adolescence* 29, no. 2 (2006): 165–76.

Sharp, Caroline. "Developing Young Children's Creativity through the Arts: What Does Research Have to Offer?" National Foundation for Education Research, 2001. https://www.nfer.ac.uk/publications/44420/44420.pdf.

Shavit-Pesach, Tamar. "*Tiyul acharei tzeva: lamah anakhnu o'sim et zeh?*" ["After army trip: why we do it?"]. *Clalit*, November 4, 2014. http://www.clalit.co.il/he/lifestyle/travel/Pages/why_do_you_travel.aspx.

Shay, Izhar, and Shir Shay. Interview by Shira Rivelis. July 2016.

Shepherd, Dean A., Trenton Williams, Marcus Wolfe, and Holger Patzelt. *Learning from Entrepreneurial Failure: Emotions, Cognitions, and Actions*. Cambridge: Cambridge University Press, 2016.

Sherer, Moshe. "Rehabilitation of Youth in Distress through Army Service: Full, Partial, or Non-Service in the Israel Defense Forces—Problems and Consequences." *Child & Youth Care Forum* 27, no. 1 (1998): 39–58.

Shilony, Itay. "*Yisraelism: ha-kokhot ha-m'atzavim et tarbut ha-nihul b'yisrael*" ["Israelism: the shaping factors of Israel's management culture"]. Ramat Gan: Ilmor Ltd., 2016.

Shnat Sherut for Everyone. "Year of Service." *Shinshinim*. http://www.shinshinim.org/.

Shochat, Eden. "Google I/O Talk: Geekcon & Unstructured Innovation." *Aleph*, July 30, 2014. https://aleph.vc/google-i-o-talk-geekcon-unstructured-innovation-4c853eeee95#.tj5n0tgmw.

Shulman, Shmuel. "The Extended Journey and Transition to Adulthood: The Case of Israeli Backpackers." *Journal of Youth Studies* 9, no. 2 (May 2006): 231–46.

Shulman, Shmuel, Benni Feldman, Sidney Blatt, et al. "Emerging Adulthood: Age-Related Tasks and Underlying Self Processes." *Journal of Adolescent Research* 20, no. 5 (2005): 577–603.

Slone, Michelle. "Growing Up in Israel." Chapter 4 in *Adolescents and War: How Youth Deal with Political Violence*, edited by K. Brian Barber. Oxford: Oxford University Press, 2010. http://www.oxfordscholarship.com.proxy-ub.rug.nl/view/10.1093/acprof:oso/9780195343359.001.0001/acprof-9780195343359-chapter-4.

Small Business BC. "Five Benefits of Networking." January 16, 2018. http://smallbusinessbc.ca/article/five-benefits-networking/.

Smith, Marc. "Importance of Failure: Why Olympians and A-Level Students
   All Need to Fail." *Guardian*, August 16, 2012. https://www.theguardian
   .com/teacher-network/2012/aug/16/a-level-student-success-failure.

Space IL, http://www.visit.spaceil.com/. Accessed March 2019.

Start-Up Nation Finder. "Start-Up Nation Finder: Explore Israeli Innovation." https://finder.startupnationcentral.org/.

Sugarman, Eli. "What the United States Can Learn from Israel about Cybersecurity." *Forbes*, October 7, 2014. http://www.forbes.com/sites/eli
   sugarman/2014/10/07/what-the-united-states-can-learn-from-israel-about
   -cybersecurity/#9f0ae8c2ad05.

Sun, Lijun, Kay W. Axhausen, Der-Horng Lee, and Xianfeng Huang. "Understanding Metropolitan Patterns of Daily Encounters." *Proceedings of the
   National Academy of Sciences* 110, no. 34 (2013): 13774–79. https://static1
   .squarespace.com/static/55b64ce8e4b030b2d9ed3c6a/t/55c116f6e4b01e6
   2831610a2/1438717686708/encounter.pdf.

Swed, Ori, and John Sibley Butler. "Military Capital in the Israeli Hi-tech
   Industry." *Armed Forces & Society* 41, no. 1 (2015): 123–41.

Taggar, Simon. "Individual Creativity and Group Ability to Utilize Individual Creative Resources: A Multilevel Model." *Academy of Management
   Journal* 45, no. 2 (2002): 315–30.

Tognoli, Jerome. "Leaving Home." *Journal of College Student Psychotherapy*
   18, no. 1 (2003): 35–48.

Tyler, Kathryn. "The Tethered Generation." Holy Cross Energy Leadership
   Academy. *HR Magazine*, May 1, 2007. https://www.shrm.org/hr-today
   /news/hr-magazine/pages/0507cover.aspx.

Tzarfati, Shira, et al. "Queen of the Yard: An Interview with Malka Haas."
   Hazman Hayarok, January 22, 2009. http://www.kibbutz.org.il/ito-
   nut/2009/dafyarok/090122_malka_has.htm. Accessed July 11, 2015.

Tzuriel, David. "The Development of Ego Identity at Adolescence among Israeli
   Jews and Arabs." *Journal of Youth and Adolescence* 21, no. 5 (1992): 551–71.

United Nations on Trade and Development (UNCTAD). *World Investment Report 2018: Investment and New Industrial Policies*. Blue Ridge Summit, PA:
   United Nations Publications, 2018.

United Nations Statistics Division. "International Migration." 2017. https://
   unstats.un.org/unsd/demographic/sconcerns/migration/migrmethods
   .htm.

Urdan, Timothy C., and Frank Pajares, eds. *International Perspectives on Adolescence*. Greenwich, CT: Information Age Publishing, 2003.

US Army. "Becoming a U.S. Military Officer." http://www.goarmy.com/careers
   -and-jobs/become-an-officer.html.

US Department of State, "2014 Investment Climate Statement." *Diplomacy in
   Action*, June 2014. https://www.state.gov/e/eb/rls/othr/ics/2014/.

Useem, Jerry. "The Secret of My Success." *United Marine Publications* 20,
   no. 6 (1979).

Van der Kuip, Isobel, and Ingrid Verheul. *Early Development of Entrepreneurial Qualities: The Role of Initial Education.* Zoetermeer: EIM, Small Business Research and Consultancy, 1998.

Waite, Sue, Sue Rogers, and Julie Evans. "Freedom, Flow and Fairness: Exploring How Children Develop Socially at School through Outdoor Play." *Journal of Adventure Education and Outdoor Learning* 13, no. 3 (2013): 255–76. http://www.tandfonline.com/doi/abs/10.1080/14729679.2013.798 590#.V2KVQrt97IU.

Wakkee, Ingrid, Peter Groenewegen, and Paula Danskin Englis. "Building Effective Networks: Network Strategy and Emerging Virtual Organizations." In *Transnational and Immigrant Entrepreneurship in a Globalized World*, edited by Benson Honig, Israel Drori, and Barbara Carmichael, chapter 4, 75–79. Toronto: University of Toronto Press, 2010.

Walker, Tim. "How Finland Keeps Kids Focused through Free Play." *Atlantic*, June 30, 2014. http://www.theatlantic.com/education/archive/2014/06/how-finland-keeps-kids-focused/373544/.

Waters, Jane, and Sharon Begley. "Supporting the Development of Risk-Taking Behaviours in the Early Years: An Exploratory Study." *Education* 35, no. 4 (2007): 365–77. http://www.tandfonline.com/doi/abs/10.1080/03004270701602632.

Weick, Karl E. "Introductory Essay—Improvisation as a Mindset for Organizational Analysis." *Organization Science* 9, no. 5 (1998): 543–55.

Weinreb, Gali. "The Black Box: Who Are the Teenagers of 2012?" (Ha'Kufsa Ha'Shehora: Mihem Bnei Hanoar Girsat 2012) *Globes*, June 2012. https://www.globes.co.il/news/article.aspx?did=1000759126.

Weitzman Institute of Science. "WISe." 2017. https://www.weizmann.ac.il/entrepreneurship/wise-program.

Wells, Ke'Tara. "Recess Time in Europe vs America." *Click2Houston*, March 10, 2016. http://www.click2houston.com/news/recess-time-in-europe-vs-america.

Williams, Lawrence E., and John A. Bargh. "Experiencing Physical Warmth Promotes Interpersonal Warmth." *Science* 322, no. 5901 (2008): 606–7. http://www.ncbi.nlm.nih.gov/pmc/articles/PMC2737341/.

Williams, Louis D. *The Israel Defense Forces: A People's Army.* New York: Authors Choice Press, 2000.

World Economic Forum. *The Future of Jobs: Employment, Skills and Workforce Strategy for the Fourth Industrial Revolution.* Global Challenge Insight Report, January 2016.

———. *The Global Competitiveness Report: 2015–2016.* Edited by Klaus Schwab. Geneva: World Economic Forum, 2016.

———. *The Global Competitiveness Report: 2017–2018.* Edited by Klaus Schwab. Geneva: World Economic Forum, 2017.

World Finance. "Israeli Innovation Drives Foreign Investment." Interview by Eyal Eliezer. February 3, 2017.

Yin, David. "Out of Israel, into the World." *Forbes*, December 19, 2013. https://www.forbes.com/sites/davidyin/2013/12/19/out-of-israel-into-the -world/#3ed5e9e2367d.

Yorumlar. "The Importance of Business Networking for Entrepreneurs." *Startupist*, November 7, 2014. http://www.startupist.com/2014/11/07/the -importance-of-business-networking-for-entrepreneurs/.

Zacarés, Juan Jose, Emilia Serra, and Francisca Torres. "Becoming an Adult: A Proposed Typology of Adult Status Based on a Study of Spanish Youths." *Scandinavian Journal of Psychology* 56, no. 3 (2015): 273–82.

Zilber, Amnon, and Michal Korman. "The Junkyard as Parable." *Magazine of the Design Museum Holon*, 2014.

INDEX

Inbal Arieli (born and raised in Israel on hummus and chutzpah) garnered her entrepreneurial skills during her mandatory military service, serving as a lieutenant in the elite Israel Defense Forces' Intelligence Unit 8200—the equivalent of the NSA.

After fulfilling her military duties, and for the past twenty years, Inbal Arieli embraced leading executive roles in the flourishing Israeli tech sector, as well as founding a series of programs for innovators. She is currently co-CEO of Synthesis, a leadership assessment and development company, whose products and services are jointly developed by veteran experts in the Israel Defense Forces, US-based executive coaches, and true, one of the foremost talent search companies in the world. She also serves as a board member and senior adviser to various programs and organizations such as Start-Up Nation Central, Birthright Israel Excel, WISe Program of the Weizmann Institute of Science, SCOLA–Startup Comprehensive Learning, and the 8200 Entrepreneurship and Innovation Support Program.

Inbal Arieli has been featured as one of the hundred most influential people in Israeli high-tech and as one of the top hundred women speakers on technology and business in the world. She lectures worldwide on Israeli innovation and its start-up ecosystem to business and government leaders. Among her most popular lectures are "The Roots of Entrepreneurship," analyzing how Israeli culture breeds entrepreneurship from a very young age, and "From Special Forces to the Board Room," demonstrating how the mind-set of military special forces units can, and should, be successfully applied to businesses.

She holds an LL.B. in law, a BA in economics, and an MBA in entrepreneurship and strategy from Tel Aviv University.

Inbal Arieli lives in Tel Aviv with her husband and their three rambunctious boys.